D0998868

Adam Smith's politics

AN ESSAY IN HISTORIOGRAPHIC REVISION

Cambridge studies in the history and theory of politics

ADAM SMITH'S POLITICS

AN ESSAY IN HISTORIOGRAPHIC REVISION

DONALD WINCH

University of Sussex

CAMBRIDGE UNIVERSITY PRESS

Cambridge
London New York Melbourne

Published by the Syndics of the Cambridge University Press
The Pitt Building, Trumpington Street, Cambridge CB2 1RP
Bentley House, 200 Euston Road, London NW1 2DB
32 East 57th Street, New York, NY 10022, USA
296 Beaconsfield Parade, Middle Park, Melbourne 3206, Australia

First published 1978

Printed in Great Britain
at the University Press, Cambridge

Library of Congress Cataloguing in Publication Data
Winch, Donald.
Adam Smith's politics.
(Cambridge studies in the history and
theory of politics)
Bibliography: p.
Includes index.
1. Smith, Adam, 1723–1790 – Political science.
I. Title.
JC176.S63W56   320.5'092'4   77-82525
ISBN 0 521 21827 6 hard covers.
ISBN 0 521 29288 3 paperback.

To Sue

ERRATUM

p.93, para.3, lines 3-4 should read:

or age. 'Property beyond the value of two or three
days' labour' is unknown and 'universal poverty
establishes there universal equality'.[3] Even
without a regular system of

0 521 21827 6

ERRATUM

p.93, para.3, lines 3-4 should read:

or age. Property beyond 'the value of two or three
days' labour' is unknown ,and 'universal poverty
establishes there universal equality'.[3] Even
without a regular system of

0 521 21827 6

Contents

Acknowledgements

I began work on this essay in 1975 while spending a sabbatical year in the delightful surroundings and company provided by the Institute for Advanced Study in Princeton. My original intention did not involve writing on Adam Smith, except perhaps incidentally, but I am very grateful for the turn events took while in Princeton. It has introduced me to new fields of historical scholarship which have proved absorbing and, I hope, fruitful. I have made the acquaintance of those who cultivate these fields and benefited greatly from their interest, courtesy, and tolerance.

My chief debt of gratitude, undoubtedly, is to Quentin Skinner, who not only guided my early steps but has consistently provided advice and encouragement at every stage of the journey; his help, given so unselfishly, has gone well beyond the call of friendship. Indeed, I count myself extremely fortunate in having been able to rely so much on the assistance and sympathy of so many friends, old and new. John Burrow not only commented on two versions of the manuscript, but has had to bear with a large amount of discussion on the subject. Andrew Skinner was more fortunate in having to read only the earliest version, but suffered manfully through a veritable marathon of Smith talk during a memorable trip we took together to Brazil in 1976. Over a longer period David Pocock has borne with a good deal of more or less focussed conversation on this and kindred matters. I learned a great deal from my talks and correspondence with David Kettler, though I fear that I have not found answers to some of the crucial problems which he raised. I was also fortunate while at the Institute for Advanced Study in finding that Albert Hirschman was working on a related theme which enabled us to exchange notes. Felix Gilbert, Hans Aarsleff, and Michael Barnes were generous in giving me the benefit of their advice at an early stage, and I am particularly grateful to John Pocock for his general encouragement and for enabling me to meet the members of the Conference for the Study of Political Thought in Chicago in 1976. To all these friends, colleagues, and new acquaintances, my thanks are due, together with the usual disclaimer concerning their responsibility for the result. I would also like to acknowledge the assistance of Gillian Lythgoe in preparing the typescript for publication.

Abbreviations

I have used all the volumes of the Glasgow bicentennial edition of the works and correspondence of Adam Smith that were available at the time this work went to the Press, and have consequently employed the system of abbreviations suggested by the editors of this edition.

Corr.   *Correspondence*
LJ(A)   *Lectures on Jurisprudence*: Report of 1762–63.
LJ(B)   *Lectures on Jurisprudence*: Report dated 1766.
LRBL   *Lectures on Rhetoric and Belles Lettres*
TMS   *The Theory of Moral Sentiments*
WN   *Wealth of Nations*

LJ(A) references are given to the volume and page number of the original manuscript, while *LJ*(B) followed by a page number refers to the Cannan edition of these lectures. This information will also be available in the bicentennial volume of both sets of lecture notes. *TMS* VII.ii.1.17 refers to *The Theory of Moral Sentiments*, part VII, section ii, chapter 1, paragraph 17. *WN* IV.iii.b.15 refers to *Wealth of Nations*, book IV, chapter iii, section b, paragraph 15.

Since I have also made considerable use of one of the volumes associated with the Glasgow edition, namely *Essays on Adam Smith*, edited by Andrew S. Skinner and Thomas Wilson, individual essays in this collection are referred to by author and title, followed by *EAS* and the page reference. A full listing of other works cited in the text is given in the bibliography.

1

Introduction: the problem – the liberal capitalist perspective

In the two hundred years that have passed since the publication of the *Inquiry into the Nature and Causes of the Wealth of Nations*, Adam Smith's reputation as a pioneering exponent of, and leading spokesman for, the principles of liberal capitalist society has become firmly established. It is a role which qualifies him to be the founding father of classical political economy, and hence one of the chief forerunners of Marx's analysis of nineteenth-century capitalism as well as of orthodox economics. It was largely in this role that economists and others throughout the world celebrated the bicentenary of the *Wealth of Nations* in 1976, thereby upholding a tradition established in the centennial and sesquicentennial years.[1]

While I shall be concerned here with the liberal capitalist perspective on Smith, I have little to say directly about the economists' Smith – the figure cultivated by generations of historians of economic thought. Nor do I deal with Smith's *œuvre* taken as a whole. For while I shall refer to most of his writings, I am chiefly interested in an aspect of them that can be described as 'political' in the broadest sense of the term. Moreover, I shall be concerned throughout with what Smith can legitimately be said to have intended, rather than with what he might be said to have anticipated or foreshadowed. Indeed, as my sub-title suggests, this essay can be seen as a contribution to a more general argument in favour of a historical interpretation of Smith's intentions and achievements.

Much of the reading presented here takes the form of an

---

[1] For a survey of the leading themes of earlier celebrations see R. D. C. Black, 'Smith's Contribution in Historical Perspective' in Thomas Wilson and Andrew Skinner (eds.), *The Market and the State* (1976), pp. 42–63.

attempt to recover a political dimension that either seems to have been obscured or distorted by the emphasis normally given to Smith's reputation as a key figure in the tradition of economic liberalism, or to have been lost somewhere between the poles of *Das Adam Smith Problem* marked out by the *Theory of Moral Sentiments* on the one side, and the *Wealth of Nations* on the other. In choosing to speak simply about Smith's 'politics' rather than under some grander, yet apparently more specific title, such as 'Adam Smith's political philosophy' or even 'Adam Smith's political principles', I am aware that I may not, initially at least, be conveying a clear idea of my subject, or even of the range of evidence that might be relevant to the historiographic issues which I wish to pursue. Nevertheless, the choice of the least specific term is deliberate, since in the course of presenting my case it will be necessary to show just how much our view of Smith has come to depend on certain perspectives of a general nineteenth-century provenance, and to question a powerful stereotype that has grown up around the subject. For such purposes it seems best not to accept too many commitments in advance. Similarly, while I wish to present an alternative reading of some of the political themes contained in Smith's writings – one which I believe is more faithful to the eighteenth-century context within which they were conceived – my interest will chiefly be concentrated on Smith rather than on any particular tradition of discourse or school of thought to which he might be said to belong. This provides another reason for not applying a label in advance of presenting the evidence.

At the lowest level of generality, of course, the term 'politics' chiefly connotes a party affiliation or a set of political allegiances. Smith's sweeping dismissal of 'that insidious and crafty animal, vulgarly called a statesman or politician, whose councils are directed by the momentary fluctuations of affairs' is a familiar one.[1] But it would be flying in the face of what we know of Smith's career, and of the realities of social and academic life in Scotland during the eighteenth century, to use such statements as a licence for disregarding the biographical evidence relating to Smith's political sympathies and contacts.

[1] *WN* iv.ii.39.

Yet one authority has said that 'Smith is one of the most elusive modern authors of distinction that ever a biographer and historian of ideas set himself to cope with'.[1] He ordered most of his unpublished papers to be destroyed; he seems to have disliked letter-writing; and generally covered his tracks so well that many episodes of his life and facets of his personality remain a mystery. Since a new biography is being prepared for the bicentennial edition, it is to be hoped that, among other things, it will furnish us with a non-hagiological view of Smith's everyday political contacts and sympathies, undertaken in the light of more recent understanding of the complexities of eighteenth-century party labels and groupings.[2] At present, therefore, it is an open question whether biographical evidence can add significantly to our knowledge of the public stance adopted by Smith in his published writings. It may only confirm certain well-known features of political life in the eighteenth century. While I shall, of course, refer to such evidence where it seems relevant, it is by no means central to my purpose. At the risk of premature dogmatism I venture to suggest that it tells us that Smith's taste in 'public' friends was both realistic and eclectic; and that in the case of leading public men it largely arose out of his need for patronage and information, and their need to call upon his economic expertise in matters which were assuming greater political importance during the latter half of the eighteenth century.

A more common type of political label applied to Smith concerns what might be vaguely called his political stance or attitude, where such words as 'sceptical', 'quietist', and 'Burkean' are the ones most frequently employed. To the question – sceptical as to what? – the answer will invariably be: sceptical as to the motives and readiness of politicians to seek a genuine public interest when faced with the clamour of private and other special interests. Alternatively, the scepti-

[1] See Ernest C. Mossner, *Adam Smith: The Biographical Approach*, David Murray Lecture, University of Glasgow, 1969, p. 5. The main biographical authority is still John Rae's *Life of Adam Smith* (1895), as supplemented by Jacob Viner's *Guide* appended to the 1965 Kelley reprint.
[2] See, for example, Ian Ross, 'Political Themes in the Correspondence of Adam Smith', *Scottish Tradition*, No. 5 (1975).

cism centres on the pronouncements of public men and their ability to implement grandiose (and hence misguided) nostrums for reordering society's affairs. This surely is the Adam Smith we all know, the Adam Smith of the 'invisible hand', who condemned the conceited 'man of system' for his attachment to 'the supposed beauty of his own ideal plan of government' in the face of recalcitrant individual behaviour.[1] It is the Adam Smith who proclaimed in one of the earliest statements of his position that: 'Little else is requisite to carry a state to the highest degree of opulence from the lowest barbarism, but peace, easy taxes, and a tolerable administration of justice; all the rest being brought about by the natural course of things.'[2]

Scepticism or quietism can be given more pointed political significance to later generations by taking a step beyond Smith's 'system of natural liberty', and what he described as his 'very violent attack' on the mercantile system, towards the issues of economic liberalism contained in the nineteenth- and twentieth-century debate on the role of the modern state in economic affairs – epitomised, however crudely and unjustly, by such slogans as *laissez-faire*, free enterprise, and the night-watchman state. Once this step has been taken, it is possible to substitute for the admittedly defective eighteenth-century party labels the beginnings at least of a modern political spectrum. Armed with such a spectrum, it becomes possible to assimilate Smith more closely to modern concerns by locating him in terms of those 'isms' which have persisted into the twentieth century.

The substitution of the nineteenth for the eighteenth century as the relevant context within which Smith's writings should be viewed is such a well-established strategy, usually requiring little more than gifts for extrapolation based on hindsight, and what appear to be minor translations of the key terms, that it may seem pointless to question it here. When we insist on believing that Smith must be addressing him-

[1] *TMS* vi.ii.2.17.
[2] As reported by Dugald Stewart from a document no longer in existence in his *Account of the Life and Writings of Adam Smith* in his *Collected Works*, ed. Sir William Hamilton, 1858, volume x, p. 68.

4

self to our world rather than to his own, are we not simply paying homage of the kind required by all seminal figures? Surely it is idle to quarrel with what several generations have regarded as significant to their day in a protean work like the *Wealth of Nations*? By definition, and with a little ingenuity, it can be made to yield support for a variety of positions. Are these not minor issues of historiographic taste and intellectual focus, which cannot, in any event, be settled authoritatively?

I hope that my own position will become clear by the end of this essay. For the present I will simply record my belief that one of the primary responsibilities of the historian – as opposed to those who are in the business of constructing decorative or more immediately usable pasts – is to be concerned with what it would be conceivable for Smith, or someone fairly like him, to maintain, rather than with what later generations would like him to have maintained. Although I regard this as an essay in recovery rather than recruitment, I shall not have recourse to unfamiliar sources or esoteric interpretative doctrines – to claims of having decoded secret messages, uncovered darker meanings, and discovered novel 'influences'. The standard problems of Smith interpretation are sufficiently difficult without having to invent others. In fact, I shall be claiming that to understand Smith's politics it is necessary to bear in mind that he is frequently employing a well-established public language for discussing such matters – a language, the resonances of which were already well known to the educated members of his immediate audience.

This does not mean, of course, that Smith was simply responding passively to his surroundings, or that he was merely a language-*user*. In contrast to some of the more presageful interpretations of Smith's achievements criticised here, which often treat his work as an embryonic and somewhat muddled enterprise that only achieved clarity and fruition in the hands of his nineteenth-century successors, the approach I have adopted requires me to argue that it should be regarded as an extraordinarily rounded enterprise, more the brilliant culmination of a programme than an overture. It should be seen as part of a system (or set of overlapping systems) which, though not completed according to Smith's original plan, was nevertheless the most ambitious of its kind to reach near-completion. It was, in short, the achievement of a leading figure in the Scottish Enlightenment, a moral philosopher-cum-scientific observer of the changing social scene, writing according to an agenda and canons of evidence and communication that Smith himself did much to define, but which were also widely endorsed and harmonious with the intellectual tastes and values of his contemporaries.

I mention this now in order to counter any suggestion that the attempt to place Smith in an eighteenth-century context must necessarily entail belittling him. Moreover, I acknowledge that any reading of Smith will have ramifications which go beyond the confines of his own period and context. The approximate reason for my own present interest in Smith arises out of a concern with the history of the social sciences. By almost any standard, whether as a leader of the movement to write a new 'sociological' kind of history of civil society, or as 'founder' of the discipline that later became economics, Smith would be acknowledged as a crucial figure in the process of transition towards what we now gather under the umbrella of 'the social sciences'. And since his work also has a distinct bearing on the shifting relationship between economy, polity, and society, it could provide an insight into both the nature and development of these troublesome intellectual enterprises, especially their relationship to the older traditions of moral and political discourse. Much of what is said here deals with the relationship between these terms, especially polity and economy; but apart from some tentative concluding remarks, I leave for another occasion the more ambitious task of exploring the implications for the history of the social sciences of the position adopted in this essay. I mention it now only because it seems appropriate in a work purporting to deal with intention to give an indication of one of the factors conditioning my own interest.

The above may also explain why it seems logical to begin by considering the remarkable consensus that seems to have formed around some version or other of the proposition that Smith's 'politics', in any significant sense of the term, is either 'missing' or has been 'eclipsed' by the more powerful economic themes which comprise the heartland of the *Wealth of Nations*. It would hardly be an exaggeration to say that the orthodox account of Smith endorsed by political theorists of divergent persuasions still largely turns on the view that his work marks an important watershed in the history of liberal political thought as the point at which economy decisively enveloped polity; that it represents a decisive moment at which a 'scientific' conception of a self-regulating social and economic realm assumed dominance over what, for better or worse, had previously been an exclusively moral and political domain.

For the present, such wide-ranging propositions may seem opaque. Moreover, at this late stage of the art of Smith interpretation, any claim to bring a fairly new perspective to bear on the problem deserves to be treated with a good deal of reserve. It seems only prudent, therefore, to offer a review of some of the main avenues that have already been explored in the attempt to relate Smith to the leading traditions of political discourse. But before doing this it may be helpful to rehearse some of the more straightforward evidence on party labels and the place occupied by political subjects in Smith's formal plan of studies.

One of the earliest attempts to characterise and label Smith's position on the contemporary political spectrum was made by the Earl of Buchan, a former pupil and friend of sorts to Smith during the last thirty years of his life. In a memoir written a year after Smith's death, he had this to say on the subject:

[Smith] approached to republicanism in his political principles: and considered a commonwealth as the platform for the monarchy, hereditary succession in the chief magistrate being necessary only to prevent the commonwealth from being shaken by ambition, or absolute dominion introduced by the consequences of contending factions. Yet Pitt and Dundas, praising his book, and adopting its principles in parliament, brought him down from London a Tory, and a Pittite, instead of a Whig and a Foxite, as he was when he set out. Bye and bye, the impression wore off, and his former sentiments returned, but unconnected either with Pitt, Fox, or anybody else.[1]

[1] D. E. Buchan, *The Bee or Literary Weekly Intelligencer*, 8 June 1791, p. 165.

7

The reference to Pitt and Dundas presumably relates to Smith's appointment as Commissioner of Customs by the North Ministry in 1778, a position which gave more formal status to the role of occasional adviser to Townshend and Lord Shelburne on fiscal and commercial policy questions which he had occupied since the 1760s.[1] Smith's biographer, John Rae, writing towards the end of the nineteenth century, endorsed Pitt's efforts to introduce 'one great measure of commercial reform after another' in the teeth of irresponsible opposition from Fox, but was as anxious as Buchan to stress that neither the source of Smith's preferment, nor his contacts with such figures as Lord Shelburne had made any difference to his 'stout' Whig sympathies – as evidenced by the loyal support which he gave to Burke and the Rockingham Whigs during the constitutional crisis of 1782 in particular.[2]

Reviewing Rae's evidence a few years later in his *Growth of Philosophical Radicalism*, Elie Halévy remained unimpressed by Smith's Whig credentials; he gave a number of persuasive reasons for believing that if Smith really was a Whig, then, like his friend Hume, he must have been the most sceptical of Whigs.[3] Indeed Halévy felt that as a sceptic in politics Smith clearly out-Humed Hume: after all, unlike Hume, Smith had not even toyed with the idea 'that politics may be reduced to a science'. He also countered the 'republican' evidence by drawing attention to Smith's 'avowed antipathy for the American democracies with their "rancorous and virulent factions"'; and by highlighting some of Smith's less Whiggish-sounding pronouncements on general warrants and standing armies. Whereas reason could be applied to men's economic affairs with some hope of success, politics involved too large an element of arbitrariness and irrationality to yield to scientific explanation. Halévy's conclusion, therefore, en-

---

[1] The evidence on this can be found in W. R. Scott, 'Adam Smith at Downing Street, 1766–7', *Economic History Review*, VI (1935–6), 85–8; and C. R. Fay, *Adam Smith and the Scotland of His Day* (1956), pp. 103–7, 114–16.

[2] J. Rae, *Life of Adam Smith*, pp. 130, 320–3, 378–9, 389, 410.

[3] *La Formation du radicalisme philosophique*, volume I, *La Jeunesse de Bentham* (1901). It appears in the English translation published in one volume in 1934 on pp. 141–2. Part of Halévy's argument is contained in the footnotes, which were drastically cut in the English translation.

tailed driving a wedge between Smith's *science* of political
economy, and his *opinions* on political matters, with the result
that Smith was left with a political attitude called 'scepticism',
but without a philosophical position capable of embracing his
views both on politics and economics. In spite of the fact that
most historians find unacceptable the distinction between
rationalism and naturalism on which Halévy's conclusion is
based, the wedge he drove between Smith's politics and his
economics has stuck firmly. As will be shown, it is mainly a
case of the hammer now being applied to that wedge taking
on different shapes.

There is, however, a more obvious reason for the subordinate or derivative status accorded to Smith's political thought,
namely the incompleteness of his plan of studies. The boundaries and divisions of the ambitious intellectual enterprise
which Smith projected as early as the 1750s, when he first took
up his position as Professor of Moral Philosophy at Glasgow,
can now be delineated with some accuracy. Leaving on one
side the *Essays on Philosophical Subjects*, which are of great
importance to an understanding of Smith's views on the philosophy, psychology, and sociology of science, and the *Lectures
on Rhetoric and Belles Lettres*, which are also of relevance to an
understanding of his opinions on the rules governing different
modes of discourse, the works that have the closest bearing
on his 'politics' form a sequence of overlapping 'systems'
running from 'the science of ethics' at one end, to political
economy, defined as 'a branch of the science of a statesman
or legislator', at the other. The ends of this sequence are
clearly marked by the *Theory of Moral Sentiments* and the *Wealth
of Nations* respectively, but the intermediate area exists only
in the form of two sets of students' notes on Smith's *Lectures
on Jurisprudence*. Since I shall be making considerable use of
these notes, the *caveat* of most other scholars who have used
them must also be registered here. Invaluable though they are,
they remain students' notes, and on any crucial doctrinal issue
should only be given weight when supported by the position
adopted in Smith's published writings. Fortunately, in most
sensitive matters, explicit and implicit cross-referencing between the *Theory of Moral Sentiments* and the *Wealth of Nations*

permits this to be done; and where differences exist between the lecture notes and the published work, these are mentioned in what follows.

By speaking of cross-references and overlapping systems, I have implied, what most scholars now accept, that there is no Adam Smith problem in the original sense of a fundamental incompatibility between the 'sympathetic' ethic of the *Theory of Moral Sentiments* and the 'selfish' ethic of the *Wealth of Nations*. This does not mean that there are no problems involved in establishing the precise nature of the conciliation between these works, but since a frontal attack on these problems is not germane to my purpose, I shall simply adopt the findings of those scholars who appear to me to have provided the most satisfactory account of the relationship.[1] The *Theory of Moral Sentiments* contains Smith's general theory of morality or psychology; it consistently operates on a higher level of theoretical generality and with a lower degree of empirical realism than the *Wealth of Nations*. The latter work can, therefore, be regarded as a specialised application to the detailed field of economic action of the general theories of social (including economic) behaviour contained in the earlier work, which means that it can properly be used to supply background assumptions to the *Wealth of Nations*, particularly on questions involving individual motivation and social conduct. It does not provide a warrant, however, for regarding the *Theory of Moral Sentiments* as a court of higher appeal on all disputed matters. It would be as wrong, in my view, to treat the *Theory of Moral Sentiments* as being logically or philosophically prior in all respects, as it would be to use it purely as an *ad hoc* source to fill in gaps in the opinions presented in the *Wealth of Nations*. But the strongest reason for not becoming unduly embroiled in disputes about these differences of level, tone, and emphasis here is that Smith constructed a bridge between the two works based on his treatment of

[1] For example, see A. L. Macfie, *The Individual in Society* (1967), especially essays 4, 5, and 6; and T. D. Campbell, *Adam Smith's Science of Morals* (1971). An account of the relationship between Smith's various works can be found in R. H. Campbell and A. S. Skinner's editorial introduction to the bicentennial edition of *WN*, and in D. D. Raphael and A. L. Macfie's introduction to *TMS*.

justice which runs directly through the territory covered by the *Lectures on Jurisprudence.*

In the *Theory of Moral Sentiments* Smith provided a causal analysis of justice in his attempt to relate both the rules of natural justice and punishment to his statement of fundamental psychological principles. His main interest lay in commutative justice, defined as the abstention from, or prevention of, infliction of injury to the persons, property, and reputations of our fellow men. Whereas beneficence merits social approbation and reward, justice, being a negative virtue, does not. But since injustice causes positive harm, it can be made the subject of prohibitory rules of a precise and enforceable nature, which is not the case with failures of benificence. By the same token, since injustice arouses a natural resentment which engages the sympathy of the impartial spectator, there is also a legitimate social and psychological basis for the mode and extent of punishment for injurious acts. While society can exist without benificence, it cannot survive the absence of justice. 'Justice...is the main pillar that upholds the edifice. If it is removed, the great, the immense fabric of human society...must in a moment crumble into atoms.'[1]

Although men are endowed with a natural instinct to preserve society, and in consequence draw up defensive rules of justice and lend their approval to punishment for infringements of these rules, impartial enforcement and the maintenance of peaceful social relations require the collective agency of a public magistrate to prevent 'every man revenging himself at his own hand whenever he fancied he was injured'.[2] The *Theory of Moral Sentiments* culminates, therefore, in a statement of the importance of cultivating the science of jurisprudence considered as 'a theory of the general principles which ought to run through and be the foundation of the laws of nations'. It also closes with an announcement of Smith's intentions:

I shall in another discourse endeavour to give an account of the general principles of law and government, and of the different revolutions they have undergone in the different ages and periods of society, not only in what concerns justice, but in what concern

---

[1] *TMS* ii.ii.3.3–4.   [2] *TMS*, vii.iv.36.

police, revenue, and arms, and whatever else is the object of law. I shall not, therefore, at present enter into any further detail concerning the history of jurisprudence.[1]

The promise with respect to police, revenue, and arms was made good with the publication of the *Wealth of Nations*, though these objects of law were largely separated from justice more narrowly defined. Nevertheless, the whole argument of the book presupposes, where it does not actually explain the emergence of, a system for administering justice. This was one of the main duties of the sovereign, and the section dealing with the 'expence of justice' in Book v goes a good deal further into the subject than its title suggests, bringing together many of the more important ideas first adumbrated in the *Theory of Moral Sentiments* and developed in the *Lectures on Jurisprudence*. But we still have to rely on the lecture notes for an indication of the content of that part of his plan which Smith once described in a letter to Rochefoucauld written in 1785 as 'a sort of theory and History of Law and Government'.[2] We also know that as late as 1790, the year of his death, Smith was still anxious to publish his views on these matters, which implies that he had not said all he wanted to say on the subject in his other works.

There are, however, those who are inclined to argue that in spite of the existence of this evidence, Smith's politics is not merely 'missing' or incomplete, but was incapable of being completed along lines that would enable it to stand on equal terms with the science of political economy contained in the *Wealth of Nations*. This position will be encountered below, but it seems worth pointing out now – contrary to Halévy's view at least – that there is no reason to believe that Smith himself regarded 'politics' (in the sense used by Halévy) as occupying a lesser or different role from that of his science of political economy, which, to repeat, was merely '*a branch of* the science of a statesman or legislator'.[3] For as he made clear in the *Theory of Moral Sentiments*,

Nothing tends so much to promote public spirit as the study of

[1] *TMS* VII.iv.37.   [2] *Corr.*, Letter 248, 1 November 1785.
[3] *WN* IV.1. Emphasis supplied.

politics, of the several systems of civil government, their advantages and disadvantages, of the constitution of our government, its situation, and interest with regard to foreign nations, its commerce, its defence, the disadvantages it labours under, the dangers to which it is exposed, how remove the one, and guard against the other. Upon this account political disquisitions, if just, and reasonable, and practicable, are of all the works of speculation the most useful. Even the worst of them are not altogether without their utility. They serve at least to animate the public passions of men, and rouse them to seek out the means of promoting the happiness of the society.[1]

In making this statement Smith was following Hume in using 'politics' to cover 'political economy' and those other subjects which 'consider men as united in society, and dependent on each other'.[2] One of the objects of this essay will be to bring to the fore and attach historical meaning to the large remainder left after political economy proper has been set on one side. This should reveal certain themes which have been obscured or made subservient to the better-known features of Smith's political economy. The treatment of justice obviously provides an important clue, and it is important to stress at the outset the natural jurisprudential framework of Smith's views on the study of politics. But it is only a framework. It sets the formal boundaries of Smith's science of politics but does not necessarily tell us what takes place within those boundaries. For this we must rely on the detail of the *Lectures on Jurisprudence* and more especially of the *Wealth of Nations*.

Needless to say, characterisations of Smith's politics already exist in abundance, though many of them derive their coherence and rationale from the dominant perspective mentioned earlier, which is still undoubtedly that associated with the English tradition of liberal individualism reaching back to Hobbes and Locke, but with special emphasis on Locke. As the upholder of a system of natural liberty within which individuals possess certain natural rights and pursue selfish ends of an economic character, Smith occupies a crucial role in this tradition. He is the first major economic spokesman for an emerging capitalist order within which a distinctive set of

[1] *TMS* iv.1.11.
[2] See David Hume, *A Treatise of Human Nature*, ed. L. A. Selby-Bigge, 1888, p. xix.

economic or property relationships – mediated by impersonal market mechanisms – was becoming firmly established. With a stronger admixture of utilitarianism of the kind associated with the names of Jeremy Bentham and James Mill, the tradition leads on to John Stuart Mill. Without this component, but with a more powerful historical one added, it leads to Karl Marx.

The persuasive power of this lineage can be judged by the fact that it has survived recognition of the Continental natural law theorists, Grotius and Pufendorf, as the more proximate influence on Smith's plan of work, just as it has survived the evidence relating to Francis Hutcheson as the medium through which this plan of studies became available to Smith. More significantly, it has also survived the accumulated evidence of Smith's explicit rejection of specific political doctrines and methods of inquiry espoused by the seventeenth-century rationalists, notably, of course, their *a priori* and unhistorical approach to political obligation as embodied in the intellectual strategy of the social contract. Recognition of Smith's 'empiricism' merely seems to yield an economic Newton in place of the economic Locke, and both images can be made to conform to the standard portrait of Enlightenment 'social science' if Locke the political philosopher is silently conflated with Locke the epistemologist. Both images confirm the conventional portrait of Smith as an advocate of strictly limited or minimal government, which at its crudest converges on the night-watchman state of nineteenth-century polemics. Pointing out, as must and has been done, that Smith was by no means a doctrinaire advocate of *laissez-faire* has not succeeded in shifting the debate outside the confines of the liberal capitalist framework.[1] Hobbes and Locke continue to emerge as the relevant ancestors for everything pertaining to liberal individualism, thereby justifying the attention paid to them by liberal and Marxist scholars alike.

[1] Jacob Viner's classic treatment of the issue in 'Adam Smith and Laissez-Faire' first appeared nearly fifty years ago; see his *Long View and the Short* (1958), pp. 213–45; for a more recent treatment see A. S. Skinner, *Adam Smith and the Role of the State* (1974), and his 'Adam Smith on the Origin, Nature and Functions of the State', a paper given at the International Political Science Association meetings in Edinburgh (1976).

It is hardly surprising then that authors who have devoted particular attention to Smith's political ideas should consider it necessary to take their bearings from this version of the liberal inheritance. William Grampp's treatment of the subject in his two volume study of *Economic Liberalism* provides a good example. After stresssing the natural rights aspect of Smith's work he moves directly to the conclusion that for Smith the state was simply 'a passive or protective agency, not one that initiated improvements'. Government becomes a 'necessary evil' imposed by the defects of human nature, with the primary objective simply of protecting individual liberties, including, of course, 'the liberty to accumulate property'.[1]

The central feature, however, of Grampp's account of the political ideas of the classical economists from Hume and Smith onwards turns on the relationship between political and economic freedom, and more especially on the paradox which he sees in the fact that neither of these advocates of economic freedom espoused the political analogue of the free market, namely representative democracy. Since Grampp also maintains that Hume and Smith's rejection of the social contract did not constitute a decisive break with the liberal mainstream, as represented by Hobbes and Locke, he is led to the following, seductively symmetric, conclusion:

What called for more emphasis in the eighteenth century was the fostering of economic freedom. When one compares in the work of Hobbes and Locke the small part occupied by the doctrine of free exchange with the great emphasis given to political freedom and security, one can understand why in the works of Hume and Smith, writing in the next century, economic freedom receives the greatest attention while political rights are taken almost as data. The former are famous for their exposition of the political rights of man and are known hardly at all for their belief in a free market, while the latter are noted almost wholly for advocating free exchange and little at all for their political doctrine. Yet there is no essential difference in either the economic or the political doctrines of the two centuries.[2]

---

[1] William D. Grampp, *Economic Liberalism* (1965), volume II, pp. 11–12, 16, 20–2, 42–4.

[2] *Ibid.*, p. 48. Essentially the same picture emerges in H. W. Spiegel, *The Growth of Economic Thought* (1971), a textbook which consciously adopts a 'cultural approach' in attempting to relate economic and political ideas: 'In

A more subtle and influential version of this thesis was put forward by Joseph Cropsey in his book on *Polity and Economy: An Interpretation of the Principles of Adam Smith*, which was, until fairly recently, the most thoroughgoing attempt to relate the two terms contained in its title. It was also one of the first works to address itself seriously to the problem of interpretation posed by the evidence of Smith's considerable misgivings concerning certain features of commercial society. For this reason alone it will be necessary to return to Cropsey's findings later in this essay. At this juncture I simply wish to draw attention to Cropsey's primary decision as to the context within which Smith's view of polity should be viewed: he begins with nothing less than an 'axiomatic premise' to the effect 'that capitalism is the embodiment of Smithian principles'. By adding the further assumption that Smith's conception of human nature 'falls into the tradition of modern thought permeated by the spirits of Spinoza and Hobbes', he proceeds to the conclusion 'that it was by the substitution of the desire to better one's condition for the fear of violent death as the critical passion of man, that Smith accomplished the liberalization and commercialisation of the Hobbean system'.[1]

Cropsey addresses himself to a more substantial paradox than the one articulated by Grampp, though like Grampp's it has strong nineteenth-century overtones. Smith becomes an advocate of capitalism, in spite of its acknowledged inequalities and moral imperfections, precisely because it provides the best (and only?) means available for realising freedom in the larger political sense. Hence the drawbacks of capitalist society,

Locke, Smith could find clearer statements about rights of the individual against government which gave expression to the popular aspirations of the time for the protection of life, liberty, and the pursuit of happiness... When Smith made his plea for natural liberty or *laissez-faire*, he had behind him the tradition of Locke's political philosophy. The great idea that there are limitations to the legitimate functions of government he could find in Locke. On the substantive side, Locke's principal limitation would restrict legislation to that enacted for the public good. Whatever this may have meant to Locke, he was farsighted enough not to load his political philosophy with the economic preconceptions of his time. It was left to future generations to fill with specific content the notion of the public good in the light of the economic ideas of their time' (p. 233).

[1] J. Cropsey, *Polity and Economy* (1957), p. 72.

though serious and unavoidable, must be regarded as the price paid for achieving political freedom within a secular society.[1]

In a later work on Smith's political philosophy, Cropsey has shifted the focus from Hobbes to Locke, while at the same time emphasising the Marxian premonitions. It contains the following clear statement of the reasons why the liberal capitalist perspective on Smith has proved so compelling to historians and political theorists who are anxious to understand the modern world of capitalism.

Smith is of interest for his share in the deflection of political philosophy toward economics and for his famous elaboration of the principles of free enterprise or liberal capitalism. By virtue of the latter, he has earned the right to be known as an architect of our present system of society. For that title, however, he has a rival in Locke, whose writing antedated his own by roughly a century. Our thesis will be that, although Smith follows in the tradition of which Locke is a great figure, yet a distinct and important change fell upon that tradition, a change that Smith helped bring about; that to understand modern capitalism adequately, it is necessary to grasp the 'Smithian' change in the Lockean tradition; and that to understand the ground of engagement between capitalism and postcapitalistic doctrines – primarily the Marxian – one must grasp the issues of capitalism in the altered form they received from Adam Smith.[2]

It should be noted in passing that neither Grampp nor Cropsey attempt to argue the case for a Locke–Smith lineage in terms of a routine study of 'influences', making use of texts rather than a general presumption of common concern. From their standpoint such a study may seem unnecessary: it would certainly not be particularly rewarding.[3] Perhaps the answers

[1] *Ibid.*, chapter 3; see pp. 20–21, 84–6, 101, 174 below for further consideration of Cropsey's position.

[2] J. Cropsey, 'Adam Smith and Political Philosophy' in *EAS*, p. 132.

[3] Hobbes and Locke are mentioned together blandly in Smith's first published essay, the letter to the editors of the *Edinburgh Review*, along with Mandeville, Shaftesbury, Butler, Clarke, and Hutcheson, as those English philosophers who have 'according to their different and inconsistent systems, endeavoured at least to be, in some measure, original; and to add something to that stock of observations with which the world had been furnished before them' (*The Early Writings of Adam Smith*, ed. J. R. Lindgren, 1961, p. 23). Hobbes is criticised in the *Theory of Moral Sentiments, TMS* VII.iii.2, along with other authors who have deduced the principle of approbation from self-love. He features beside Grotius, Pufendorf, and Cocceii as one of the founders of the science of jurisprudence at the beginning of Smith's

are all too obvious. Quite apart from Smith's use of natural rights terminology and his endorsement of limited government in economic affairs, there seems to be an echo of Locke's labour theory of the origins of property in Smith's famous announcement that: 'The property which every man has in his labour, as it is the original foundation of all other property, so it is the most sacred and inviolable.'[1] Does Smith not argue, as Locke is said to have done, that: 'Civil government, so far as it is instituted for the security of property, is in reality instituted for the defence of the rich against the poor, or of those who have some property against those who have none at all'?[2] For good measure it might be added that Marx himself regarded Locke's philosophy 'as the basis for all the ideas of the whole of subsequent English political economy'.[3]

To those who are familiar with the writings of C. B. Macpherson on 'possessive individualism' as a major characteristic of the liberal democratic inheritance it will be clear that with appropriate emphasis on these passages linking property and civil government it is possible to take the liberal capitalist thesis in a Marxian direction.[4] There has yet to be a complete extension of the perspectives of 'possessive individualism' to Smith, but the materials are readily available, and some

lectures on the subject; and it is made perfectly clear there and elsewhere that Smith has no intention of following Hobbes's example in having recourse to the state of nature, or in adopting the rationalist approach generally to matters of law and government; (see pp. 51–3 below for further discussion of this point). The only other significant reference to Hobbes is in the *Wealth of Nations*, where he is cited disapprovingly as having defined wealth as power, *WN* i.v.3. The situation is not much better with regard to significant references to Locke. All of the direct citations in the *Wealth of Nations* are to Locke's views on currency and coinage, though Cannan, in his edition of *WN*, imputed three more to Locke's *Treatises of Government* on the basis of presumed similarities in phrasing and doctrine. There are direct references to Locke's views on government in the *Lectures on Jurisprudence*, but they are all designed to refute Locke's doctrines on the social contract, tacit consent, and the right of resistance; (see pp. 52–5 below for further comment).

1 *WN* I.x.c.12.   2 *WN* v.i.b.12.
3 K. Marx, *Theories of Surplus Value*, Moscow edition, part I, p. 367.
4 See especially C. B. Macpherson, *The Political Theory of Possessive Individualism* (1962). A non-Marxian view which embodies the same assumptions can be found in the writings of R. H. Tawney; see especially *Religion and the Rise of Capitalism* (1926) on the growth of individualism.

gestures in this direction have already been made.[1] Macpherson himself has maintained that the story of liberal political theory from Locke to Bentham and James Mill is one of 'increasing economic penetration', where Hume and Smith are seen as crucial in the movement towards establishing not merely 'the centrality of economic relations', but the essentially exploitive class basis of market relations, and hence the need for a system of government that would preserve inequality of property by protecting the rich from the poor.[2] It will, of course, be necessary to return to these questions more fully later. For the moment I simply wish to draw attention to the scope provided by the liberal capitalist framework for convergence between the liberal and Marxian positions.

The scholarly Marxian position on Smith is more strongly represented by the work of Ronald Meek, who, following up the suggestions of Roy Pascal, was originally more concerned with the forward linkages to Marx than the backward linkages to Locke.[3] In recent years, however, Meek has done a considerable amount of detective work on the origins of the version of materialist history, organised into four stages of society defined in terms of their mode of subsistence – hunting, pasturage, agriculture, and commerce – which can be found in Smith's *Lectures on Jurisprudence* and parts of the *Wealth of Nations*.[4] Apart from elucidating the 'theory of the four stages', which he regards as an 'organising principle' behind much of Smith's mature work, Meek has argued that

[1] See, for example, R. Schlatter, *Private Property; The History of an Idea* (1951), especially pp. 161, 182–4. The same idea seems to underly H. Mizuta's remark that Locke having failed, 'the task of justifying their [embryonic industrialists] activities was left to Adam Smith...'; see 'Moral Philosophy and Civil Society' in *EAS*, p. 115.

[2] See 'The Economic Penetration of Political Theory' in *Political Economy and Political Theory*, ed. C. B. Macpherson (mimeographed, Conference for the Study of Political Thought, Toronto, 1974).

[3] See R. Pascal, 'Property and Society: The Scottish Historical School of the Eighteenth Century', *The Modern Quarterly*, 1 (1938), 167–79, and R. L. Meek, 'The Scottish Contribution to Marxist Sociology' as reprinted in his *Economics and Ideology* (1967), pp. 34–50.

[4] See R. L. Meek, 'Smith, Turgot, and the "Four Stages' Theory"', *History of Political Economy*, III (1971), 9–27; and *Social Science and the Ignoble Savage* (1976), especially chapter 4.

it provided a theory of development and a 'sociology' for its eighteenth-century exponents which incorporated the traditional subject matter of political theory by treating law and government as epiphenomenal to the underlying social and economic forces producing progress. Since the subsequent career of political economy is depicted by Meek as one of emergence and emancipation from this historicist sociology, we arrive by a roundabout route at the same conclusion established by the use of Halévy's wedge.[1]

As will be maintained later in this essay, there is room for disagreement as to how far Smith commits himself to economic determinism in his use of the four stages theory, but the obvious point to note here is that the further one goes towards determinism the smaller the scope allowed for autonomous political action. An important element of cultural relativism is introduced into the picture, but as far as one meaning at least of 'politics' is concerned, the effect is the same as the conventional portrait of Smith as a believer in mechanisms which produce economic and social harmony with minimal political intervention.

Neither of what I have, perhaps rather loosely, described as the two Marxian-inspired interpretations of Smith's politics, with their respective emphases on the emergence of a distinctive bourgeois ideology, or on Smith's socio-economic determinism as the basis for a comprehensive social science, share the concern of several influential political theorists with Smith's role in the decline or deflection of classical political philosophy towards economics. As we have already noted, this is what underlies Cropsey's interest in Smith's political philosophy. Once more a particular view of Locke's significance, centring on his property doctrines, furnishes the relevant background. Locke is the essential transitional figure in the process whereby property and men's self-preserving economic relationships were, contrary to classical teaching, brought into the foreground of political philosophy. By iden-

---

[1] See the 'Afterword' to R. L. Meek, *Social Science and the Ignoble Savage* and 'Political Theory and Political Economy, 1750–1800' in *Political Theory and Political Economy*, ed. C. B. Macpherson (mimeographed, Conference for the Study of Political Thought, Toronto, 1974).

tifying itself with an account of polity which entailed 'a mere mutation of the status of pre-political man', political philosophy 'caused itself to be supplanted primarily by economics, the discipline that systematically enlarges upon the self-preserving motive of pre-civil man'.[1] The ultimate destination of this process of abdication can be found in Marx, 'when the replacement of political man by the species-animal reaches a climax'.[2] Smith stands between these two landmarks, enlarging on the implications of the self-preserving instincts of man, and showing how 'nature speaks to history in the language of economics'.[3]

Approaching the problem from a different point of view, Sheldon Wolin reaches similar conclusions in his book on *Politics and Vision*. Although the fate and preferred destination differ profoundly, like Cropsey, Wolin sees the origin of our 'present predicaments' in the progressive sublimation of politics. Again, too, Locke has a crucial role in the story of the decline of political authority by virtue of his decision to connect property with society rather than with a created political order, thereby identifying polity as a mere superstructure deriving its legitimacy from a natural social order. Wolin avoids the trap of seeing Smith as a simple-minded advocate of *laissez-faire* harmonies, but his account of the way in which the discovery of 'society' by the first generation of social scientists led to a decline in what was specifically 'political' in the classical tradition of political philosophy emphasises Smith's 'non-political model of society which, by virtue of being a closed system of interacting forces, seemed able to sustain its own existence without the aid of an "outside" political agency'.[4] The link that connects Locke, the classical economists, and later writers in the liberal tradition is not based on natural rights, property doctrines, or even selfishness, so much as on a common 'philosophy of sobriety, born in fear, nourished by disenchantment, and prone to believe that the human condition was, and was likely to remain one of pain and anxiety'.[5]

[1] J. Cropsey, 'On the Relation of Political Science and Economics', *American Political Science Review*, LIV (1960), 14.
[2] J. Cropsey, 'Adam Smith and Political Philosophy' in *EAS*, p. 138.
[3] *Ibid.*, p. 151.   [4] Sheldon Wolin, *Politics and Vision* (1960), p. 292.
[5] *Ibid.*, p. 294.

Unlike the standard Marxian interpretations, therefore, Wolin portrays the liberal conception of the state as being 'rooted in psychological anxieties rather than acquisitiveness'. Activity provided the chief means by which these anxieties could be resolved, and increasingly this came to mean economic activity, with the end result that the classical economists fashioned 'a body of knowledge which was coeval with the whole of organized social life'.[1] Smith's work stands, therefore, as an important landmark in a more complex and troubled version of the history of liberal individualism, one in which 'economy' and 'society' are replacing 'polity'.

A somewhat different range of scholarly argument has been deployed by Robert Denoon Cumming in his study of liberal thought entitled *Human Nature and History*. In common with Cropsey and Wolin, Cumming depicts the liberal sequence from Locke to Hume and Smith as one in which individualism becomes increasingly centred on economic and property considerations. It culminates in Smith's system of natural liberty as presented in the *Wealth of Nations*, where 'each individual is to be left free to consult his distinct interests and to function in the economic sphere separately from other individuals, but it equally culminates methodologically in Smith's political economy as the analysis of this system which Smith initially offers as one portion of his overall theory of human nature, but which he eventually presents as a distinct and separate science'.[2] The import of this for Cumming is that 'political economy can not be confined within traditional political theory'; it thereby severs its links with a general and humanistic theory of human nature. This is the *real* departure marked by the *Wealth of Nations*, in contrast to Meek's view that political economy was escaping from 'sociology'.[3] The shift of focus accomplished by Smith entailed a movement

[1] *Ibid.*, p. 300.
[2] R. D. Cumming, *Human Nature and History; A Study of the Development of Liberal Political Thought*, 1969, volume II, p. 116; see also pp. 138–40, 171, 174–5, 213–20.
[3] See R. D. Cumming, 'The Four Stages' Theory', a comment on R. L. Meek's 'Political Theory and Political Economy, 1750–1800', in *Political Theory and Political Economy*, ed. C. B. Macpherson (mimeographed, Conference for the Study of Political Thought, 1974).

away from concern with subjective individual intentions and differences towards objective and unintended social consequences, economic structures and regularities. Cumming believes that Smith had attended to the former group of considerations in his *Theory of Moral Sentiments,* and that there are traces of the same psychological concerns left in the *Lectures on Jurisprudence.* The decision to separate the economic sections of these lectures for enlarged treatment opened up an unbridgable gap 'where Smith's treatment of political problems should have come'.[1] Thus it is Cumming's view that Smith's project for a 'theory and History of Law and Government' was incapable of being completed rather than simply incomplete.

This abbreviated account of three interpretations of Smith's contribution to the career of political philosophy raises more issues than can be tackled squarely here. Each of the writers mentioned has his own conception of 'political' and 'theory', and his own view of the consequences attached to the process of decline which they collectively describe. My purpose in drawing attention to their positions is simply to illustrate the underlying agreement on the lineage and on the liberal capitalist context within which the problem of Smith's politics should be situated. It is part of a much larger story in which the strength and autonomy of a socio-economic realm variously threatens, limits, or deflects the realm of the political. It is conceivable that according to certain definitions of 'political', the trajectory which they describe or deplore can be justified. Whether or not this is the case is not my immediate concern, though I shall question the historical basis of some of the judgements registered. It would clearly be folly on my part to claim that, contrary to the positions outlined above, Smith is a *political* philosopher in every significant sense of the term. Nevertheless, I do wish to maintain that Smith has a 'politics' which is far from being trivial. The rejection of one form of understanding does not, of course, imply that its replacement lacks value, still less autonomy.

Returning in conclusion of this brief survey to somewhat less rarified contemporary evidence of the kind mentioned earlier,

[1] R. D. Cumming, *Human Nature and History,* volume II, p. 219.

it will be obvious that, with or without Lockean pedigree, Smith's image as a political thinker is irrevocably bound up with his scepticism and antipathy towards positive government, particularly in economic affairs. Moreover, in addition to the standard themes of economic non-interventionism, some commentators, notably Friederich Hayek, have emphasised the anti-rationalist implications of Smith's version of individualism, wherein social outcomes are explained as the result of human action but cannot be attributed to human design.[1] In Hayek's case the preferred political destination appears to be defined by Edmund Burke; and there is, by now, a sizeable body of literature emphasising the 'conservative' intellectual affinities between Smith and Burke which takes the argument well beyond the establishable facts of their friendship.[2] While it seems a pointless exercise to attempt to establish the *degree* of conservatism shared by the two men, especially when, as is often the case, no account is taken of the crucial divide marked by the French Revolution, there is a good deal of shared ground in their common interest in the historical or conventional basis of social and political institutions.

More credence should perhaps be accorded to a contemporary version of the 'conservative' hypothesis, namely that to be found in Dugald Stewart's *Account of the Life and Writings of Adam Smith*, which first appeared in 1793, three years after Smith's death. In speaking of Smith's 'science of politics', of which the *Wealth of Nations* formed part, Stewart drew attention to its comparative modernity and went on to stress that it aimed at improving society 'not by delineating plans of

---

[1] See F. A. Hayek, *Individualism and Economic Order* (1948), pp. 1–32; *The Constitution of Liberty* (1960), chapter 4; and *Studies in Philosophy, Politics, and Economics* (1967), chapters 5 and 6.

[2] For the facts alone see J. Rae, *Life of Adam Smith*, pp. 144–5, 389–90, 393–6; and *Corr.*, Letters 38, 145, 216, 217, 226, 263 and 265. The literature on affinity is much larger; see, for example, W. L. Dunnes, 'Adam Smith and Burke: Complementary Contemporaries', *Southern Economic Journal*, VII (1941), 330–46; D. Barrington, 'Edmund Burke as an Economist', *Economica*, XXI (1954), 252–8; C. R. Fay, *The World of Adam Smith*, chapter 1; and the works by Hayek cited in the previous note. For less enthusiastic views of the closeness of intellectual relations between the two men see L. Robbins, 'Hayek on Liberty', *Economica*, XXVIII (1961), 66–81; and J. Viner, *Guide to John Rae's Life of Adam Smith*, pp. 23–33.

new constitutions, but by enlightening the policy of actual legislators'. In what is possibly an oblique reference to recent events across the Channel, he also stated that the science demonstrated 'that the happiness of mankind depends, not on the share which the people possess, directly or indirectly, in the enactment of laws, but on the equity and expediency of the laws that are enacted'. Stewart thereby cast Smith as an 'expert' – albeit a rather speculative one – operating within established forms of government, and chiefly concerned with the quality of specific laws and regulations. Moreover, he went out of his way to underline the élitist implications of this position.

Such speculations, while they are more essentially and more extensively useful than any others, have no tendency to unhinge established institutions, or inflame the passions of the multitude. The improvements they recommend are to be effected by means too gradual and slow in their operation, to warm the imaginations of any but of the speculative few; and in proportion as they are adopted, they consolidate the political fabric, and enlarge the basis upon which it rests.[1]

The introduction of political 'conservatism' into the discussion could be as misleading as the application of some usages of 'liberal', 'democratic', or 'radical'. It encourages the dubious assumption that there is a clearly-defined and graded political spectrum possessing sufficient claims to intertemporal generality to be applicable at any chosen point in the past. But there is another way of expressing Stewart's summary view of the tendency of Smith's politics which bypasses this trap. It was best expressed, among Smith's contemporaries, by Adam Ferguson, who has in turn been echoed by Nicholas Phillipson, a modern commentator on the cultural and political significance of that aspect of the Scottish Enlightenment of which Smith, together with Hume, was such a striking representative. Ferguson criticised Smith (and Hume) for going too far in the direction of encouraging an attitude of aesthetic distance and mandarin scepticism towards public affairs. Such teachings threatened to undermine the capacity for autonomous political action which Ferguson considered essen-

[1] D. Stewart, *Collected Works*, ed. Sir William Hamilton, volume x, p. 56.

tial to counteract other debilitating tendencies in modern society. It strengthened the private, contemplative, scientific, and spectatorly qualities at the expense of those of the public actor, the man capable of undertaking an act of political will.[1] This also appears to be what Nicholas Phillipson has in mind when he says of the Edinburgh literati during the second half of the eighteenth century that they created a substitute for political action in 'the collective will to understand'.[2]

Dugald Stewart and Adam Ferguson undoubtedly captured something of the flavour of Smith's politics which has eluded many later commentators. Nevertheless, in what follows I should like to indicate in a systematic way how the picture can be made to appear in a different and less artificial light by taking account of recent work that has considerably modified our view of Anglo-American political thought in the period which runs, roughly, from the Whig Settlement in 1689 to the Philadelphia Convention convened by the American founding fathers in 1787. The following chapter will, therefore, be devoted to an account of my understanding of the significance of this remarkable body of revisionist literature.

My object in subsequent chapters will be to show that Smith employs a consistent method or style of political analysis in his writings and lectures which cannot readily be encompassed within the categories of the liberal capitalist perspective. I hope thereby to implant the notion that Smith's politics is more problematic than it has been made to appear; and that we shall need to approach that problem from a less proleptic point of view than has frequently been the case so far. Finally, it will be necessary to consider whether Smith's well-known antipathy to positive government, and what has been described as a mixture of complacency and scepticism on political matters,

[1] My understanding of Ferguson's differences from Smith is due to David Kettler, who has argued the matter through in considerable detail in 'History and Theory in the Politics of Adam Ferguson: A Reconsideration', in *The Year 1776 in the History of Political Thought*, ed. J. G. A. Pocock (mimeographed, Conference for the Study of Political Thought, Chicago, 1976).

[2] See N. Phillipson, 'Culture and Society in the Eighteenth Century Province: The Case of Edinburgh and the Scottish Enlightenment' in L. Stone (ed.), *The University in Society* (1974), volume II, pp. 407–48.

carry with them the implication that he constructed an intellectual system in which politics is epiphenomenal to the more profound economic forces at work in modern commercial society, a mere derivative (the discarded husk?) of the better known economic system.

2

Republicanism and sceptical Whiggism

Those political theorists and historians who are committed, for one present-minded reason or another, to the enterprise of constructing a genealogy of liberal or bourgeois individualism which is continuous from Locke to the nineteenth century and beyond have suffered a major casualty as a result of recent research on eighteenth-century political thought and ideology. That casualty is no less a figure than Locke himself, the 'founder' of liberal constitutionalism. The following statements by Leslie Stephen neatly encapsulate, albeit in caricature, the view that has been exploded by recent scholarship.

Happy is the nation which has no political philosophy, for such a philosophy is generally the offspring of a recent, or the symptom of an approaching, revolution. During the quieter hours of the eighteenth century Englishmen rather played with political theories than seriously discussed them.

Locke expounded the principles of the Revolution of 1688, and his writings became the political bible of the following century.[1]

It is now some years since the painstaking detective work of Peter Laslett on the dating of the composition of the *Two Treatises of Government* effectively disposed of the idea that Locke wrote in order to justify the Glorious Whig Revolution.[2] Further research on Locke, most notably by John Dunn, has shown the predominantly theological character and restricted local engagement of Locke's political sympathies and writings. It would seem that Locke's reputation, like that of Adam

---

[1] L. Stephen, *History of English Thought in the Eighteenth Century*, Harbinger edition, volume II, pp. 101–11, 114.
[2] See P. Laslett's introduction to his edition of *John Locke: Two Treatises of Government*, revised edition (1963).

Smith, has acquired many gratuitous qualities over the years, which tell us more, perhaps, about our need for stories with heroes or evil geniuses than strict attention to the historical facts of the case might otherwise allow.[1] Far from acting as the bible for a complacent century which lacked an autonomous interest in political theory, recent scholarship converges on the conclusion that Locke's *Two Treatises* was of strictly limited significance to many of the most lively as well as profound developments which took place in Anglo-American political thought during the eighteenth century.

This has been demonstrated most effectively and completely with regard to the American Revolution, where Locke's influence on the colonists was once thought to have reigned supreme.[2] But this negative conclusion with regard to Locke is merely a byproduct of the remarkable historiographic upheaval which has occurred in the last ten to fifteen years on the subject of the American Revolution. The revisionist literature has led to a major reappraisal of the nature and qualities of Anglo-American political thought between 1688 and 1776, and during the post-revolutionary period in which the constitution of the new republic was being formed. It is deservedly referred to as an Anglo-American phenomenon because one of the main conclusions of the literature turns on the essential unity of this political culture. As the colonists increasingly felt their liberties as true-born Englishmen to be threatened by the corrupting encroachment of Parliament and Crown, so their appeal to a tradition of English oppositional writers, and its contemporary exponents, grew in fervour and shrillness. By means of this appeal they articulated an ideology designed to preserve established liberties by securing a restitution of what they regarded as the original principles of the English constitution. While there was much that was merely eclectic, opportunist, and ritualistic in this appeal, it was given shape and form by its eager acceptance of, and coalescence around,

---

[1] See J. Dunn, *The Political Thought of John Locke: An Historical Account of the 'Two Treatises of Government'* (1969).

[2] See C. Rossiter, *Seedtime of the Republic: The Origin of the American Tradition of Liberty* (1953), pp. 139–47; and J. Dunn, 'The Politics of Locke in England and America in the Eighteenth Century', in J. W. Yolton (ed.), *John Locke: Problems and Perspectives* (1969), pp. 45–80.

a distinct body of ideas which can be variously described as belonging to a radical Whig canon, a 'Commonwealth' tradition, or a 'Country' ideology. Each of these descriptions carries with it distinct 'republican' overtones, though since 'republican' was a term of eighteenth-century art, its meaning will require further explication here.

The existence of a classical republican strain in English political thought, as represented by the first generation of Commonwealthmen – Milton, Marvell, Neville, Harrington, and Algernon Sidney – has long been recognised.[1] It was through the writings of these men that a theory of mixed government based on classical and renaissance models and ideals of citizenship was both translated into an English setting and kept alive. The theory has a lineage which goes back to Aristotle, Polybius, Cicero, and Machiavelli, and revolves around the idea that each of the pure forms of polity – monarchy, aristocracy, and democracy – was subject to its own characteristic form of degeneration – tyranny, oligarchy, and anarchy. A mixture of pure forms might prove more stable, and hence have greater chances of survival, but like all polities, mixed governments were subject to the processes of decay. One of the chief means by which decay occurred was through loss of balance as a result of the encroachment by one of the constituent elements comprising the polity on the others. Although decay could take many forms, the generic terms used to describe the process were 'corruption', 'enfeeblement', and 'loss of virtue'. Corruption was both a political condition and a moral affliction suffered by the citizenry at large. Indeed, the chief antidote to corruption was preservation or renewal of the public spirit or 'virtue' of the citizenry, typically by subordinating private concerns to the public good, encouraging active participation in public affairs, and preventing the pursuit of personal luxury from undermining such essential citizenly qualities as martial valour. Once the process of corruption had been allowed to reach a critical point, however, the only means of arresting further decay was via a return to the original principles of the republic's constitution; and during such crises a major role could be played by

---

[1] The main study on the subject is Z. S. Fink, *The Classical Republicans* (1945).

the sagacious or prudent legislator, possessing the character of a Lycurgus or Solon.

In her study of *The Eighteenth-Century Commonwealthman,* first published in 1959, Caroline Robbins showed how successive groups of 'Real Whigs' kept alive the republican principles and ideals of the first generation of Commonwealthmen, while adapting them to serve as the basis for radical comment upon, and opposition to, the constitutional developments which took place after the English Revolutionary Settlement.[1] Her pioneering study has now been extended in a number of directions, chiefly as a result of work by Bernard Bailyn and John Pocock. It was Bailyn's study of *The Ideological Origins of the American Revolution* in 1967 that demonstrated the importance of the radical Whig tradition to colonial political culture, and its significance in determining the nature of the eventual revolution.[2] More perhaps than any other single work, Bailyn's book has done much to revitalise the study of the revolutionary movement, and to reveal its political and psychological characteristics; it stands at the centre of a historiographic movement which has produced a number of important studies on American constitutional and political thought.[3]

John Pocock has extended Caroline Robbin's findings in a different, though closely related, direction. The early heroes of the Robbins story, and now of the pre-revolutionary debate in America – Moyle, Molesworth, Fletcher, Toland, Trenchard, and Gordon – reappear in Pocock's studies of the same theme as 'neo-Harringtonians'.[4] This shift of focus not only

---

[1] C. Robbins, *The Eighteenth-Century Commonwealthman,* revised edition (1968). See also the introduction to her edition of *Two English Republican Tracts* (1969).

[2] See B. Bailyn, *The Ideological Origins of the American Revolution* (1967), and *The Origins of American Politics* (1968).

[3] See, for example, G. S. Wood, *The Creation of the American Republic, 1776–1787* (1969), and G. Stourzh, *Alexander Hamilton and the Idea of Republican Government* (1970). A useful appraisal and anthology of writing on the American Revolution can be found in J. P. Greene (ed.), *The Reinterpretation of the American Revolution, 1763–1789* (1968). See also the review article by J. G. A. Pocock, 'Virtue and Commerce in the Eighteenth Century', *Journal of Interdisciplinary History,* III (1972), 119–34.

[4] See especially J. G. A. Pocock, 'Machiavelli, Harrington and English Political Ideologies in the Eighteenth Century', originally published in 1965, but reprinted as chapter 4 of *Politics, Language and Time* (1971).

emphasises Harrington's role as the chief translator of classical–renaissance republicanism or civic humanism into English historical and constitutional categories – largely by identifying the landed freeholder with the independent and virtuous republican citizen – but broadens the oppositional camp to include Bolingbroke as 'the most spectacular of the neo-Harringtonians'. The inclusion of Bolingbroke, the scourge of Walpole's Ministry during the period 1726 to 1734, and the main upholder of the doctrine that the extensive network of influence created and manipulated by Walpole had systematically corrupted Parliament by undermining its independence, moves the inquiry beyond the various Whig categories on to a spectrum best described as 'Court' versus 'Country'. In opposition to the Court, or official Whig position, the spokesman for the Country ideology argued that the balance within the English mixed system of government rested on the independence of the component parts of the constitution. The maintenance of this balance was the main bulwark of traditional English liberties; and the only effective way of curtailing the inevitable encroachment of executive of Court power was to maintain the autonomy of Parliament by protecting the independence of the men of landed property who were its members.

Walpole's success in expanding the civil and military establishment was widely attributed to the creation of new forms of public borrowing. The threat posed by this expansion expressed itself in the influence exerted over Parliament through the offer of places and pensions, and through the close and corrupting relationship which had grown up between the executive, place-men, and the amorphous new groups associated with the National Debt and the licensed joint stock companies. The latter comprised a sinister 'moneyed interest' supporting the Court, and hence opposed to Country, or independent landed, interests. Another major element in the Country opposition to corruption and executive tyranny centred on the fear of a standing army, largely because it remained outside Parliamentary control, but also because it was thought of, potentially at least, as posing a direct threat of tyranny. Just as frequent Parliaments and the separation of the executive and judiciary powers were the standard remedies for executive encroachment, so the alternative to a standing army was the creation of a vigorous militia.

Pocock has expounded what he calls the 'Court–Country ambivalence' in eighteenth-century political debate with considerable finesse, and has now capped his earlier studies by publishing *The Machiavellian Moment* – a magisterial survey of the entire civic humanist tradition from its Florentine roots to its later development in Anglo-American political thought before and after the American Revolution. In this book he has also expanded on a number of hints contained in his earlier work concerning the applicability and significance of the civic humanist perspective to the study of those eighteenth-century authors who occupy a special position as the leading philosophical commentators on social, economic, and political affairs, notably Montesquieu, Hume, Ferguson, Smith, and Millar.[1]

This brief account of the revisionist literature conveys little idea of its richness and subtlety. It is designed simply to mark out the boundaries of the discussion, to introduce a few of the key names and terms, and to direct the reader's attention to some of the secondary sources that form a background to the argument of this essay. In what follows, I shall largely take the existence of this literature for granted, merely appropriating any specific findings that seem particularly relevant to my case. Before going any further, however, it may be useful to answer some questions that may have been forming in the reader's mind.

Even if it is accepted that the new literature has added to our understanding of eighteenth-century political ideology, by showing just how deeply contemporary debate in England and America was imbued with 'republican' terminology and ideas, what possible relevance could it have for the study of thinkers of the stature and independence of Montesquieu, Hume, and Smith? What bearing can the existence of a lively polemical tradition, thoroughly normative and moralistic in outlook, and chiefly designed to activate or legitimate specific courses of political action, have on the work of writers who were self-

[1] See J. G. A. Pocock, *The Machiavellian Moment* (1975), especially chapter 14.

consciously seeking to construct a *science* of politics – to sustain a philosophical position on social and economic affairs? Quite apart from the epistemological questions surrounding the claim – primarily associated with Hume – to be engaged in the construction of an 'experimental' or Newtonian approach to the sciences of man in society, the gulf between a mode of discourse which emphasised the socially and historically relative character of economic and political institutions, and one that was largely static in its appeal to ancient practice and 'first principles' would seem to be enormous. Is it not the case that one of the leading characteristics of the 'experimental' approach to politics was revealed in its rejection of the classical–renaissance idea that successful forms of government depended on the existence of distinctive political virtues?[1] 'Machiavellian moralism' has frequently been counterposed against the hard-headed realism and historical awareness of eighteenth-century 'social science', one of whose characteristic triumphs was the successful demolition of such republican myths as that of the all-wise 'legislator' or founder of states.[2] Surely, too, one of the primary features of the work of the early 'social scientists' was their commitment to understanding those novel economic forces connected with commercial activities which provided the basis for the essential 'modernity' of contemporary civilisation – a stance which would hardly seem compatible with the nostalgia and agrarian bias that has sometimes been portrayed as one of the main characteristics of the Country ideology.[3]

Much of the rest of this essay will be devoted, explicitly or implicitly, to providing answers to these questions – in so far

[1] This position has been argued fully in relation to Hume by J. Moore in 'Hume's Political Science and the Classical Republican Tradition', in *The Year 1776 in the History of Political Thought*, ed. J. G. A. Pocock (mimeographed, Conference for the Study of Political Thought, 1976).

[2] See, for example, Duncan Forbes's statement that: 'The Legislator myth flourished in the eighteenth century, for a number of reasons, and its destruction was perhaps the most original and daring *coup* of the social science of the Scottish Enlightenment' in his introduction to A. Ferguson, *An Essay on the History of Civil Society* (1966), p. xxiv. See also G. Stourzh, *Alexander Hamilton and the Idea of Republican Government* (1970), pp. 177–8.

[3] The nostalgic qualities are stressed by Isaac Kramnick in his study of *Bolingbroke and his Circle* (1968). For further comment on this see pp. 122, 126 below.

as they relate to Smith's politics. Some of the lines on which answers might be constructed are suggested in Pocock's work, though Smith mainly features there in the margins of the argument. I shall be following up some of Pocock's suggestions here, but with my own purposes in mind. At this juncture I shall simply record in fairly peremptory fashion the initial reasons for believing that the findings of the historiographic movement described so far could have a bearing on the historical understanding of Smith's politics.

It will probably be accepted that evidence with regard to those political conceptions around which a great deal of contemporary debate continued to revolve could provide valuable information on the historical background to the *agenda* of Smith's politics and the language in which that agenda was couched. For this purpose it is not necessary to accept a commitment to establish decisive 'influence', still less 'membership'; and it follows *a fortiori* that nothing so crude as a proof of party allegiance or class ideology is entailed. A well-defined tradition of political discourse with a significant, or even merely vociferous, group of exponents becomes a part of the contemporary culture which any judicious observer and analyst must come to terms with, whether by explanation or rebuttal. The claim involved here is so modest – even flatly so – that it will probably be disputed only by those who adopt the purist notion that Smith's thought somehow belongs on an ethereal and timeless plane of abstract discourse.

A second, and more ambitious reason lies in one of the most attractive qualities of the new literature, namely that it offers a means of constructing a *via media* between the streamlined motorway histories of liberalism (or, for that matter, of the social sciences), which glide swiftly over the surrounding historical countryside, often carrying heavy warnings and messages to the present, and those low roads that aimlessly twist and turn through all the minor personal and factional intrigues of eighteenth-century politics. Much of the interest that now attaches to the study of eighteenth-century political thought derives from the productive tension and interplay that existed between the polemical and philosophical levels of discourse. With a largely unhistorical Locke removed from the centre of the stage, it becomes possible to do justice to the full range of political ideas available to eighteenth-century commentators, and to give more attention to an established, largely secular, language of political discourse which owes far less to Locke's concern with questions of obligation, original contract, and natural rights than was originally thought to be the case. Ironically enough, Locke himself recognised that: 'Politics contains two parts, very different the one from the other. The one, containing the original of societies, and the rise and extent of political power; the other, the art of governing men in society.'[1] This distinction was well understood by eighteenth-century writers, where the first part was concerned with the moral principles of right and obligation, while the second dealt with the historical and empirical conditions underlying forms of government, their reasons for success or failure.[2] Like everything else, the distinction has classical roots, but Machiavelli and Harrington were considered to be the leading exponents of the second, more empirical, approach to 'the art of governing men in society'.

With the publication of *The Spirit of the Laws* in 1748, Montesquieu supplanted and modernised the role previously occupied by Machiavelli as the leading representative of the empirical approach to political inquiry. Montesquieu's concern with those conditions, physical and moral, which accounted for the viability of different systems of law and government; his interest in the *ésprit general* of nations, defined in terms of the prevailing constellation of manners and customs; his inquiry into how power was exercised in different forms of government, and into those underlying principles or passions which activated them while they remained in a healthy condition – all this was sufficient to establish his credentials as the most influential eighteenth-century exponent of what Pocock has called the 'sociology of civic ethics'.[3] It was

[1] See *Some Thoughts Concerning Reading and Study for a Gentleman*, 1693, as reprinted in the 1823 edition of Locke's *Works*, volume III, p. 296.

[2] On this distinction see G. Stourzh, *Alexander Hamilton and the Idea of Republican Government* (1970), pp. 3–5.

[3] See J. G. A. Pocock, *The Machiavellian Moment*, p. 484.

also sufficient for his nineteenth-century French successors, Comte and Durkheim, to bestow somewhat patronising praise on him as a progenitor of sociology in the 'positivist' mould.[1] By the same token, however, and with far greater historical justification, it is possible to regard Montesquieu as the pivotal figure in the history of the eighteenth-century science of comparative politics. On the one hand, he can be seen as the last major exponent of a classical–renaissance tradition of concern with the cultivation of distinctive political qualities, and on the other, as one of the first of the 'moderns' in his recognition that the changes in society associated with commerce could furnish a basis for a new plan of liberty, and a substitute for virtue in the ancient sense.[2] Montesquieu's observations on the *sui generis* qualities of England's social and constitutional arrangements were fundamental to the connections which he made between commerce and liberty, as well as to his better-known, though mistaken, views on the significance of the separation of judicial, legislative, and executive powers. The mistake in itself provides a link with the English oppositional literature mentioned earlier, for there is persuasive evidence to show that Montesquieu derived the notion of the separation of powers from Bolingbroke's partisan idealisation of the English constitution.[3]

Whatever might be said on the subject of Montesquieu's own intellectual obligations, however, there can be no doubt as to the pervasive influence of *The Spirit of the Laws* on all serious political speculation during the second half of the eighteenth century. This was as true of the Scottish writers on civil society as it was of the framers of the American republic, for whom Montesquieu's work remained a kind of textbook of alternative forms of polity. Of the Scots, Adam Ferguson was the

[1] See A. Comte, *The Positive Philosophy of Auguste Comte*, freely translated and condensed by H. Martineau, 1854, volume II, pp. 56–60; and E. Durkheim, *Montesquieu and Rousseau*, Ann Arbor Paperback edition (1965), pp. 1–61.

[2] See D. Lowenthal, 'Montesquieu and the Classics: Republican Government in *The Spirit of the Laws*' in J. Cropsey (ed.), *Ancients and Moderns* (1964), pp. 258–87. The most convenient source now available for studying Montesquieu's political thought is Melvin Richter, *The Political Theory of Montesquieu* (1977).

[3] See R. Shackleton, 'Montesquieu, Bolingbroke, and the Separation of Powers', *French Studies*, III (1949), 25–38.

happiest to confess his debt to Montesquieu;[1] and his work
contains the strongest influence of the Machiavellian themes
of virtue, spirit, and corruption, as they were transmitted by
Montesquieu.[2] It may have been the excessive attention paid
to these themes that was partly responsible for Hume's disapproval of Ferguson's *Essay on the History of Civil Society* – and
since there are many similarities between Smith's and Hume's
political and intellectual stance, there may be a clue here to
Smith's position.[3] Nevertheless, John Millar's frequently
quoted statement with regard to the history of civil society –
'The great Montesquieu pointed out the road. He was the Lord
Bacon in this branch of philosophy. Dr Smith is the Newton'
– cannot be ignored by being treated as ritual obeisance.[4]

But if the influence on Smith of Montesquieu's science of
politics cannot be ignored, compared with that exercised by
his friend, David Hume, it was diffuse rather than specific.
Hume's science of politics has been the subject of considerable
debate, with many competing assessments being offered on
such questions as the epistemological status of this science;
Hume's precise location on the political spectrum, whether
contemporary or modern; and his intentions as a political
commentator and historian.[5] With regard to the last of these
questions in particular, there is now a major new study by
Duncan Forbes of *Hume's Philosophical Politics*. In addition to
its merits as the most close-textured historical reading of

[1] 'When I recollect what the President Montesquieu has written, I am at a
loss to tell, why I should treat of human affairs...In his writings will be
found, not only the original of what I am now, for the sake of order, to
copy from him, but likewise probably the source of many observations,
which in different places, I may, under the belief of invention, have
repeated, without quoting their author': see A. Ferguson's *Essay on the
History of Civil Society*, ed. Duncan Forbes (1966), p. 65.

[2] The best complete assessments of Ferguson can be found in D. Kettler, *The
Social and Political Thought of Adam Ferguson* (1965), and in Duncan Forbes's
introduction to his edition of Ferguson's *Essay* cited in the previous
note.

[3] On the possible reasons for Hume's disapproval see D. Kettler, *The Social
and Political Thoughts of Adam Ferguson*, pp. 57–60, 76.

[4] See J. Millar, *An Historical View of the English Government*, 1812 edition,
volume II, pp. 429–30n.

[5] A useful brief survey and bibliography can be found in J. Moore, 'Hume's
Political Science and the Classical Republican Tradition', in *The Year 1776
in the History of Political Thought*, ed. J. G. A. Pocock (mimeographed,
Conference for the Study of Political Thought, 1976).

Hume's politics currently available, Forbes's approach to Hume has a distinct bearing on Smith – a bearing which Forbes himself has done a great deal to demonstrate.[1]

At the heart of Forbes's approach to Hume's politics lies his distinction between 'sceptical' or 'scientific Whiggism' on the one side, and various forms of 'vulgar Whiggism' on the other.[2] As a philosophical observer of the historical and contemporary political scene, Forbes argues, Hume was attempting to sustain a sceptical, detached, and comparative view, not only of English political institutions, but of the alternative European and Asian polities as well. The espousal of this clinical and non-parochial perspective was essential to Hume's claims for a science of politics; and it could only be achieved in the circumstances of the day by distancing himself from vulgar Whiggism – a capacious category designed to encompass a great number of popular beliefs about the nature of the English constitution and its history. Making use of this distinction, Forbes has, for example, shown how Hume's failure to endorse the congratulatory Whig interpretation of the 'matchless constitution' was responsible for the contemporary charges brought against him for having written a 'Tory' history of England.[3] Forbes has also attacked attempts to portray Hume's career as that 'of a sceptical Whig in process of becoming a candid Tory' by maintaining that the use of any simple Whig–Tory spectrum misconceives the very nature of Hume's philosophical enterprise, especially when the portrait has to be based so much on biographical evidence, derived from letters.[4]

One of the parochial implications of the vulgar Whig in-

[1] A number of incidental comparisons between Hume and Smith are made in D. Forbes, *Hume's Philosophical Politics* (1976), but the main source of Forbes's view on Smith is his 'Sceptical Whiggism, Commerce, and Liberty', in *EAS*, pp. 179–201.

[2] Forbes's earliest use of this distinction can be found in an article which he wrote as early as 1954 entitled 'Scientific Whiggism: Adam Smith and John Millar', *Cambridge Journal*, VII (1954), 653–70.

[3] An earlier statement of Forbes's views on Hume as a historian can be found in his introduction to the Penguin edition of D. Hume's *History of Great Britain* (1970).

[4] See D. Forbes's review of Giuseppe Giarrizzo's *David Hume politico e storico* (1962) in *The Historical Journal*, VI (1963), 280–95; and D. Forbes, *Hume's Philosophical Politics*, chapter 5.

terpretation of the English constitution was that no other form of government, certainly not that to be found in absolute monarchies like France, was capable of achieving and guaranteeing liberty. Perhaps Forbes's most valuable contribution to our understanding lies in his careful dissection of the variety of contemporary meanings attached to such basic terms as 'liberty', 'freedom', and 'free governments'. His main contention is that for both Hume and Smith, 'liberty' chiefly connoted personal or civil liberty in the sense of security under the rule of law. Personal liberty, seen as the regular and impartial administration of justice and the security of property and contracts, was compatible with many different forms of government, except those that were purely despotic and arbitrary. Hence it was possible for monarchies, especially civilised monarchies like France, to guarantee liberty even if they could not be classified as 'free governments'. Forbes also suggests that Hume and Smith regarded public, or what we would call political liberty – a quality that *did* depend on the form of government, and the share which some or all of the people have in it – as having an instrumental importance only in so far as it reinforced personal liberty.

Bearing in mind the indiscriminate use made of 'liberty' in discussions of Smith's economic and political 'liberalism' over the years, it is clear that in this respect alone Forbes has provided a powerful antidote to those anachronistic interpretations which silently equate 'liberty' with democratic freedoms. On this matter Forbes's conclusion reinforces another derived from the work on the Anglo-American oppositional literature mentioned earlier, namely that even for the most radical of eighteenth-century Whigs, there is a world of difference between a thorough-going 'republican' antagonism towards royal or executive tyranny, and those sympathies which, particularly after the French Revolution, are properly called 'democratic' in the modern sense.[1]

Forbes's work embodies an original and penetrating per-

---

[1] See, for example, B. Bailyn, *The Ideological Origins of the American Revolution*, pp. 282–3; C. Robbins's introduction to *Two English Republican Tracts*, pp. 42–3; and Franco Venturi, *Utopia and Reform in the Enlightenment* (1971), pp. 62 and 90.

spective on Smith's politics. I shall have occasion to refer to it at several points later in this essay. There is a great deal to be said for regarding Smith as a 'scientific Whig', borrowing from and sharing many ideas with Hume. The distinction between 'sceptical' and 'vulgar' Whiggism is also particularly well adapted to the negative purpose of showing just how trivial and misleading the conventional party labels can be when applied to those who were self-consciously engaged on the construction of a systematic philosophical enterprise. Hume has suffered more from this labelling than Smith, largely because he wrote a great deal more that was overtly political in every sense of the word. Moreover, Smith wrote fewer letters of a lively and indiscreet kind, a fact much regretted by his friends, no doubt, though one which has left fewer hostages to biographical fortune. If anything, the problem with Smith is the paucity of materials relevant to a historical understanding of his science of politics, which may account for the freedom with which anachronistic 'isms' continue to be applied. For this reason it seems necessary to be more responsive to some of the more commonplace eighteenth-century political resonances to be found in his work than an *early* application of Forbes's forceful distinction might allow.

One of the main features of vulgar Whiggism with which both Hume and Smith dispensed, was, of course, Locke's version of the social contract and his theory of consent. In this respect at least, Forbes's approach is in accord with other recent literature which has shown the limited number of eighteenth-century doors of any interest that can be opened by reference to Locke's political writings alone. But Forbes, quite understandably for his purpose, also includes 'Commonwealthmen, republicans or democratic radicals or even Tories' in the vulgar category, and claims that his distinction runs deeper than any Court–Country divide.[1] This enables him, for example, to dismiss the meagre evidence, largely derived from the unreliable Earl of Buchan, to the effect that Smith 'approached to republicanism in his political principles'.[2]

[1] D. Forbes, 'Sceptical Whiggism, Commerce and Liberty', in *EAS*, p. 180.
[2] For the full version of Buchan's testimony see the citation on p. 7 above. Forbes's dismissal of the 'republican' argument is in the essay cited

The charge of teaching republican principles in his lectures at Glasgow was one that John Millar, Smith's pupil, was seriously called upon to defend himself against during the constitutional crisis of 1784, but there is no equivalent evidence relating to Smith.[1] The term 'republican' had acquired a fairly elastic meaning during the second half of the eighteenth century. For bolder spirits it might mean the replacement of the Crown by some kind of elected magistrate, while for others it simply denoted those who were opposed to specific policies or developments which appeared to be shifting the balance within the mixed constitution too heavily in favour of the monarchy.

The elasticity of contemporary usage can be illustrated briefly by reference to what appears to have been Millar's position and Hume's reaction to it. Millar was anxious to show that he had not meddled 'with the local and partial politics of the day', and said that he had eliminated some parts of his lectures which might give rise to this suspicion. His chief aim had been 'to recommend that system of limited monarchy which was introduced at the Revolution'. The stress here could be on 'limited'. One of his pupils, Francis Jeffrey, had heard Millar lecture when he was not under suspicion; and it was Jeffrey's opinion that 'though sincerely attached to the limited form of monarchy established at the Revolution, [Millar] seems to have thought that the monarchy itself was the least valuable part of the system, and that most of its advantage might have been secured under another system of administration'.[2] This would, of course, be a statement of theoretical

in the previous note, pp. 195–8. The evidence relating to Buchan's eccentricity and general unreliability can be found in J. Viner's *Guide to John Rae's Life of Adam Smith*, 1965, pp. 22–3. Added to this is the fact that Buchan's own sympathies were decidedly 'republican'; he was the author of a ludicrously enthusiastic portrait of Andrew Fletcher, one of the best-known Scottish figures in the commonwealth canon (see D. E. Buchan, *Essays on the Lives and Writings of Fletcher of Saltoun and the Poet Thomson*, 1792), and he joined the multitude of oppositional writers in condemning standing armies (see *Letters on the Impolicy of a Standing Army*, 1793).

[1] Millar's reply to the charge of republicanism can be found in his letter to Edmund Burke, then Rector of the University of Glasgow, reprinted in W. C. Lehmann, *John Millar of Glasgow* (1960), pp. 71–2.

[2] Review of J. Millar's *Historical View of the English Government*, *Edinburgh Review*, III (1803), 155.

preference, and as such was open to the following response by Hume.

> I cannot but agree with Mr Millar, that the Republican Form of Government is by far the best. The antient Republics were somewhat ferocious, and torn internally by bloody Factions; but they were still much preferable to the Monarchies or Aristocracies which seem to have been quite intolerable. Modern Manners have corrected this Abuse; and all the Republics in Europe, without Exception, are so well governd, that one is at a Loss to which we should give the Preference. But what is this general Subject of Speculation to our Purpose? For besides, that an establishd Government cannot without the most criminal Imputation, be disjointed from any Speculation; Republicanism is only fitted for a small State: And any Attempt towards it can in our Country, produce only Anarchy, which is the immediate forerunner of Despotism. Will he tell us what is that form of a Republic which we must aspire to? Or will the Revolution be afterward decided by the Sword: One great Advantage of a Commonwealth over our mixt Monarchy is, that it would considerably abridge our Liberty, which is growing to such an Extreme, as to be incompatible with all Government. Such Fools are they, who perpetually cry out Liberty: and think to augment it, by shaking off the Monarch.[1]

There is a good deal of indirect evidence to suggest that Smith was closer to Hume than Millar on this matter. As Forbes has shown, Smith displayed little admiration for existing republics (less than Hume?), and appears to have agreed with Hume that this form of government was unsuited to large commercial societies and empires.[2] Smith's position is perhaps best caught in an off-hand, and remarkably neutral, statement in the notes of his *Lectures on Jurisprudence*, to the effect that monarchies 'now set the fashion'.[3]

This said, it is still important to bear in mind that however dubious the term 'republican' might be as a political label, the monarchy–republic dualism was an essential framework of political analysis for Smith, just as it was for Montesquieu and Hume. Thus, in his *Lectures*, Smith combined the ideas of Montesquieu and Hume by following the former in describing

---

[1] See *Letters of David Hume*, ed. J. T. Y. Greig, 1932, volume II, p. 306.

[2] See D. Forbes, 'Sceptical Whiggism, Commerce, and Liberty', in *EAS*, pp. 196–7.

[3] *LJ*(B), p. 55; see also p. 274.

both aristocracy and democracy as republican forms of government, and the latter in equating monarchies and republics with the two psychological principles of political obligation, namely authority and utility, respectively. Since the English government was a mixture of these two forms – Montesquieu described it as a republic disguised as a monarchy – the two major factions, Tory and Whig, could also be related to the monarchical regard for authority and the democratical enthusiasm for what Smith called 'a sense of public utility'.[1] Moreover, as Franco Venturi has reminded us, for men of the Enlightenment, not only did the republican intellectual tradition provide a link with a classical past, but even the remaining, much-weakened, European republics constituted an alternative to the modern monarchies, though 'as a form of life, not as a political force'.[2] Smith was following a well-established eighteenth-century pattern in expressing 'an intention of writing a treatise upon the Greek and Roman republics', even though, unlike Montesquieu, Ferguson, and Gibbon, he did not complete the project.[3] Venturi's statement certainly fits those parts of Smith's *Lectures* and the *Wealth of Nations* where he considers the peculiarities of the Dutch and Venetian republics.

While there may be much that was simply rhetorical and modish about the invocation of classical examples and styles during the eighteenth century, it would seem unwise to ignore the underlying humanistic roots on the grounds that the surface is littered with minor neo-classical enthusiasms and allusions. What might otherwise be a somewhat vague injunction is given added force by the resurgence of republicanism which took place after 1776, as a result of the American

[1] See p. 52 below for further comment.
[2] See F. Venturi, *Utopia and Reform in the Enlightenment*, pp. 70–1 and passim. See also F. C. Lane, 'At the Roots of Republicanism', *American Historical Review*, LXXI (1966), 403–20.
[3] The informant is Millar as reported in D. Stewart's *Account of the Life & Writings of Adam Smith*, in *Collected Works*, volume x, p. 000. On Smith's admiration for Greece and Rome see also W. R. Scott, *Adam Smith as Student and Professor* (1937), p. 325 n. The best recent study of those eighteenth-century historiographic conventions which culminated in Edward Gibbon's *Decline and Fall of the Roman Republic* is J. W. Johnson's *The Formation of English Neo-Classical Thought* (1967).

Revolution, an event which was, by many standards, the most important political development to occur in Smith's lifetime. The fact that Hume's political writings were called upon as notable contributions to the modern science of politics, and hence as a guide to wise constitutional practice, by the founders of the fledgling American republic, may be fortuitous, but it adds a little spice to the idea that contemporary republicanism, in its various forms, might provide a useful perspective on Smith. There is certainly something to be said for a science of politics which finds itself with work to do, rather than simply standing as the monument to a philosophical stance.

3

Hutcheson and Smith: Real Whig versus sceptical Whig

The sketch of the ground-plan of Smith's ambitious scheme of studies given in the first chapter of this essay makes it plain that the most obvious place to begin consideration of his science of politics is with the *Lectures on Jurisprudence*. The two sets of notes on these lectures enable us to form an impression of the line of approach Smith was pursuing in the 1760s, prior to his decision to develop the material on police, revenue, and arms into a separate work on the *Wealth of Nations*. It is well known that the general pattern, and sometimes the order, if not emphasis, of Smith's teaching at Glasgow was closely modelled on Frances Hutcheson's lectures; and that in choosing to deal with economic subjects within the context of his duties as a Professor of Moral Philosophy, Smith was following Hutcheson and the Continental natural law theorists, Grotius and Pufendorf.[1] In view of the prominence rightly accorded to Hutcheson in the standard treatments of 'influence', it is surprising how little attention has been paid to Hutcheson's political ideas. On these matters at least, the 'never-to-be-forgotten' teacher seems to have been allowed to slip from memory. It is all the more surprising when one remembers that Hutcheson features prominently in Caroline Robbins's study of *The Eighteenth-Century Commonwealthman* as one of the leading Scottish representatives of the radical or Real Whig position.[2] He was a member of the Dublin coterie that

[1] See E. Cannan's introduction to the *Lectures on Justice, Police, Revenue and Arms* (1896); W. R. Scott, *Francis Hutcheson* (1900), pp. 230–45; and, for a recent review of the evidence, W. L. Taylor, *Francis Hutcheson and David Hume as Predecessors of Adam Smith* (1965), pp. 18–28.

[2] See C. Robbins, *The Eighteenth-Century Commonwealthman*, pp. 185–96; see also C. Robbins, '"When is it that Colonies may turn Independent"; An

formed around Molesworth in the 1720s, and it was through Molesworth that Hutcheson became acquainted with the work of Shaftesbury.[1] Although Hutcheson is now chiefly remembered as an influential exponent of the moral sense view of ethics, Robbins stated that 'his most original contribution to eighteenth-century thought was undoubtedly made in the field of politics'.[2] The significance of his political views was certainly not lost on his contemporaries, for as his colleague, William Leechman, stated:

As he had occasion every year in the course of his lectures to explain the origin of government, and compare the different forms of it, he took peculiar care, while on that subject to inculcate the importance of civil and religious liberty to the happiness of mankind: as a warm love of liberty, and manly zeal for promoting it, were ruling principles in his own breast, he always insisted upon it at great length, and with the greatest strength of argument and earnestness of persuasion: and he had such success on this important point, that few, if any, of his pupils, whatever contrary prejudices they might bring along with them, ever left him without favourable notions of that side of the question which he espoused and defended.[3]

When Hutcheson's lectures were published posthumously as *A System of Moral Philosophy* in 1755, the book was reviewed by Hugh Blair, a friend of Adam Smith's. On the question of 'civic relations' Blair maintained that,

[Hutcheson] shows himself a warm friend to the cause of liberty, and discovers a just abhorrence of all slavish principles. He boldly asserts the rights of resisting in the people, when their fundamental privileges are invaded; whilst, at the same time, he inculcates the advantages of regular subjection and due regard to laws even under faulty administrations. Besides the moral considerations of government, our author gives also the political view of it, after the manner of Harrington and Machiavelli, in a comparison of the different

Analysis of the Environment and Politics of Francis Hutcheson (1669–1746)', *William and Mary Quarterly*, XI (1954), 214–51.
[1] See W. R. Scott, *Francis Hutcheson*, pp. 26–36, 182, 211. Hutcheson acknowledged the patronage and support of Molesworth in his first book, *An Inquiry into the Original of Our Idea of Beauty and Virtue* (1725).
[2] C. Robbins, *The Eighteenth-Century Commonwealthman*, p. 188.
[3] See Leechman's account of the life and writings of Hutcheson as prefixed to F. Hutcheson, *A System of Moral Philosophy* (1755), pp. xxxv–xxxvi.

forms and plans of politics, and of the respective advantages and disadvantages that attend them.[1]

John Rae, Smith's biographer, speculated that the 'deep strong love of all reasonable liberty which characterised [Smith] must have been, if not first kindled, at any rate quickened by contact with Hutcheson'.[2] Parallels have been drawn between Hutcheson's mention of natural liberty in economic affairs, and Smith's famous 'system of natural liberty', though it is generally accepted that Hutcheson's interpretation of the scope of economic liberty was far more circumscribed.[3] But it also seems worth stressing that even if master and pupil could be shown to be at one on this matter, this would have a bearing on the *role* of government in economic affairs, but not necessarily on the more general 'moral' and 'political' themes underlying obligation and preferred *forms* of government. On the latter questions especially, Hutcheson had a great deal more to say than Smith, and his views were expressed with more fervour than we have learned to associate with his pupil. Robbins found Smith's position 'much more difficult to delimit and describe than that of his beloved teacher', and she concluded that 'he was not by disposition a revolutionary, nor was he moved to eloquence, as were so many of the Real Whigs, by the political considerations of the social contract, or of justice'.[4] Although this statement underplays Smith's interest in justice, there is a good deal to be said for the general verdict it registers. Nevertheless, without denying the problems of delimitation, it now seems possible to say a little more on the subject. In attempting to do so, however, I shall not be concerned to apply a label or even to establish Hutcheson's 'influence' in the conventional sense of the term. Rather I shall be attempting to demonstrate the *availability* to Smith of a particular way of discussing politics, which happened in this case to come from an impec-

---

[1] H. Blair, *Edinburgh Review*, No. 1 (1755), 22–3.

[2] J. Rae, *Life of Adam Smith*, p. 13.

[3] This point was first established by W. R. Scott, *Adam Smith as Student and Professor* (1937), pp. 112–14; the evidence is reviewed in W. L. Taylor, *Hutcheson and Hume as Predecessors of Adam Smith*, pp. 42–4.

[4] C. Robbins, *The Eighteenth Century Commonwealthman*, p. 196.

cable source. For this purpose I shall be comparing Smith's lectures with the version of Hutcheson's lectures contained in the *System*, there being no significant changes in this book from the position adopted in his earlier works.[1]

Hutcheson's treatment of political obligation begins in the middle of Book II of the *System* with a deductive account of the laws of nature and the duties of life as they exist in the 'state of liberty' prior to the establishment of civil government. In common with his predecessors, Carmichael and Pufendorf, he denies Hobbes's view of this condition as being one of war; rather it is one in which men possess various sacred rights and are endowed with a moral faculty which gives rise to 'natural bonds of beneficence and humanity to all'. The mere fact that men are capable of acting contrary to their natures by injuring one another proves nothing about the true condition of the state of liberty, 'since all the laws and obligations of that state enjoin peace and justice and beneficence'.[2] Nor is the natural state a solitary condition; it is simply one in which men have 'no common superior or magistrate, and are subject to God, and the law of nature'.[3] The remainder of Book II is devoted to a taxonomy of perfect and imperfect rights 'according as they are more or less necessary to be maintained for the public interest'. The entire discussion is conducted under a strong assumption of natural equality in the enjoyment of rights, and contains an attack on all forms of slavery as well as a denial of any right to govern based solely on superior abilities or riches.

Property is dealt with under 'adventitious rights'. Having criticised Locke's labour theory of the origin of property, Hutcheson explains that his own inquiry is directed towards discovering the moral justification for the institution of property; and this amounts to an inquiry into its social utility in encouraging industry by securing to men the fruits of their labour.[4] Hutcheson criticises the communism of Plato and Sir

---

[1] F. Hutcheson, *A System of Moral Philosophy*, as reproduced in Volumes V and VI of the Georg Olms Verlagsbuchhandlung edition of Hutcheson's *Collected Works* (1969). All references will be to this edition, and will be given as *SMP* followed by the book, chapter, and page reference.

[2] *SMP* II.iv.281.   [3] *SMP* I.iv.283.   [4] *SMP* II.vi.318–22.

Thomas More, but acknowledges the justice of 'agrarian laws' to prevent immoderate acquisition. He also endorses the case for allowing communal access to 'such things as are inexhaustible and answer the purposes of all'; and the right of prescription by the community where property is neglected.[1]

It is only after considering a wide variety of legal and economic topics, from contracts and criminal law to coinage, that Hutcheson returns to the problem of political obligation – though he clearly fails to stick to his intention in dealing with the state of liberty of confining his attention to 'the rights and duties founded in nature previous to any adventitious states or lasting relations introduced by some institution, contract, or deed of men'. Experience of the uncertainties and inconveniences of the state of liberty – now called 'anarchy', but with no implied disapprobation – induces men to agree to submit to the direction of others. The weakness and imperfection of men, their difficulties in settling disputes without violence, and the impossibility of obtaining 'concurrence in any great and noble designs of distant advantage to whole nations' are recognised as legitimate motives for forming civil governments.[2] But while acknowledging the benefits of regular government, Hutcheson is anxious to avoid the conclusion that 'the very worst sort of polity is better than the best condition of anarchy';[3] his aim is to maintain a balance between the two conditions in order to underline his repeated reference to the right of resistance to despotic governments. There may be other reasons why government is established, such as force and oppression, but Hutcheson sidesteps these by saying that he is inquiring into 'the just and wise motives to enter into civil polity. . . and not into points of history about facts'.[4]

For similar reasons perhaps he states that 'the only natural method of constituting or continuing civil power must be some deed or convention of men'.[5] In common with Locke he argues that the original contract is binding on successive generations who make use of the advantages of the political

---

[1] *SMP* II.vi.322–4, 327, 335–9.   [2] *SMP* III.iv.212–17.
[3] *SMP* III.iv.218.   [4] *SMP* III.iv.224–5.
[5] *SMP* III.iv.226.

union, notably by exercising the right of inheritance. While consent is the obvious method of constituting political authority, it is also possible to envisage a state being formed and imposed by a powerful paternal figure for reasons later accepted by the community at large, though Hutcheson is quick to add that 'absolute hereditary monarchy cannot be settled upon this pretence'.[1] By the same token the people retain the right to revoke any contract which proves to have pernicious consequences.

Smith's contrasting treatment of the same themes in his *Lectures on Jurisprudence* is made apparent at the outset. After referring to Grotius, Hobbes, Pufendorf, and Cocceii as his predecessors, he curtly dismisses the idea of dealing with laws in the state of nature on the simple historical grounds that 'there is no such state existing'.[2] He describes the various categories of natural and acquired rights possessed by man *qua* man, member of a family, and as citizen, which it is the object of justice to protect. In the 1762–3 *LJ*(A) notes he followed Hutcheson's precedent in proceeding directly to a detailed treatment of these rights, though in the later version, *LJ*(B), he seems to have had second thoughts about this procedure. Whereas the origin of natural or personal rights – those that concern life, limb, and reputation – was 'quite evident', the 'acquired rights such as property require more explanation'. The reason given for this is that: 'Property and civil government very much depend on one another. The preservation of property and the inequality of possession first formed it, and the state of property must always vary with the form of government.'[3] This was to be one of the main themes of Smith's historical account of progress, though it should be noted that, contrary to more deterministic interpretations, the relationship envisaged between government and property is a reciprocal one.[4] My surmise – no more – would be that Smith

---

[1] *SMP* III.iv.231.   [2] *LJ*(B), p. 2.
[3] *LJ*(B), p. 8.
[4] Smith's meaning is caught by Duncan Forbes's aphorism distancing Ferguson from earlier Marxist interpretations: 'When Ferguson says that property is a matter of progress, he is not saying that progress is a matter of property'; see Forbes's introduction to A. Ferguson, *Essay on the History of Civil Society* (1966), p. xxv.

became more anxious to give early prominence to those parts of his lectures in which he had something new to add to the natural law tradition inherited from Hutcheson. Whether or not this is true, the effect of the *LJ*(B) arrangement of topics, by introducing 'the original principles of government' before private jurisprudence, is to emphasise the break with the social contract theory and to undercut most of the normative and libertarian emphasis of Hutcheson's endorsement of Locke's version of this theory.

In rejecting Locke's theory of voluntary contract and tacit consent, Smith was merely following in Hume's footsteps. The resemblance is further underlined, as was noted earlier, by Smith's equation of the principles of obligation that he wishes to substitute for the contract idea, namely authority and utility, with monarchy and democracy, and the Tory and Whig factions respectively.[1] It is at this point, according to *LJ*(A) at least, that Smith provides a mild and ambivalent hint of a preference for the Whigs. They are described as 'the bustling, spirited, active folks, who can't brook oppression and are constantly endeavouring to advance themselves', whereas the Tories are 'the calm contented folks of no great spirit, and abundant fortunes which they want to enjoy at their ease'.[2] As far as the principle of authority is concerned, Smith had elaborated on Hume's ideas in the *Theory of Moral Sentiments*. It is not surprising, therefore, to find him referring his listeners to that work for a fuller discussion of the social and psychological origins of the distinction of ranks.[3] *LJ*(A) also confirms Forbes's view that Smith, like Hume, was anxious to stress the parochial or Anglo-centric character of the contract theory.

...this doctrine of freedom as founded on contract is confined to Britain, and has never been heard of in any other country, so that there it cannot be the foundation of the obedience of the people; and even here it can have influence with a very small part of the people, such as have read Locke etc. The far greater part have no notion of it. And nevertheless they have the same notion of the obedience due to the sovereign power, which cannot proceed from any notion of contract.[4]

[1] *LJ*(B), p. 11.
[3] *LJ*(B), p. 9.
[2] *LJ*(A), volume v, p. 63.
[4] *LJ*(A), volume v, p. 59.

On the same psychological grounds, tacit consent is given equally short shrift.

Every moral duty must arise from something which mankind are conscious of. The case is the very same as in that of approbation and disapprobation; as no one can draw a conclusion or agree to one without knowing the premises, so no one can have a notion of any duty from a principle of which they not at least some confused conception: for it is very seldom that one has a distinct notion of the foundation of these duties, but have merely a notion that they have such and such obligations. All have a notion of the duty of allegiance to the sovereign, and yet no one has any conception of a previous contract, either tacit or express.[1]

Similarly with Locke's right of resistance to a monarch who raises taxes without consent, Smith points out that consent is not a feature of absolutist governments and is 'but a very figurative metaphorical' notion in England, still more so in Scotland, where so few have voting rights.[2]

When every allowance is made for the nature of the source, namely lecture notes, what seems striking is the remarkably matter-of-fact way in which psychological empiricism is employed to dismiss a form of argument that was not merely popular but had received the *imprimatur* of distinguished predecessors in the natural law tradition. Hume's conclusions are appropriated, but without his concession to the logic if not historical realism of the contractarian position.[3] There is not even a nod in the direction of recognising the instrumental merits of an explicitly normative inquiry into political obligation. On this matter at least, Smith does not acknowledge any distinction between what Hutcheson described as 'the just and wise motives to enter into civil polity' and 'points of history about facts', though he had done so in parallel case in the *Theory of Moral Sentiments* when noting the difference between the rules of natural justice and systems of positive law considered simply as 'the records of the sentiments of mankind in different ages and nations'.[4] The main consequences of

---

[1] *LJ*(A), volume v, p. 65. [2] *LJ*(A), volume v, p. 68.
[3] Thus Smith does not make the concessions to the idea of an original 'promise' and 'consent' which Hume made in his early essay 'On the Original Contract'. On Hume's view see D. Forbes, *Hume's Philosophical Politics*, p. 76.
[4] *TMS* vii.iv.36.

rejecting consent arising out of contract as an account of the origins of government and its powers over the citizenry are, first, a special emphasis on 'sentiment' or 'opinion', and secondly, that particular importance is attached to a form of inquiry that Hutcheson did not undertake, namely that based on the view that government is a product of 'the natural progress which men made in society'.[1]

The effect of Smith's change of strategy on one of the leading themes of Hutcheson's *System* – the citizen's rights of resistance – is quite striking. Readers of the *Theory of Moral Sentiments* would not have been surprised to learn that Smith was decidedly cautious in his approach to this question in his lectures. In his book he had written at length on the source of our 'habitual sense of deference' in our greater capacity to sympathise with 'the passions of the rich and powerful' than with those of our social equals and inferiors. It was this that provided a firm foundation for the distinction of ranks and 'the peace and good order of society'.

Even when the order of society seems to require that we should oppose [the rich and powerful], we can hardly bring ourselves to do it. That kings are the servants of the people, to be obeyed, resisted, deposed, or punished, as the public conveniency may require, is the doctrine of reason and philosophy; but it is not the doctrine of Nature. Nature would teach us to bow down to their exalted station, to regard their smile as a reward sufficient to compensate any services, and to dread their displeasure, though no other evil were to follow from it, as the severest of mortification.[2]

There could hardly be a clearer contrast with Hutcheson's stance towards the rich and powerful:

'Tis in vain to talk of invading the liberty of the rich, or the injury of stopping their progress in just acquisitions. No publick interest hinders their acquisitions as much as is requisite for any innocent enjoyments and pleasures of life. And yet if it did, the liberty and safety of thousands or millions is never to be put in the ballance with even the innocent pleasures of a few families; much less with their vain ambition, or their unjust pleasures, from their usurped powers or external pomp and grandeur.[3]

---

[1] *LJ*(A), volume iv, p. 9.   [2] *TMS* i.iii.2.3.
[3] *SMP* iii.vi.248.

Although Smith later modified his view on this matter, to the extent of acknowledging that the disposition to admire and sympathise with the rich and powerful was based on a corruption of our moral sentiments, he did not retract the comments on the social utility of this psychological disposition.[1] The comments on rights of resistance in the lectures are also extremely mild. Such rights are acknowledged to be lawful 'whatever the principle of allegiance...because no authority is altogether unlimited'. Violent abuses of power call for violent counter-measures, but both the natural tendency in men to submit to authority and the principle of utility enjoin support for the established powers, whatever the form of government, and in spite of the prevalence of certain abuses. In *LJ*(A) it is conceded that 'whenever the confusion, which must arise from the overthrow of the established government is less than the mischief of allowing it to continue, then resistance is proper and allowable'.[2] But the compatible conclusion reported in *LJ*(B) seems to catch Smith's mood better: 'No government is quite perfect, but it is better to submit to some inconveniences than make attempts against it.'[3]

The contrast between Smith and Hutcheson can also be seen in what Blair called the 'political' as opposed to 'moral' view of government, where Hutcheson relies a great deal on Harrington's views on power and property. Hutcheson provides a detailed but a-historical treatment of preferred forms of government which is based almost exclusively on the classical–renaissance theory of mixed government. He argues that the three classical types of polity are unstable, though he seems to have felt that democracy could be made more secure by means of an agrarian law which enabled property to be so diffused among the populace that no cabal 'shall have a fund of wealth sufficient to support a force superior to that of the rest'.[4] Nevertheless, a comparison of the advantages and disadvantages of the purer forms of polity leads him to favour a stable mixture of all three. Agrarian laws may still be neces-

---

[1] For the modification of Smith's view see the chapter added to the 6th edition of *TMS* I.iii.3.

[2] *LJ*(A), volume v, p. 58.   [3] *LJ*(B), p. 72.

[4] *SMP* III.vi.247.

sary to preserve the democratic element, but 'without any such laws some mixed states are safe, provided the lords can sell their estates, and trade and manufactures flourish among the plebeians; and they have access to the places of greatest profit and power. By these means, without any law, wealth may be sufficiently diffused.'[1] The popular assembly should be elected by means of ballot to prevent bribery, and should be entrusted with the major responsibility for legislation. The senate should be equipped with various deliberative, checking, and appelate judicial powers, but like the popular assembly should be elected. All civil and military offices should be rotated to prevent the formation of cabals, and to ensure a wider degree of participation and diffusion of experience among the populace. The monarchy, either elected or hereditary, should be entrusted with executive functions and the power to act as umpire; but it should not be allowed any 'other foundation of wealth than what depends on the law, or the grants of the popular assembly'.[2] The account is rounded off with a lengthy discussion of the right of resistance to monarchs or senates who usurp or assume powers contrary to those originally entrusted to them.

Smith also employs the classical tripartite division of polities – monarchy, aristocracy, and democracy – but in the form attributable to Montesquieu, namely with the last two being classified as republican forms of government. He also uses Montesquieu's version of the division of the powers of the state into legislative, judicial, and executive functions, the last being concerned with the power of making peace and war.[3] Once more though, instead of confining himself to a static taxonomy of constitutional mechanisms, as Hutcheson had done, he immediately proceeds to deal with these forms of government historically.

A great deal has been written in recent years on Smith's role as one of the leading 'sociological' historians of civil society, most of it under the heading of the 'theory of four stages',

[1] *SMP* III.vi.259.
[2] *SMP* III.vi.263.
[3] *LJ*(A), volume IV, p. 1; *LJ*(B), p. 17.

where Ronald Meek and Andrew Skinner have led the way.[1] There is room for differences of interpretation as to how important the four stages are as an organising principle behind Smith's mature work taken as a whole, and as to how far his use of this 'theory' establishes his credentials as an economic determinist or materialist historian along lines later associated with the name of Marx.[2] For the moment, however, it is not necessary to enter into these questions. I shall first give a summary account of the political characteristics of the history of civil society presented in the *Lectures*. This should not – initially at least – be controversial, if only because even those who adopt the view that Smith is a full-blooded economic determinist will presumably concede that law and government were the *subject* of the bulk of the *Lectures*.

The four stages are employed when explaining the development of those parts of private jurisprudence that relate to property, and in the sections on public jurisprudence which deal with man as citizen. It is with the latter that I shall chiefly be concerned here. According to the standard natural law approach to these questions, as expounded by Hutcheson, there are only two 'stages' of society, the states of liberty and civil government, neither of which are seen as historical entities. Only the first of Smith's stages – the society of hunters – approximates to the state of liberty, since 'they have no regular form of government, and consequently live according to the laws of nature'. What government there is will be

[1] See the references to Meek's work on p. 19 n. 4 above. For Skinner's treatment of the same themes see 'Economics and History: The Scottish Enlightenment', *Scottish Journal of Political Economy*, XII (1965), 1–22; 'Natural History in the Age of Smith', *Political Studies*, XV (1967), 32–48; and more recently and fully in 'Adam Smith: An Economic Interpretation of History' in *EAS*, pp. 154–78.

[2] See for example R. D. Cumming's criticisms of Meek's position on the four stages theory in *Political Theory and Political Economy*, ed. C. B. Macpherson (mimeographed, Conference for the Study of Political Thought, 1974). Skinner discusses Smith's catholicism as a historian, and draws attention to the qualifications that must be made to the economic determinist interpretation in 'Adam Smith: An Economic Interpretation of History', *EAS*, pp. 169–78. Meek's qualifications to his interpretation can be found in R. L. Meek, *Social Science and the Ignoble Savage*, pp. 120–1. For a recent, though none too well defined, affirmation of Smith's status as a full-blooded economic determinist see D. A. Reisman, *Adam Smith's Sociological Economics* (1976).

'democratical': judicial and executive functions will be exercised by the people in common, and there will be little need for any legislative function.[1] It is only with the move towards pasturage, and the consequent establishment of property in the form of herds and flocks, that inequalities arise which make regular government necessary. The wording of this is more blunt in *LJ*(A) than in the previously-known versions.

> Laws and government may be considered in this, and indeed, in every case, as a combination of the rich to oppress the poor, and preserve to themselves the inequality of goods, which would otherwise be soon destroyed by the attacks of the poor, who, if not hindered by government, would soon reduce the others to an equality with themselves by open violence. The government and laws hinder the poor from ever acquiring wealth by violence, which they would otherwise exert on the rich; they tell them they must either continue poor, or acquire wealth in the same manner as they have done.[2]

Here we have a splendid hook on which to hang an extension to Smith of C. B. Macpherson's theory of 'possessive individualism', with Locke standing as the obvious predecessor. Unlike Locke, however, Smith maintains that material forms of property hardly exist before government, still less property *rights*, which require the establishment of civil governments. In so doing Smith was simply adhering to the Roman Law distinction between natural or personal rights and adventitious rights such as property which only come into existence under regular legal systems. The alternative link through Locke's labour theory of the *origins* of property is no stronger. The essential text derives from the *Wealth of Nations*: 'The property which every man has in his labour, as it is the original foundation of all other property, so it is the most sacred and inviolable'.[3] In view of the fact that the context within which this statement appears is a discussion of the oppressive effects on the poor of the apprenticeship laws, it is scarcely a sound basis on which to rest an interpretation of Smith's views of the *origins* of property rights, especially those which entail heavy emphasis on physical as opposed to personal property. When Smith deals with *this* question in the *Lectures*

---

[1] *LJ*(A), volume IV, pp. 2–3; *LJ*(B), p. 15.
[2] *LJ*(A), volume IV, p. 11; *LJ*(B), p. 260. [3] *WN* I.x.c.12.

he adopts the standard approach of the Continental natural law theorists in assigning property rights to occupation, accession, prescription, succession, and voluntary transference. In so doing he was following Hutcheson, who specifically rejected the Lockean view as arising 'from some confused imagination that property is some physical quality or relation produced by some action of men'.[1] Smith also criticises this theory, and makes use of his doctrine of the impartial spectator to show that whatever right exists, derives, in Dugald Stewart's words, from 'the general sympathy of mankind with the reasonable expectation which the occupant has formed of enjoying unmolested the object he has got possession of, or of which he was the first discoverer'.[2]

The inequality of property in shepherd societies confers great power on the rich over the poor: '[The rich] have no possible means of spending their property, having no domestic luxury, but by giving it in presents to the poor, and by this means they attain such influence over them as to make them, in a manner, their slaves.'[3] A system of patriarchal chieftains arises, whose authority becomes hereditary. Where the shepherds live in villages or towns, judicial functions may still be exercised by the people at large; the private influence of the rich need not infringe on democratical forms of government. Once the business of society becomes more complex, however, the detailed administration of justice increasingly falls into the hands of the richer chieftains or princes, though the legislative function remains at a rudimentary stage of development. Larger settlements will be possible among shepherds than among hunters, and hence larger collective enterprises can be undertaken. Where the shepherds adopt migratory or marauding habits, it may be possible for them to assemble large and powerful armies, as was the case with those formed by Tamerlane, Genghis Khan, and Mahomet.[4]

The next development comes with the formation of regular settlements, though whether it takes place depends on the

---

[1] *SMP* II.vi.318 and II.viii.346.
[2] See D. Stewart, *Collected Works*, ed. Sir W. Hamilton, volume VIII, p. 263.
[3] *LJ*(B), p. 16; see also *LJ*(A), volume IV, p. 4.
[4] *LJ*(A), volume IV, pp. 18–20.

existence of geographical conditions favourable to agriculture and defence. Thus the Tartars remain at the marauding shepherd stage, while Attica becomes 'the country which first began to be civilized and put into a regular form of Government'.[1] For defensive purposes, cities like Athens are constructed. Within such towns powerful men gradually lose some of their pre-eminence through luxury and the diffusion of wealth. Democratical forms of government are restored, with slavery making it possible for freemen to attend to the business of government.[2] At this stage then, Smith's story concerns the rise and fall of the ancient republics, divided between the defensive republics of Greece, and the conquering republics of Rome and Carthage. The former lose their liberty as a result of 'refinement' – improvements in the arts and commerce which reduce the number of men willing to, or capable of, bearing arms. Mercenaries and the rabble have to be employed, especially by the smaller non-slave-owning republics; and this places them at a disadvantage because of the difficulties such armies have in mastering the complex arts of seige warfare. The conquering republics succumb more to the internal threat posed by standing armies commanded by ambitious men of the stamp of Marius, Sulla, Caesar, and Pompey, who thereby establish military monarchy and imperial government. Although military monarchies are capable of administering justice impartially, they too fall prey to refinement and the consequent decline in the martial virtues of the populace.[3]

In this way Smith clears the ground for a consideration of the forms of government 'now in force in Europe', beginning with the allodial period which followed on from the invasion of the Roman empire by the shepherd nations of Northern Europe. Once more, great inequalities of property appear, this time associated with settled forms of agriculture, with the allodial lords acquiring large numbers of dependants in the form of retainers and tenants. Since monarchs are unable to exercise full jurisdiction, these lords retain considerable

[1] *LJ*(A), volume IV, p. 28; *LJ*(B), pp. 22–4.
[2] *LJ*(A), volume IV, pp. 29–30, 32–4.
[3] *LJ*(A), volume IV, pp. 36–56; *LJ*(B), pp. 26–30.

powers, modified only by such weak instrumentalities as a popular court system with a Witenagemot at its apex.[1]

The power of the lords in their frequent disputes with one another and the king depends on the number of tenants and retainers they can call to arms. Constant warfare makes it necessary for them to give more favourable and secure leases to their tenants in order to obtain military service. By a parallel process the lords exchange their independent allodial status for a hereditary feudal relationship to the king in return for his protection.[2] The more orderly system of government introduced under feudalism entails placing greater power in the hands of the monarch and the more powerful lords who comprise his court. Initially, therefore, feudalism results in the creation of 'aristocratical monarch' and the extinction of those democratical vestiges, like the Witenagemot, which existed under the allodial system. But the next phase in the process leads to absolutism, and is brought about by the decline in the power of the feudal lords relative to the king as a result of the introduction of commerce and luxury.

Alongside the move to absolutism, though after it in point of time, is the rise of the power of the Commons. This was the result of the need of kings for financial and military support in cases of internal and external conflict. It had led them to grant special privileges to the inhabitants of towns and to curry favour with the people at large by granting their requests in return for subsidies and additional taxes. By this point Smith's story has started to become an English one, with the Tudors representing a high water mark in the move towards absolutism before the power of the Commons was firmly established. This is the general rule throughout Europe, since 'the power of the nobles has always been brought to ruin before a system of liberty had been established, and this, indeed, must always be the case'.[3] But whereas absolutism remained the rule elsewhere in Europe, with the exception of Germany where the extent of territory and an elected monarchy had left considerable wealth and power in the hands of

---

[1] *LJ*(A), volume IV, pp. 56–9; *LJ*(B), pp. 34–6.
[2] *LJ*(A), volume IV, pp. 58–66; *LJ*(B), p. 37.
[3] *LJ*(A), volume IV, p. 81.

princes, the course of political development in England was unique. This was largely as a result of being an island free from the threat of foreign invasion, especially after Scotland was subdued. No standing mercenary army was necessary in England, 'and consequently the King had no power by which he could overawe either people or parliament'.[1] Elizabeth I had sold royal demesne lands rather than raise taxes, thereby obliging her Stuart successors to have recourse to Parliament to finance their extravagance. This had enabled the Commons to whittle away the royal prerogative and to exercise strict control over military spending, the size of the civil list, and the other uses of revenue derived from taxes and the public debt. The legislative function had thereby been divided between the king, lords, and Commons.

In the later lecture notes this account of the rise of the English Parliament concludes with the establishment of that 'happy mixture of all the different forms of government properly restrained, and a perfect security to liberty and property'.[2] The earlier notes are no less confident, but they mention the possibility that this 'happy mixture' might be overturned:

The Civil List is so considerable that in the hands of designing, vigorous, and ambitious princes, it might give them an influence far superior to that which the dependents of a few officers about the palace can bestow. But customs of this sort are very difficultly [sic] changed by any prince. The standing army might also without doubt be turned against the nation, if the King had attained great influence with it. But there is one security here also. Many of the persons of chief rank and station in the army have also large estates of their own, and are members of the House of Commons. They have in this manner an influence and power altogether independent of the King. It would never be their interest to join with the King in any design to enslave the nation, as no consideration he could bestow on them would be able to turn their interest to his side.[3]

This passage has been quoted at length because, however crudely rendered, it gives an indication of Smith's views in 1762–3 on the sensitive issues posed by the standing army, royal

[1] *LJ*(A), volume IV, p. 83; *LJ*(B), p. 44.   [2] *LJ*(B), pp. 45, 71–2.
[3] *LJ*(A), volume IV, p. 88.

influence, and the independency of Parliament. It is clear that he adopted a fairly complacent position on these matters, for while he did not dismiss the fears expressed by oppositional writers, neither did he endorse them – a characteristic Smithian stance, as we shall see. Although the English system of liberty was unique, it was not fragile. Judges were independent of the Crown; Ministers could be impeached; and *habeas-corpus* provided security against arbitrary imprisonment. Smith noted the effect of the Septennial Act in lengthening the life of Parliaments, and hence in reducing the dependence of members on their constituents, but seems to have considered the English system of elections a sufficient guarantee of liberty. It was certainly better for being less dominated by the aristocracy than the Scottish system. The same congratulatory tone pervades Smith's account of the development of the English judicial system given in both sets of lecture notes, as well as his brisk retelling of how the papist machinations of James II led to his rightful rejection and replacement by the Protestant succession.[1]

Smith's political and religious sympathies are less important than his historical preoccupations. The brief summary given above does not convey Smith's talent for detailed illustration, but it should show just how much of the story revolves around political and military events. The four economic stages provide only a loose framework, and modes of subsistence exert an influence on the pattern of events, if at all, only when coupled with other factors, which include favourable geographical conditions, historical accidents, and even the personalities of monarchs. The last of these factors has a particularly important role to play in the special case of the English political and legal establishments.

There is also a clear political pattern of a cyclical kind operating within the unilinear economic stages. The clue to this pattern is provided by Smith's echo of Hutcheson's concluding section in the *System* on the 'seeds of decay' contained within every state – when he speaks of the 'fatal dissolution that awaits every state and constitution whatever'.[2]

---

[1] *LJ*(A), volume v, pp. 64–6, 72–6; *LJ*(B), pp. 71–2.
[2] *LJ*(B), p. 32. For Hutcheson's views on 'seeds of decay' see *SMP* III.xi.

The theme of the famous set-piece analysis of the decline in the power of the barons which later appeared in Book III of the *Wealth of Nations* features not once but three times in the *Lectures*. It occurs first in the case of the chieftains when the early republics come into being; it happens to the allodial lords when they opt for a feudal relationship with the king and exchange domestic luxury for direct power over their dependants; and it brings the downfall of the feudal barons. A modified version of the same argument is deployed to explain how the English Crown became dependent on parliamentary taxes rather than on the revenue from its estates. Similarly with the effects of commerce and 'refinement' on military strength; they bring down the ancient republics and later the imperial power of Rome when faced with barbarian invaders. In other words, commerce is more than a stage of society; it is a constant cause producing the same effects at all stages. Marius, Sulla, and Caesar are mentioned as examples of the dangers to liberty of standing armies, and the fact that Smith brings in Cromwell at the same time makes it clear that the pattern is capable of repeating itself in modern times, though Britain's 'peculiar advantage' in relying on sea power rather than a standing army is given as a reason why she may be exempt from the general rule, particularly since parliamentary liberty was established *before* a standing army.

These political and military themes are interwoven with, and frequently override, the economic processes of transition; they cannot, therefore, be treated simply as epiphenomenal illustrations of these processes. And since Smith's narrative juxtaposes ancient and modern examples, moving easily from past to present, a didactic political purpose should be anticipated here as in his economic writings. No less than Hume, Smith is engaged on an 'experimental' inquiry into the science of politics, making use of ordinary (i.e. not conjectural) historical material to provide evidence of regularity, or constant contingency, in a world of apparent diversity and change. Liberty, dependence, power, and influence take various forms, but there are also regular underlying contrapuntal relationships between them which are not relative to the given state of society. They provide a foundation for the exercise of 'scientific' judgement and advocacy by the philosopher.

The evidence of the *Lectures* is, of course, partial and inadequate. It may be wise to follow Forbes's advice in treating some of the more vulgar Whiggish asides as a lecturer's 'green plums' rather than as his mature conclusions.[1] We certainly know that Smith regarded it as 'the chief purpose of history, to relate events and connect them with their causes, without becoming a party on either side', from his praise of Machiavelli as 'of all the modern historians the only one [before Hume?] who has contented himself' with this aim.[2]

The transition from Hutcheson's *System* to Smith's *Lectures* involves a marked change of style from one that is predominantly normative to one that is more 'experimental' and coolly historical – a transition which accords well with the normal picture of the shift towards 'social science'. Employing Smith's terminology, it is possible to describe the change as one in which Smith sides with 'Nature' whereas Hutcheson relies on 'reason and philosophy', provided that we bear in mind that Smith makes full use of the ambivalence of the word 'Nature' to cover both what can be explained and what can be morally justified. Such ambivalence should not be disturbing unless we are anxious to press the modern distinction between 'science' and 'philosophy' on Smith, and hence expect him to distinguish normative and positive propositions with the compulsiveness attempted by some of his nineteenth-century successors.

The contrast with Hutcheson's Real Whig version of the commonwealth themes has served mainly to increase the distance, in terms of both style of argument and conclusions, between teacher and pupil. For while the general shape and order of treatment given to such subjects as public, private, domestic, and international law belong to a common pattern established by the Continental natural law theorists, the content of Smith's *Lectures* reveals a pervasive change, leaving only isolated echoes of Hutcheson's original position. Moreover, there is

[1] See D. Forbes, 'Sceptical Whiggism, Commerce and Liberty', *EAS*, pp. 181–2.
[2] *LRBL*, ed. J. R. Lothian, pp. 110–11.

one further and major distancing factor which only emerges fully when Smith turns to the subject of 'Police', and more especially to the duties of the magistrate to provide security from crimes and other disturbances to good order, and to achieve 'cheapness or plenty, or, which is the same thing, the most proper way of procuring wealth and abundance'.[1]

It was, of course, in these parts of his lectures that Smith dealt with the importance of the division of labour to society and a number of other subjects that were to appear in magnified form in the *Wealth of Nations*. The emergence of commercial society from within the interstices of the predominantly agricultural society of feudal Europe is prefigured in this part of the *Lectures*. This material was to provide a foundation for Smith's history 'of the different progress of opulence in different nations' in Book III of the *Wealth of Nations*, where it was linked with the more purely economic analysis contained in the earlier books on the division of labour, capital accumulation, and the distinction between productive and unproductive labour. Hutcheson had dealt with some of these economic questions in his lectures, and has been credited with having laid a foundation for Smith's treatment of the division of labour. There are also similarities in the order of treatment given to these questions by both men. But Hutcheson's account is neither consecutive nor anywhere near as elaborate as even the rudimentary treatment Smith accords these subjects in his lectures. More to the point, Hutcheson does not deal with the special characteristics of a form of society deeply penetrated by commerce and manufacturing; and his comments on the relationship between economy and polity are virtually confined to a few Harringtonian propositions concerning the need for an agrarian law to bring power and property into equilibrium.[2]

It would run counter to the spirit of Smith's historical enterprise, within which there is an evolving relationship between property and power, to invoke anything as static and crudely interventionist as an agrarian law. The nearest

[1] *LJ*(B), p. 157.
[2] See e.g. *SMP* III.vi.245–6 and the remarks on the agrarian law cited on pp. 55–6 above.

equivalent might appear to be Smith's consistently hostile attitude towards large land holdings and such feudal remnants as the laws of primogeniture and entail which made them possible. For in this case Smith suggested that legislation might be in order to remove these surviving relics of an earlier stage of society.[1] But speculation on this is no longer necessary because the new lecture notes furnish us with an explicit statement of Smith's position on the Harringtonian issue of the agrarian law.

...though an agrarian law would render all on an equality, which has indeed something very agreeable in it, yet a people who are all on an equality will necessarily be very poor, and unable to defend themselves in any pressing occasion. They have nothing sound which can give them relief in time of need. But when goods are manufactured, a very small quantity of them will procure an immense one of another country...So that, in the present state of things, a man of great fortune is rather an advantage than of disadvantage to the state, providing that there is a gradual descent of fortunes betwixt these great ones and others of the least and lowest fortune. For it will be shown hereafter that one who leaps over the heads of all his countrymen is of real detriment to the community. This is not the case in England, where we have fortunes gradually descending from £40,000 to £200 or £300.[2]

Taken by itself, this statement may not seem particularly enlightening. Nevertheless, it contains a powerful hint of several ideas that had already been developed in Hume's essays on commerce and related matters, and were later to feature strongly in the *Wealth of Nations*. Smith's treatment of the relationship between commerce and liberty, and the changing forms which it takes as society improves in civilisation by moving from an agricultural to a commercial basis, is already quite well developed in the economic sections of the *Lectures*. Further comment on this theme, as well as some of the other topics first considered in the *Lectures*, will be reserved to the succeeding chapters of this essay. But one final observation seems in order. In dealing with police, revenue, and arms in the *Lectures*, Smith returns to some of the earlier historical material on law and government, particularly in

[1] See *LJ*(B), pp. 228–30 and its development in *WN* III.i.2–8.
[2] *LJ*(A), volume III, 67–8.

those parts concerned with 'the slow progress of opulence'. In so doing, as befits the subject matter, the four stages reappear in augmented form. It is here, for example, when speaking of the 'natural wants of mankind' that Smith gives what is perhaps his strongest statement of the importance of the economic factor to the history of civil society:

> The whole industry of human life is employed not in procuring the supply of our three humble necessities, food, clothes, and lodging, but in procuring the conveniences of it according to the nicety and delicacy of our taste. To improve and multiply the materials, which are the principal objects of our necessities, gives occasion to all the variety of the arts...Law and government, too, seems to propose no other object but this; they secure the individual who has enlarged his property, that he may peaceably enjoy the fruits of it. By law and government all the different arts flourish, and that inequality of fortune to which they give occasion is sufficiently preserved. By law and government domestic peace is enjoyed and security from the foreign invader. Wisdom and virtue too derive their lustre from supplying these necessities. For as the establishment of law and government is the highest effort of human prudence and wisdom, the causes cannot have a different influence from what the effects have. Besides, it is by the wisdom and probity of those with whom we live that a propriety of conduct is pointed out to us, and the proper means of attaining it. Their valour defends us, their benevolence supplies us, the hungry is fed, the naked is clothed, by the exertion of these divine qualities. Thus according to the above representation, all things are subservient to supplying our threefold necessities.[1]

This passage brings together several characteristic Smithian arguments, partly derived from the *Theory of Moral Sentiments* (the insatiable quest by men for conveniences in excess of basic needs, the social setting required for propriety, as well as the providential overtones), and partly foreshadowing the *Wealth of Nations* emphasis on the division of labour and 'the constant, uninterrupted desires on the part of every man to better his condition'. The set-piece on 'natural wants' does not appear in the same prominent introductory position in the *Wealth of Nations*, but it is possible to see in the passage quoted the justification for an enlarged inquiry into the economic basis

---

[1] *LJ*(B), pp. 160–1; *LJ*(A), volume VI, pp. 8–11.

of commercial or civilised society.[1] This part of the *Lectures*, more than the earlier parts on public and private jurisprudence, corresponds with John Millar's statement to the effect that Smith was concerned 'to point out the effects of those arts which contribute to subsistence, and to the accumulation of property, in producing correspondent improvement or alterations in law and government'. Although Millar thought that this was part of the unfinished book on jurisprudence, it would be hard to find a better description of the commerce and liberty theme dealt with in Book III and parts of Book V of the *Wealth of Nations*.

[1] It is an interesting sign of the effect of different approaches to Smith that the passage cited is particularly important to Ronald Meek because of its *economic* emphasis, whereas R. D. Cumming regards it as significant as the last moment when economic questions were given a *psychological* foundation. See R. L. Meek, *Social Science and the Ignoble Savage*, pp. 125–6, and R. D. Cumming, *Human Nature & History*, volume I, pp. 174–5.

4

Commerce, liberty and justice

The *Wealth of Nations* can be accurately, if not very fully, described as an extended treatise on the reciprocal relationship between commerce and liberty. Unfortunately, the success story which revolves around Smith as the founding father or evil genius of 'economic liberalism' has concentrated attention on one side of this relationship – the examination of the benefits of a regime of economic liberty for the growth and diffusion of commercial prosperity. Smith's interest in the other side of the relationship – the effect of the emergence of commercial society in producing a regime of liberty and justice – has suffered by contrast. 'Economic liberal' is essentially a nineteenth-century label, though one which most commentators have been happy to retain. It focusses attention on the role of the state in the economic affairs of individuals, but does not give due recognition to the historical framework of Smith's inquiry into the interrelationship of commerce and liberty. Nor does it adequately characterise the larger social and political dimensions of that inquiry. On both counts, therefore, it leads to neglect of one of Smith's main claims to have advanced the understanding of his contemporaries.

Smith was not, of course, alone in dealing with the commerce and liberty theme. Its early delineation by his predecessors, Montesquieu and Hume, forms one of the bases for their claim to speak decisively for the 'moderns' against the 'ancients' on this matter. The theme also appears as a *leitmotiv* in the writings of other Scottish historians of civil society, notably those of Lord Kames, Adam Ferguson, William Robertson, and John Millar. But while recognition of the pervasive changes in modern society generated by commerce constitutes a common bond among all these writers, they were by no means united on every aspect of their appraisal of its consequences. Thus Smith, in the course of giving more prominence to the subject, also introduced a number of significant changes of emphasis which entail a shift towards a more complex and qualified story than the one to be found in the pages of Montesquieu and Hume: it is certainly told with a detachment which frequently borders on cynicism. Some of Smith's qualifications and reservations were shared by Kames, Ferguson, and Millar; they comprise an attitude which has been described as one of 'historical pessimism', though 'historical realism' might be more appropriate. In either case it constitutes a major modification to the older portrait of these writers, and of Smith in particular, as optimistic celebrants of social progress. At a later point in this chapter and its successor it will be necessary to provide an interpretation of Smith's 'pessimism' or 'realism', and to take issue with some of the secondary literature that has grown up around it in recent years.

The most natural approach to Smith's treatment of commerce and liberty is via the writings of Montesquieu and Hume. Montesquieu had discussed 'the spirit of commerce' at two points in *The Spirit of the Laws*, the first when dealing with the ancient trading republics, and the second when dealing with the subject at greater length in Books IX to XXII, where the first of these books contains a thinly-disguised commentary on England's political characteristics as a commercial and free nation. In the ancient case, he argued that 'when a democracy is founded on commerce, private people may acquire vast riches without a corruption of morals', because 'the spirit of commerce is naturally attended with that of frugality, economy, moderation, labour, prudence, tranquillity, order and rule'.[1] In the later books he attempted to explain the relationship of commerce to different forms of government, its effect in controlling 'the great and sudden arbitrary acts of the sovereign', and as 'the cure for the most destructive prejudices'. It was the source of 'agreeable

---

[1] C. S. Montesquieu, *The Spirit of the Laws*, Hafner edition, p. 46.

manners' and a major influence acting in favour of peace between nations.[1]

While there were many fertile hints in Montesquieu, it was to Hume's political essays and historical writings that Smith gave generous credit when he wrote his account of 'how the commerce of the towns contributed to the improvement of the country'. Hume was, Smith said, 'the only writer who, so far as I know, has hitherto taken notice of' the way in which 'commerce and manufactures gradually introduced order and good government, and with them, the liberty and security of individuals, who had before lived almost in a continual state of war with their neighbours, and of servile dependency upon their superiors'.[2] It has been pointed out that by the time the *Wealth of Nations* was published in 1776, it would have been possible for Smith to cite a number of authors, mostly Scottish, who had dealt with the commerce and liberty theme at length. Since he had lectured on this subject as early as the 1750s, this apparent lack of generosity could be attributed to his claims to priority over most of his fellow Scottish historians.[3]

Although the establishment of claims to priority is not the main concern of this essay, it also seems worth recording, if only in passing, that the eighteenth-century interest in the wider gains and losses associated with commerce was by no means confined to the philosophers and historians mentioned so far. Quite apart from the political arguments advanced by various authors in the mercantile tradition, and by Sir James Steuart in his *Principles of Political Oeconomy* in 1767, all the leading representatives of the Augustan literati – Addison, Swift, Pope, and Johnson – had written extensively on the connections between commerce, luxury, and modern 'civilised' or 'polished' society, laying particular stress on the compatibility of the new economic pursuits with ancient conceptions of private and public virtue. Although much of this literature belongs to an earlier period and phase of the discussion, it seems worth mentioning here in view of the

[1] *Ibid.*, see especially pp. 316–19, 364–6. For an excellent account of Montesquieu's role in formulating and transmitting these ideas see A. O. Hirschman, *The Passions and the Interests* (1977), pp. 70–81.
[2] *WN* III.iv.4.
[3] See the editorial note attached to the previous reference.

continuing importance of the concept of virtue and Smith's familiarity with the Augustan literature. His knowledge of, and general sympathy with the neo-classical tastes and standards of these authors is abundantly clear from the evidence provided by the notes on his *Lectures on Belles Lettres and Rhetoric*. We also know that he was well acquainted with the most infamous of the Augustan attempts to explode both the jeremiads on loss of virtue and the genteel apologetics for commerce penned by Addison and Steele, namely Bernard de Mandeville's *Fable of the Bees*. A more comprehensive eighteenth-century reading of Smith would certainly have to encompass this body of earlier writing.[1]

Hume's political essays include several that are of considerable importance to historians of economic thought, who have tended to search them for evidence of Hume's originality as an economic theorist and his credentials as an economic liberal in the nineteenth-century sense of the term. The latter task generally entails emphasising those ideas which reveal where Hume rejected, or failed to reject, characteristic mercantile 'errors' with regard to the wisdom of state intervention in economic affairs. Two of the economic essays, 'Of Commerce' and 'Of Luxury', can, however, be grouped with 'Of the Rise and Progress of the Arts and Sciences' and 'Of Civil Liberty' to form a sequence of arguments on the political theme of commerce and liberty. They support Forbes's conclusion that 'it is an unquestioned assumption of Hume's social and poli-

---

[1] The paragraph that precedes this note is highly compressed, and I will simply list some of the secondary works that have been most useful to me in appreciating the writers and groups mentioned. On the politics of mercantilism see M. Kammen, *Empire and Interest*, 1970. On Steuart see A. Skinner's introduction to the Scottish Economic Classics edition of the *Principles*. On Addison see E. A. Bloom and L. D. Bloom, *Joseph Addison's Sociable Animal* (1971). On Johnson see J. H. Middendorf 'Johnson on Wealth and Commerce' in *Johnson, Boswell and their Circle* (1965), pp. 49–64. On Pope and Swift see I. Kramnick, *Bolingbroke and His Circle* (1968), chapter 8. On Pope in particular see H. Erskine-Hill, *The Social Milieu of Alexander Pope* (1975). On Mandeville see two papers by M. M. Goldsmith, 'Mandeville and the Spirit of Capitalism', in *Political Economy and Political Theory*, ed. C. B. Macpherson (mimeographed, Conference for the Study of Political Thought in Toronto, 1974); and 'Public Virtue and Private Vices: Bernard Mandeville and English Political Ideologies in the Early Eighteenth Century', *Eighteenth-Century Studies*, IX (1976), 477–510.

tical theory that the good life is dependent on economic progress'; and his contention that they show Hume 'at his least sceptical'.[1] Indeed, the emphasis on economic progress forms an essential part of Hume's campaign against the backward-looking cast of much contemporary political theory.

Hume's language and mode of conducting his argument in these essays can also be described in terms of the civic humanist perspective discussed in Chapter 2. The essays revolve around a comparison between the practices of ancient and modern states, with their respective attitudes to commerce and luxury being treated as the touchstone. Since ancient practice is, of course, that of the ancient republics, the comparison largely involves consideration of the differences between these republics and modern monarchies. Hume is inquiring into the compatibility of commerce and luxury with the maintenance of stability, power and independence – and he opens 'Of Commerce' with a statement of the 'modern' position on this matter. 'In general', he says,

> The greatness of a state, and the happiness of its subjects, how independent soever they may be supposed in some respects, are commonly allowed to be inseparable with regard to commerce; and as private men receive greater security, in the possession of their trade and riches, from the power of the public, so the public becomes powerful in proportion to the opulence and extensive commerce of private men.[2]

Commerce and manufactures increase the resources available both for private consumption and to meet the expenses of the sovereign, though the two uses are always in competition with one another. The policy of the ancient republics, and notably of Sparta, in curbing commerce and private luxury was 'violent and contrary to the more natural and usual course of things'. In the absence of manufactures the bulk of the people are employed in agriculture, and will become slothful and barbaric for lack of the incentives and opportunities with which to satisfy their natural demands for pleasure and vanity. The populace of a nation in which manufactures and the

[1] D. Forbes, *Hume's Philosophical Politics*, p. 87.
[2] D. Hume, *Essays, Moral, Political and Literary*, eds. T. H. Green and T. H. Grose, volume I, pp. 288–9.

mechanical arts are cultivated becomes lively and skilful, capable of meeting additional taxation from its superfluities, and of supplying manpower to the state in time of war. Innocent luxury is not incompatible with virtue; rather it may be a condition for its realisation. Wherever industry and the arts flourish there is scope for vigour and the enlargement of the human faculties, intellectual and social, as well as mechanical. Mildness of temper and moderation are encouraged, but this does not undermine the martial spirit: contrary to ancient belief, men become more able and willing to defend their country and their own liberties. The peasantry become independent of their feudal landlords, and a new middling rank is recruited from the tradesmen and merchants, jealous of liberty, and with less disposition to submit to the authority of tyrants, whether monarchical or aristocratic. Commerce, therefore, helps to maintain free governments, just as – in common with the arts and sciences – it is more likely to thrive under free rather than absolute governments.

The sequence is by now a familiar one. Parts of it can be found in Montesquieu, and we have already noted the similarity between Hume's position and that adopted by Smith in his *Lectures* when speaking about the redundancy of agrarian laws.[1] The only point of giving a brief summary here is to draw attention to the nature of the questions being addressed, and to the way in which the modern monarchy/ancient republic dualism provides a structure for the argument. A form of political rhetoric is being employed, though this does not mean that the questions are purely rhetorical. Hume only says that the sequence is true 'in general'. There may be circumstances in which commerce and luxury 'instead of adding strength to the public, will serve only to thin its armies, and diminish its authority among the neighbouring nations'.[2] The ancient policies, though violent, 'may *sometimes* have no other effect than to render the public more powerful'.[3] Luxury can be vicious and debilitating, though it is generally to be favoured over sloth and idleness.[4]

[1] See p. 67 above.
[2] D. Hume, *Essays*, volume I, p. 289.
[3] *Ibid.*, p. 292 (italics in original).   [4] *Ibid.*, p. 309.

Moreover, it is possible for such inequality to arise in commercial states that the rich 'enjoy all the power, and will readily conspire to lay the whole burthen on the poor'.[1] There was in addition one major feature of commercial society in Britain that troubled Hume deeply, namely the growth of the National Debt – a subject which will be taken up in detail later.[2]

In the account of 'the progress of opulence' given in Book III of the *Wealth of Nations*, Smith expanded on his treatment of the same theme under 'Police' in the *Lectures on Jurisprudence*. This involved concentrating on the emergence of commercial society from the later feudal period of the agricultural phase of social development. The earlier material in the *Lectures* considered in the previous chapter – especially those parts dealing with hunters, shepherds, the rise and fall of the ancient republics, and the emergence of the English Parliament and court system – was not used as part of a single narrative, though the hunters and shepherds, and some of the material on English courts, reappear in Book v when dealing with justice and arms.[3] Republics of a kind, however, emerge as the cities and towns within feudal kingdoms: hence even if the story of the journey *from* republics to monarchies disappears, republics *within* monarchies remain and have an important part to play. For it is in the towns that commerce and manufacturing flourish, and the story of political and economic liberty is made to turn on the evolving relationship between town and country, with the sovereign increasingly to be found in alliance with town-dwellers against the feudal landowners. Although the military theme is no longer as prominent as it was in the *Lectures*, the ability of cities to become 'a sort of independent republics', to maintain discipline, and to form effective militias is still important to their capacity to remain independent and collaborate with the king against his lords. It should also be noticed that the development of the towns beyond 'what the improvement and cultivation of the territory in which they were situated could

[1] *Ibid.*, p. 297.   [2] See pp. 124–8.
[3] For a detailed account of the relationship between *LJ*(A), *LJ*(B), and *WN* see the editorial notes to *WN*, especially III.II.i.

support' was attributed to 'human institutions'. If the countryside had not been badly governed, and if the towns had not been granted special privileges by the Crown, the 'natural order of things' would have led to improvement in agriculture *before* the development of foreign commerce and manufacture for distant sale. In other words, political factors had taken precedence over natural economic forces.[1]

Prior to the rise (or rather recovery) of the towns – that is, after the fall of Rome but before the introduction of commerce and manufacturing – the allodial, and subsequently feudal, lords controlled large tracts of land. Having few opportunities to spend their incomes on goods, the bulk of their surplus is devoted to the maintenance of dependants. By necessity and inclination these large landowners engage in warfare rather than agricultural improvements; and the powers which they exercise over their dependants give little incentive to villains or tenants-at-will to carry out improvements.[2] The dependants are, in fact, only slightly better off than under complete slavery, an institution based on a psychological disposition in man, namely his 'love to domineer' when provided with opportunities to do so.[3]

Initially at least, the inhabitants of the towns are also subject to the harassment and exactions of the masters of the surrounding countryside. They achieve a measure of autonomy and liberty by being granted various corporate privileges by the monarch in return for financial and military support against the barons. Once 'order and good government' are established in the towns, the security which this affords encourages the accumulation of capital and more ambitious economic activities, especially in those towns with easy access to foreign markets and sources of raw material.[4] Manufacturing either begins on an imitative basis, having been stimulated by foreign commerce, or in order to capitalise on the existence of a domestic raw material.

Once established, commerce and manufacturing provide an expanding market for the produce of the country, while at the same time mercantile wealth looks for profitable investment

[1] See *WN* III.3.9.   [2] *WN* III.ii.8–20.
[3] *WN* III.ii.10.   [4] *WN* III.iii.13.

outlets through the ownership and improvement of land.[1] But the 'revolution of the greatest importance to public happiness' chiefly occurs as a result of the new opportunities furnished by commerce and manufacturing for landowners to expend their surpluses on alternatives to 'rustick hospitality' and the maintenance of large bodies of retainers. They also acquire an incentive to increase the size of their surpluses, and to this end are prepared to alter the system of land tenure by granting greater security to their tenants. By so doing the feudal barons exchange their military and judicial powers for luxury, thereby undermining their own standing in relation both to their dependants and the monarch.

The tenants having in this manner become independent, and the retainers being dismissed, the proprietors were no longer capable of interrupting the regular execution of justice, or of disturbing the peace of the country. Having sold their birth-right, not like Esau for a mess of pottage in time of hunger and necessity, but in the wantonness of plenty, for trinkets and baubles, fitter to be the play-things of children than the serious pursuits of men, they became as insignificant as any substantial burgher or tradesman in a city. A regular government was established in the country as well as in the city, nobody having sufficient power to disturb its operations in the one, any more than in the other.[2]

The revolution wrought by commerce was an unintended consequence of the pursuit of vanity by the barons coupled with the cupidity of merchants. It is favourable to liberty because it destroys a source of arbitrary power and a parti-cularly degrading form of dependence. The new tenant far-mers and merchants and artificers have a purely market relationship to their social superiors, and Smith emphasises the difference between this form of 'dependence' and the older, more oppressive, type of subordination.

In the present state of Europe, a man of ten thousand a year can spend his whole revenue, and he generally does so, without directly maintaining twenty people, or being able to command more than ten footmen not worth the commanding. Indirectly, perhaps, he maintains as great or even a greater number of people than he could have done by the ancient method of expence. For though the quantity of precious productions for which he exchanges his great revenue

---

[1] *WN* III.iv.1–3.   [2] *WN* III.iv.15; see also 10.

by very small, the number of workmen employed in collecting and preparing it, must necessarily have been very great. Its great price generally arises from the wages of their labour, and the profits of all their immediate employers. By paying that price he indirectly pays all those wages and profits, and thus indirectly contributes to the maintenance of all the workmen and their employers. He generally contributes, however, but a very small proportion to that of each. Though he contributes, therefore, to the maintenance of them all, they are all more or less independent of him, because generally they can all be maintained without him.[1]

This distinction is closely related to the one made in the *Theory of Moral Sentiments* and repeated in the *Lectures*, namely between a natural or psychologically-based habit of deference, and the cruder, more utilitarian, notion of economic dependence.

Our obsequiousness to our superiors more frequently arises from our admiration for the advantages of their situation, than from any private expectations of benefit from their goodwill. Their benefits can extend but to a few but their fortunes interest almost everybody.[2]

Although independence is only one aspect of the new relationships which come into being in commercial societies, Smith gives it a crucial place in determining the improvement in manners: 'Nothing tends so much to corrupt mankind as dependency, while independency still increases the honesty of the people.'[3] Hence the greater prevalence of crime in court and other non-commercial cities, where the bulk of the population are employed as retainers and menial servants.[4] The fact that Smith also regards probity and punctuality as qualities associated with commercial nations brings us back to Montesquieu's list of benefits connected with the spirit of commerce. But in Smith's case the benefits go well beyond *mœurs* and *manières*, however widely interpreted, because the new set of social relationships is linked with economic progress through

[1] *WN* III.iv.11; see also v.i.b.7.
[2] *TMS* I.iii.2.3. In *LJ*(B) the same idea is expressed when speaking of wealth as a title to authority: 'This proceeds not from any dependence that the poor may have upon the rich, for in general the poor are independent, and support themselves by their labour, yet, though they expect to benefit from them, they have a strong propensity to pay them respect.' (p. 9.)
[3] *LJ*(B) p. 155; see also *LJ*(A) volume VI, pp. 2–4.
[4] *WN* II.iii.12.

the crucial doctrine contained in the distinction between productive and unproductive labour, which is expounded at length in Book II on the accumulation of capital. The proportion of the total work-force employed 'productively' is one of two main determinants of the rate of economic growth, the other being the extent of the division of labour; it also 'determines in every country the general character of the inhabitants as to industry or idleness'.[1]

At this point, therefore, we make decisive contact with the better-known economic themes of the *Wealth of Nations* – with the 'frugality and good conduct' which is an essential background to the restless 'desire of bettering our condition', the keynote of the 'economic' chapters. Commercial society is not merely one in which more people are engaged in producing capital goods, though this may be one of its concomitants; it is one in which more people are drawn into the wider circle of commercial relationships. It is the situation arrived at once the division of labour has been thoroughly established, and men can supply only a small part of their needs from their own produce. It is that form of society in which 'every man...lives by exchanging, or becomes in some measure a merchant'.[2]

It is precisely at this point too that we encounter the full complexity of Smith's treatment of the relationship between commerce and liberty, between economic progress and its moral and political consequences for society. For not only does Smith's account of the emergence of commercial society have a strong flavour of Mandevillian cynicism about it, with its stress on the unintended public benefits derived from blind selfishness, but the new form of society is marked by several major defects of a moral and civic character. The revolution associated with commerce and manufacturing eliminates certain gross forms of dependency and domination, but it does not abolish oppression and social conflict. On the contrary, in some crucial respects it widens the scope for contest and envy, and creates new arenas and forms of conflict between individuals, between the different orders of society, and be-

[1] *WN* II.iii.12. [2] *WN* I.iv.1.

tween private and public interests. Moreover, it is well known that Smith treated the harbingers of commercial society, the merchant and manufacturing classes, with considerable reserve, especially as regards their collective capacity to combine against the public interest.

These summary statements will only be surprising to those who still subscribe to the myth that Smith is an economic determinist of an optimistic disposition, believing in Progress and preaching a simple doctrine of the harmony of egoisms through *laissez-faire* market behaviour. While most serious commentators now regard this as a myth, there is still scope for considerable disagreement as to the importance of Smith's 'reservations', and as to the way in which the Smithian 'paradoxes' should be resolved or clarified. In what follows I shall criticise some of the ways in which these paradoxes have been posed, while at the same time attempting an exposition and interpretation of my own. But there is one basic fallacy that needs to be disposed of at the outset. It is essential to distinguish between Smith's views on the general attributes of *commercial* societies and their associated defects, and his criticisms of the effects of the 'mercantile' system and the specific abuses connected with the 'monopolizing spirit'. There are occasions on which Smith uses the words 'commercial' and 'mercantile' interchangeably, but this should not be allowed to obscure the fact that under a 'system of natural liberty' – the antithesis of the mercantile system – the usual results of commerce remained 'mutual communication of knowledge and all sorts of improvements', and 'among nations, as among individuals, a bond of union and friendship'.[1]

The optimistic qualities of Hume's account of the relationship between commerce and liberty have already been noted: there are virtually no flaws in it – unless the controversial essay on public credit is brought into the reckoning, and a few disgruntled remarks about the overgrowth of cities like London are inflated. By contrast, Smith, in his earliest treatment of the relationship in the *Lectures*, draws special attention to various 'inconveniences' and 'disadvantages' associated with the commercial spirit. In brief summary these

---

[1] *WN* IV.iii.c.9.

were that: 'The minds of men are contracted and rendered incapable of elevation. Education is despised, or at least neglected, and heroic spirit is almost utterly extinguished'.[1] The evidence of the *Lectures* is sufficient to dispose of the view that these ideas were an after-thought, though the fact that the equivalent passages in the *Wealth of Nations* appear in Book v, whereas the treatment of the advantages derived from the division of labour appears in Book I, has brought forth a sizeable literature seeking to reconcile the 'contradictions', 'conflict', or 'tension' between the two books. By a premonitory association with Marx, which has become more compelling since the rediscovery of the 'humanist' Marx of the early philosophical manuscripts, this literature appears under the headline of 'alienation'. Indeed, it has become one of the newest ways of transposing Smith into a nineteenth- or twentieth-century setting. I shall later argue that 'alienation' is not the most appropriate term or concept – unless, of course, one is interested in influences on, or hints of, Marx. It is not only more faithful to Smith's language but to his intentions as well to retain the generic eighteenth-century term used to describe such phenomena, namely 'corruption'. But whatever code word is used, there is no doubt that Smith's argument deserves serious attention, especially in view of the fact that it also features in the writings of other Scottish historians of civil society.[2]

Whereas Hume associated the 'quick march of the spirits' with commerce and manufacturing, according to Smith 'the employment of the far greater part of those who live by labour' on simple tasks reduces their capacity for invention and renders them

> ...as stupid, and ignorant as it is possible for a human creature to become. The torpor of his mind renders him, not only incapable of relishing or bearing a part in any rational conversation, but of conceiving any generous, noble, or tender sentiment, and conse-

---

[1] *LJ*(B), pp. 255–9, 261.
[2] See e.g. Lord Kames, *Sketches of the History of Man*, 1774, volume I, pp. 112–15, 396–416; volume II, pp. 109–51, 289–311, 326–40; volume III, pp. 116–33; A. Ferguson, *An Essay on the History of Civil Society*, ed. D. Forbes, IV.i. pp. 182–3. J. Millar, *Historical View of English Government*, 1812 edition, volume IV, pp. 144–56.

quently of forming any just judgement concerning many even of the ordinary duties of private life. Of the great and extensive interests of his country he is altogether incapable of judging; and unless very particular pains have been taken to render him otherwise, he is equally incapable of defending his country in war. The uniformity of his stationary life naturally corrupts the course of his mind, and makes him regard with abhorrence the irregular, uncertain, and adventurous life of a soldier. It corrupts even the activity of his body, and renders him incapable of exerting his strength with vigour and perseverance, in any other employment than that to which he has been bred. His dexterity at his own particular trade seems, in this manner, to be acquired at the expence of his intellectual, social, and martial virtues. But in every improved and civilized society this is the stage into which the labouring poor, that is, the great body of the people, must necessarily fall, unless government takes some pains to prevent it.[1]

There can surely be no question of glossing over such a set of charges; it represents a major flaw in commercial or civilised society, undermining many of those virtues and mechanisms of 'sympathy' which Smith had maintained in the *Theory of Moral Sentiments* were essential to social harmony and benificence. The only question which seems to require attention is how, if at all, the charges can be reconciled with what Smith says elsewhere in making the division of labour one of the prime sources of economic progress. But this requires an answer to a prior question, namely within what kind of context should the problem and its solution be posed? Thus by concentrating on one central economic aspect of the problem – 'the determinants of inventive capacity' – Nathan Rosenberg has successfully demonstrated that there is no conflict between Books I and V. Smith's position allows for an improvement in the *collective* intelligence of society, and hence continued capacity for technical improvement, even though the individual capacities of workers may undergo deterioration.[2]

Others, following a broader approach, largely dictated by the pursuit of Marx's concept of alienation, have attempted to link the crucial passage in Book V with Smith's earlier

---

[1] *WN* v.i.f.50.
[2] See N. Rosenberg, 'Adam Smith on the Division of Labour: Two Views or One?', *Economica*, XXXII (1965), 127–39; see also S. Hollander, *The Economics of Adam Smith* (1973), pp. 215, 266.

observations on what they regard as 'class conflict' and 'his exploitation theories of wages, profits, and rent'. By such methods it is possible to arrive at a composite picture of Smith as Marx's anticipator on almost every aspect of 'alienation'. Smith's 'modern factory workers' and 'detail factory labourers' were not merely 'self-estranged', but powerless and isolated to boot.[1] Alternatively, by attempting to relate alienation to a Ricardianised version of Smith's concept of the stationary state, an equally gloomy but far less radical portrait of Smith's predictions for the future of capitalism emerges – one that can be safely condemned by twentieth-century standards as 'hobbled by a class-bound social vision'.[2]

One of the great virtues of Joseph Cropsey's *Polity and Economy: An Interpretation of the Principles of Adam Smith* was its early and wholehearted recognition of the problem posed by Smith's condemnation of certain aspects of commercial society, and its attempt to relate economy and polity in Smith's writings in the light of this fact. Cropsey took the tough-minded view that Smith not only found commerce an inadequate substitute for virtue, but could suggest no adequate remedies to compensate for the losses entailed. Nevertheless, it was still justifiable to regard Smith as a determined advocate of capitalism because he endorsed it as the only system capable of ushering in a secular and free form of society. Since 'commerce generates freedom and civilisation', it must be embraced in spite of its defects.[3]

Cropsey's position has deservedly been an influential one,

---

[1] See R. Lamb, 'Adam Smith's Concept of Alienation', *Oxford Economic Papers*, XXV (1973), 275–85. With a little more ingenuity it should soon be possible to demonstrate that Smith's workers also suffered from 'normlessness' and 'meaninglessness', thereby completing the Marxian hand of cards as depicted, for example, by M. Seeman, 'On the Meaning of Alienation', *American Sociological Review*, XXIV (1959), 783–91. Lamb's article is largely in the form of a reply to one by E. G. West which minimizes the Marxian anticipations; see E. G. West, 'The Political Economy of Alienation, Karl Marx and Adam Smith', *Oxford Economic Papers*, XXI (1969), 1–23; see also West's earlier article 'Adam Smith's Two Views of the Division of Labour', *Economica*, XXXI (1964), 23–32. For his most recent views on the subject see 'Adam Smith and Alienation' in *EAS*, pp. 540–52.

[2] See R. L. Heilbroner, 'The Paradox of Progress: Decline and Decay in the *Wealth of Nations*' in *EAS*, pp. 524–52.

[3] J. Cropsey, *Polity and Economy*, p. 95.

though it has recently been challenged on substantial as well as insubstantial grounds. Taking the latter first, Cropsey's concept of 'freedom' has been contested on the basis of Smith's remarks about the lower orders' 'incapacity for self government'. If this is the case: 'These are surely weak soldiers to whom to entrust the defense of liberty. Yet unless liberty is to be protected by the labouring man himself, it will be nothing more than a cloak for exploitation.'[1] It should first be noted that in the relevant passage on the lower orders there is no mention of 'self-government'. What Smith actually says is that 'though the interest of the labourer is strictly connected with that of the society, he is incapable either of comprehending that interest, or of understanding its connexion with his own'.[2] As both earlier and later references to the same subject make clear, Smith's point is that the common people, though 'jealous of their liberty', do not appreciate correctly 'wherein it consists'.[3] Cropsey does not in fact shirk this evidence on lack of understanding, nor does his argument require liberty to be entrusted to these 'weak soldiers'. But it is easy to see how an interpretation of Smith's intentions which presumes a largely post-eighteenth-century conception of political freedom seems open to a blatantly twentieth-century response based on the notion that liberty must be equated with participatory democracy. At any moment, one feels, the argument is about to turn into a discussion of universal suffrage – an issue which was not even academic for Smith.

Cropsey's position is not only proof against such feeble challenges but has the additional quality, lacking in several recent interpretations of Smith's 'contradictions', that it does not have recourse to such supposititious dualisms as the following: between 'Smith's conflicting positive and normative economic theories'; between 'an abstract theory of capitalism' and a 'socialist criticism of existing society';[4] between Smith as the objective economist, and Smith as subjective sociologist

---

[1] R. L. Heilbroner, 'The Paradox of Progress...', *EAS*, p. 535.
[2] *WN* I.xi.p. 9.   [3] *WN* I.x.c.59 and v.i.f.50–3.
[4] See R. Lamb, 'Adam Smith's Concept of Alienation', *Oxford Economic Papers*, xxv (1973), 279–80; see also the same author's 'Adam Smith's System: Sympathy not Self-Interest', *Journal of the History of Ideas*, xxxv (1974), 671–82.

who regrettably allowed his feelings to lead him 'to overstate his case against the factory system so wildly as to contradict the more objective findings of the economic analysis of the division of labour'.[1] If any of these dualisms fail it is always possible to fall back on the tautologous idea that the whole business is 'no more than a contemporary and perhaps modish piece of authorship'.[2]

Much of the coherence of Cropsey's interpretation derives from its fundamental assumption that the issue must be placed within the context of the liberal capitalist perspective described earlier. Duncan Forbes's historical approach enables him to lay the groundwork for a more substantial criticism of this position. By emphasising Smith's concern with the degree of civilisation attained, rather than with forms of government, and by drawing attention to the justiciary qualities of Hume and Smith's interest in liberty, rather than the narrower question of political liberty or 'free governments', Forbes demonstrates the cosmopolitan nature of their concern with the theme of commerce and liberty. Furthermore – and this is more crucial – he is able to show that Smith did *not* maintain that there was a *necessary* connection between economic progress and freedom. The singular characteristics of English history cannot be described as a law deducible from Smith's science of politics: 'One cannot have freedom without commerce and manufactures, but opulence without freedom is the norm rather than the exception.'[3]

Another way forward, carrying us beyond the categories imposed by the liberal capitalist perspective and its Whiggish tendency to search for clues as to what later opponents or defenders of liberal capitalism and Marxian socialism have considered relevant, has been provided by John Pocock's work on the eighteenth-century career of civic humanism. In addition to showing just how the civic humanist tradition survived and continued to inform political debate in the eighteenth century, he has suggested that in spite of the pro-

[1] See E. G. West, 'Adam Smith's Two Views of the Division of Labour', *Economica*, XXXI (1964), 32.
[2] This is one of the alternatives proposed by E. G. West in 'Adam Smith and Alienation', *EAS*, p. 550.
[3] D. Forbes, 'Sceptical Whiggism, Commerce, and Liberty', in *EAS*, p. 201.

gressive economic assumptions subscribed to by the Scottish historians of civil society, there is still an important sense in which they employed the Machiavellian language of virtue and corruption to describe the dangers to moral identity and citizenship posed by the advance of commercial society.[1] My acceptance of this fertile suggestion may be clear already, but in order to examine its implications for a reading of Smith's politics, Smith's method of analysing political problems will have to be considered in more detail. This will be undertaken in the next three chapters, but first it is necessary to give a fuller account of Smith's balance sheet of progress by taking note of his views on inequality and justice.

When viewed in long historical perspective, and under favourable circumstances, commerce may be productive of liberty, bearing in mind Forbes's explication of what liberty meant to Hume and Smith. It may also generate private and public opulence and be accompanied by improved standards of honesty, punctuality, and probity. But these benefits do not, in themselves, make commercial society a harmonious or a just society.

According to the account of the division of labour given in the *Lectures*, in an early draft of the *Wealth of Nations*, and in the book itself, the advance of civilisation goes hand in hand with an improvement in the standard of material comfort enjoyed by the labouring classes, who comprise the bulk of society. Smith explicitly stated that such standards, and not merely rising *per capita* incomes, were the most appropriate measure of economic welfare.[2] He also defended the 'liberal reward of labour' as one of the best methods of increasing productivity; and he showed that improvement in the economic condition of the 'greater part of every political society'

---

[1] J. G. A. Pocock, *Politics, Language and Time*, pp. 101–3, 146; and *The Machiavellian Moment*, pp. 498–504.

[2] '...what improves the circumstances of the greater part [of political society] can never be regarded as an inconveniency to the whole. No society can surely be flourishing and happy, of which the far greater part of the members are poor and miserable. It is but equity, besides, that they who feed, cloath and lodge the whole body of the people, should have such a share of the produce of their own labour as to be themselves tolerably well fed, cloathed and lodged.' *WN* I.viii.36.

was most likely to be achieved in 'progressive' commercial states. That Smith held these views is not a matter of dispute.[1] The difficulties of interpretation arise when other factors are brought into the reckoning, namely Smith's recognition (sometimes amounting to insistence) that neither the tasks nor the benefits are divided equitably in civilised societies, and his portrayal of a large number of instances in which conflict and injustice appear to be the order of the day.[2]

Smith appears to have been intrigued by, and hence may have set out to emphasise, the paradoxes associated with commercial progress. In the *Lectures*, for example, the initial account of the economic benefits of the division of labour is followed immediately by a reminder that 'he who...bears the burden of society, has the fewest advantages'.[3] The early draft of the *Wealth of Nations* was a good deal more explicit on this subject:

In a Civilized Society the poor provide both for themselves and for the enormous luxury of their Superiors. The rent, which goes to support the vanity of the slothful Landlord, is all earned by the industry of the peasant. The monied man indulges himself in every sort of ignoble and sordid sensuality, at the expence of the merchant and the Tradesman, to whom he lends out his stock at interest. All the indolent and frivolous retainers upon a Court, are, in the same manner, fed and clothed and lodged by the labour of those who pay the taxes which support them...with regard to the produce of the labour of a great Society there is never any such thing as a fair and equal division. In a Society of an hundred thousand families, there will perhaps be one hundred who don't labour at all, and yet, either by violence, or by the orderly oppression of law, employ a greater part of the labour of the society than any other ten thousand in it. The

[1] See e.g. A. W. Coats, 'Changing Attitudes to Labour in the Mid-Eighteenth Century', *Economic History Review*, II (1958), 35–51; and S. Hollander, *The Economics of Adam Smith*, chapter 8; and P. J. McNulty, 'Adam Smith's Concept of Labour', *Journal of History of Ideas*, XXXIV (1973), 345–66.

[2] As far as conflict is concerned see the comprehensive list of instances compiled by J. Viner in 'Adam Smith and *Laissez–Faire*' as reprinted in his *Long View and the Short*, pp. 228–30.

[3] *LJ*(B) pp. 162–3. Later on there is a cryptic comment along the same lines: 'They who are strongest and, in the bustle of society, have got above the weak, must have as many under as to defend them in their station. From necessary causes, therefore, there must be as many in the lower stations as there is occasion for, there must be as many up as down, and no division can be overstretched.' (*Ibid.*, pp. 167–8.)

division of what remains after this enormous defalcation, is by no means made in proportion to the labour of each individual. On the contrary those who labour most get least.[1]

This was clearly a well-rehearsed set-piece, leading up to the following question: 'In the midst of so much oppressive inequality in what manner shall we account for the superior affluence and abundance commonly possessed even by this lowest and most despised member of Civilized Society, compared with what the most respected and active savage can attain to'. The answer was that 'so great a quantity of everything is produced, that there is enough both to gratify the slothful and oppressive profusion of the great, and at the same time abundantly to supply the wants of the artisan and the peasant'. The surprising thing about this set-piece is that it does not appear in the *Wealth of Nations*, and we are left to speculate why these passages should have been left out, while the substance of the answer was included. Mandevillian cynicism seems to be the source of the stylistic extravagance; and it may be that Smith realised he was overplaying his hand. Nevertheless, there are still enough pejorative statements in the *Wealth of Nations* – drawing attention to oppression, the idle rich, cupidity, conflict, and the widespread propensity to dominate or deceive – to suggest that the answer given with respect to the division of labour should not be allowed to diminish the force of the question posed in the early draft.

It is reasonable to suppose that those who are inclined to see the glimmerings of an exploitation theory in Smith's treatment of wages, profits, and rent, and in the labour theory of value, would have regarded their license as having been extended if the earlier passages had been incorporated into the final text. Both in the *Lectures* and in the early draft, Smith underlined the contrast created by the division of labour by stating that in savage states 'every one enjoys the whole fruit of his own labour'. Extra force can be given to this statement by invoking the dictum that: 'The property which every man has in his labour, as it is the original foundation of all other property, so it is the most sacred and inviolable.' While, for reasons given earlier, it does not seem correct to interpret this

[1] As reprinted in W. R. Scott, *Adam Smith as Student and Professor*, pp. 326–8.

dictum as evidence of Smith's acceptance of Locke's labour theory of the *origins* of property, it does contain echoes of the labour theory of value in one or other of its much-disputed forms. Without becoming embroiled in disputes as to whether, and in what sense, Smith can be regarded as a 'true' labour theorist, it must be pointed out that all simple interpretations of Smith as an upholder of a labour theory of the *causes* (as opposed to *measure*) of value have to overcome the inconvenient fact that he disposed of the subject in a couple of pages. Moreover, rightly or wrongly, he expressly limited the application of the theory 'to that early and rude state of society which precedes both the accumulation of stock and an appropriation of land'.[1] Steering clear of the open-ended question of whether Smith might or might not be said to have 'foreshadowed' later theories of exploitation, it would seem abundantly obvious that such a theory did not form part of his intentions. The entire object of the omitted passages was to show that the gains derived from civilisation and the division of labour are achieved *in spite of* the existence of injustice.

More interesting problems of interpretation are posed by Smith's views on the distinction of ranks, and by the slighting references to material enjoyments, and hence to inequalities in the means of acquiring them, which are to be found in the pages of the *Theory of Moral Sentiments*. Smith not only depicted the distinction of ranks as an essential feature of well-ordered societies, but regarded wealth, particularly of the established variety, as one of the strongest claims to deference and authority, despite his later recognition that such claims were based

---

[1] *WN* I.vi.i. One of the earliest suggestions that Smith's theory of value 'almost inevitably gave rise to the doctrines of the post-Ricardian socialists and to the labour theory of value and the exploitation theory of Karl Marx' was made by P. H. Douglas, 'Smith's Theory of Value and Distribution' in J. M. Clark *et al.*, *Adam Smith, 1776–1926* (1928), p. 77. J. A. Schumpeter also maintained that while Smith did not uphold an exploitation theory, he 'foreshadowed' all the nineteenth-century versions; see J. A. Schumpeter, *History of Economic Analysis* (1954), pp. 111, 190–1, 264–5, 331–4. R. Lamb, 'Adam Smith's Concept of Alienation', *Oxford Economic Papers*, XXV (1973), 279, simply assembles these references to Schumpeter, without further argument, to show that Smith held an 'exploitation theory of wages, profits, and rent'. For a recent exposition of what positions Smith did in fact hold on all these matters see M. Bowley, *Studies in the History of Economic Theory before 1870* (1973), pp. 120–1, 183–206.

on a corruption of men's sentiments. We have also noted his views on agrarian laws and on the usefulness of graded inequality given in the *Lectures*.[1] One answer to the problems posed by these opinions has been mentioned already when pointing out that deference to authority and economic dependence belong to separable (if not always separate) realms, with a 'natural' or social psychological basis being given to the former, while the latter is considered in terms of the moral and social consequences of particular historic forms of economic relationship. The great advantage of commercial over feudal society, for example, was that direct political power of an arbitrary or personal kind was no longer the *necessary* concomitant of economic power.[2]

But this does not entirely explain Smith's frequent references to the opportunities for oppression in modern commercial societies in which feudal dependence has been removed, especially when one considers various complacent remarks on inequality made in the *Theory of Moral Sentiments*. Smith's scepticism towards material enjoyments is a major feature of this work, and is by no means absent in the *Wealth of Nations*. Beyond certain 'necessities and conveniences of the body' Smith maintained that the pursuit of material benefits was in large measure delusory to the individuals involved. By comparison with the effort entailed, the actual results were in 'the highest degree contemptible and trifling'. The economic fruits of ambition and emulation were an illusion, because 'power and riches appear then to be, what they are, enormous and operose machines contrived to produce a few trifling conveniences to the body'. The main object of ambition, therefore, is to acquire respect and admiration, the satisfaction of our desire to emulate those above us in the social ladder, and the gratification of our vanity and craving for social esteem. But Smith acknowledged that the illusion, though derived from a corruption of our moral sentiments, was an important one to society because it 'rouses and keeps in continual motion the industry of mankind'.[3] Moreover, he

---

[1] See p. 67 above.
[2] This was the basis of Smith's criticism of Hobbes for having confused wealth with power; see *WN* I.v.3.
[3] *TMS* IV.1.

went on to argue that the division of society into rich and poor was not accompanied by many of the supposed detriments of inequality. It was possible for 'fair play' to be infringed in 'the race for wealth, and honours, and preferment', but those who succeeded in the race were unable either to consume more of the necessities of life, or to derive more happiness from their consumption than the 'meanest peasant'. In spite of their 'natural selfishness and rapacity', they were forced by the limitations of personal consumption of real goods to 'divide with the poor the produce of all their improvements'.

[The rich] are led by an invisible hand to make nearly the same distribution of the necessaries of life which would have been made, had the earth been divided into equal proportions among all its inhabitants; and thus, without intending it, without knowing it, advance the interest of the society, and afford means to the multiplication of the species. When Providence divided the earth among a few lordly masters, it neither forgot nor abandoned those who seemed to have been left out in the partition. These last, too, enjoy their share of all that it produces. In what constitutes the real happiness of human life, they are in no respect inferior to those who would seem so much above them. In ease of body and peace of mind, all the different ranks of life are nearly upon a level, and the beggar, who suns himself by the side of a highway, possesses that security which kings are fighting for.[1]

Such complacent 'providentialism' is not, of course, uncharacteristic of the picture of the universe presented in the *Theory of Moral Sentiments*. Echoes of the same fatalistic stance can also be found in the *Wealth of Nations*, together with extended use of the underlying doctrine of unintended and unforeseen benefits. Without labouring the reference to the 'invisible hand', there is a clear parallel between the static mechanism of redistribution described in the passage just cited and the social dynamic depicted in Book III of the *Wealth of Nations*, whereby the pursuit of vanity by the feudal barons brings a chain of unintended social benefits in its train. On this showing alone we are not faced with the dual personality seemingly required by many of the original statements of *Das Adam Smith Problem*. But we should be prepared for Smith to be more content in the *Theory of Moral Sentiments* with the

---

[1] *TMS* IV.i.10.

aesthetic satisfactions afforded by the contemplative spectator's stance, even though he was aware that such a position
was not likely to be adopted or appreciated by the ordinary
participants in the rough and tumble of the social drama. By
the same token, as Jacob Viner pointed out over fifty years
ago, we should expect Smith in the *Wealth of Nations* to give
a more detailed and realistic account of the way in which
economic harmony does or does not result from particular
forms of behaviour, institutional arrangements, and legislative
intervention.[1] It is, therefore, still necessary to ask how Smith
conceives the emerging relationship between commerce and
justice, the object of which was to protect 'every member of
society from the injustice or oppression of every other member
of it'.[2]

To this question Smith gives a lengthy answer in the section
on justice in Book v of the *Wealth of Nations*, which is a
development of parts of the *Lectures* and contains one of the
tightest expositions of the four stages theory of progress. It
is also significant that this section provides the most extensive
account of the origins of ranks and subordination to be found
outside the pages of the *Theory of Moral Sentiments*.

In the most primitive hunting stage of society, subordination
and authority derive entirely from superior personal qualities
or age. Property beyond 'the universal poverty establishes
there universal equality'.[3] Even without a regular system of
justice, a limited harmony can be created on the basis of
respect for person and reputation. In such societies, envy,
malice, and resentment bring no real advantages, and are
consequently more amenable to a natural prudential restraint.
The crucial change occurs in the shepherd stage when inequality of possessions introduces new sources of subordination
and releases less controllable passions.

---

[1] See J. Viner, 'Adam Smith and *Laissez-Faire*' in *Long View and the Short*, pp.
228–31. As the editors of *TMS* have pointed out in their introduction, the
changes made by Smith in the 6th edition indicate that as Smith grew older
there was a move towards greater emphasis on those virtues, such as
prudence, which underly motivation in the more realistic world of the
Wealth of Nations; see *TMS*, pp. 18–19.
[2] *WN* v.i.b.1.   [3] *WN* v.i.b.7.

...avarice and ambition in the rich, in the poor the hatred of labour and the love of present ease and enjoyment, are the passions which prompt to invade property, passions much more steady in their operation, and more universal in their influence. Wherever there is great property, there is great inequality. For one very rich man, there must be five hundred poor, and the affluence of the few supposes the indigence of the many. The affluence of the rich excites the indignation of the poor, who are often both driven by want, and prompted by envy, to invade his possessions. It is only under the shelter of the civil magistrates that the owner of that valuable property, which is acquired by the labour of many years, or perhaps of many successive generations, can sleep a single night in security... The acquisition of valuable and extensive property, therefore, necessarily requires the establishment of civil government.[1]

Smith explains how birth and fortune enable the chieftains in shepherd societies to command military support from their retainers, and hence to acquire a protective and judicial role in all domestic or inter-clan disputes. In turn, the chieftain receives the support of those beneath him in the social scale, who see that 'the maintenance of their lesser authority depends upon that of his greater authority'.[2] This form of civil government, with its related system of judicial authority, has some similarity with that which exists during the allodial period of the agricultural stage of society, where a number of territorial lords share (or more often dispute) power with a single sovereign.

It is only after the erosion of the power of the lords by the process described in Book III that modern centralised monarchies are established in which judicial authority is concentrated in the hands of sovereign and his agents. In the *Lectures* Smith asks why the improvement in the arts associated with commerce does not have the same effect on the authority of the king as it has on his nobles, the answer being that:

[The king] is possessed of a million, while none of his subjects can spend above thirty or forty thousand pounds, and therefore he can spend it in no other way, but by maintaining a great number of people. Luxury must therefore sink the authority of the nobility, whose estates are small in proportion to that of the king; and as this continues unaffected, his power must become absolute.[3]

---

[1] *WN* v.i.b.2.   [2] *WN* v.i.b.12.
[3] *LJ*(B), p. 43.

The initial effect of commerce, therefore, is to establish royal absolutism. Smith was consistently more critical of arbitrary and oppressive rule by the feudal aristocracy than he was of military or absolute monarchies.[1] As Forbes has demonstrated, it was partly this that enabled Smith to avoid 'vulgar' Whiggism by speaking of '*civilized* monarchies' even when they were not 'free governments'.[2] Absolute monarchies, like that of France, were capable of achieving a large measure of liberty, defined as security under the law, simply by means of strict and impartial administration of justice. The risk of absolutism becoming despotism increased when discretionary powers were conferred by the executive on subordinate bodies. On this subject Smith echoes Montesquieu's fears pertaining to France when he defined despotism as a situation in which 'the authority of the executive power gradually absorbs that of every other power in the state, and assumes to itself the management of every branch of revenue which is destined for any public purpose'.[3]

Smith also follows Montesquieu in endorsing the separation of the judiciary from the executive as 'the great advantage which modern times have over ancient, and the foundation of that great security which we now enjoy, both with regard to liberty, property, and life'.[4] In so doing he not only accepts the doctrine of the separation of powers, but reveals how high security under law stands in his scale of political values.

When the judicial is united to the executive power, it is scarce possible that justice should not frequently be sacrificed to, what is vulgarly called, politics. The persons entrusted with the great interests of the state may, even without any corrupt views, sometimes imagine it necessary to sacrifice to those interests the rights of a private man. But upon the impartial administration of justice depends the liberty of every individual, the sense which he has of his own security. In order to make every individual feel himself perfectly secure in the possession of every right which belongs to him, it is not only necessary that the judicial should be separated from the

[1] See, for example, *LJ*(A), volume IV, pp. 81–2: '...the nobility are the greatest opposers and oppressors of liberty that one can imagine. They hurt the liberty of the people even more than an absolute monarch.'
[2] See D. Forbes, 'Sceptical Whiggism, Commerce, and Liberty' in *EAS*, pp. 187–90.
[3] *WN* v.i.d.16.   [4] A. Smith, *LRBL*, ed. J. R. Lothian, p. 170.

executive power, but that it should be rendered as much as possible independent of that power. The judge should not be liable to be removed from his office according to the caprice of that power.[1]

In this passage Smith is clearly engaging in direct advocacy, even though he attributes the origin of the separation of powers to the impersonal processes of progress and historical accident.[2] When 'the private estate of the sovereign had become altogether insufficient for defraying the expence of the sovereignty', and a regular system of taxation had to be introduced, the judges were granted fixed salaries, and the services of the courts were no longer paid for by presents to the sovereign. This is the exact judicial equivalent of the sovereign's dependence on Parliament for taxation, another major bulwark of liberty – in England at least.

Once more then, viewed in long historical perspective, and especially under favourable circumstances like those to be found in England, commercial civilisation, with all its inequalities and opportunities for oppression, is capable of generating an improved system of administering justice in which the benefits of the division of labour are extended to the separation of the judiciary and executive powers of government. Given the importance which Smith attached to this innovation as a guarantee for personal liberty under the rule of law, it must be firmly incorporated into the commerce and liberty theme, though the fact that it had only been fully achieved in England obviously limits its significance. It should also be added, as an antidote to the view that sees Smith as chiefly concerned in this section and Book v generally with suggesting methods of keeping public expenditure in check, that he said of the payment of judges' salaries that 'regular payment. . .should not depend upon the goodwill, *or even the good economy* of the executive power'.[3]

---

[1] *WN* v.i.b.25.

[2] 'The separation of the judicial from the executive power seems originally to have arisen from the increasing business of the society, in consequence of its increasing improvement' (*WN* v.i.b.24). See also the statement in *LRBL*, that the separation was 'introduced only by chance to ease the supreme magistrate of the most laborious and least glorious part of his power, and has never taken place until the increase of refinement and the growth of society have multiplied business immensely' (p. 170).

[3] *WN* v.i.b.25 (italics supplied).

But if commerce brings improvement in the machinery of justice, there is also a sense in which commercial society depends more crucially on a precise system of justice, partly as a result of the accumulation of property, and partly as a result of the nature and complexity of the social dealings between its members. It expands the circle within which individuals are free to pursue vanity and social esteem through economic activity. It creates a world which is increasingly regulated by a sense of utility rather than the older forms of authority, though these are constantly being renewed and modified through pursuit of the objects of ambition. Montesquieu had observed that:

...in countries where the people move only by the spirit of commerce, they make a traffic of all the humane, all the moral virtues; the most trifling things, those which humanity would demand, are there given, only for money.

The spirit of trade produces in the mind of a man a certain sense of exact justice, opposite, on the one hand, to robbery, and on the other hand to those moral virtues which forbid our always adhering rigidly to the rules of private interest, and suffer us to neglect this for the advantage of others.[1]

Smith had something very similar in mind when he spoke of justice having a special role to play in societies no longer regulated by beneficence: 'Society may subsist among different men, as among different merchants, from a sense of its utility, without any mutual love or affection; and though no man in it should owe any obligation, or be bound in gratitude to any other, it may still be upheld by a mercenary exchange of good offices according to an agreed valuation.'[2]

Smith's decided preference for the 'system of natural liberty' is obviously relevant here. On most occasions where economic ends are sought, it is the system which is both just and expedient; it respects important rights and is the most effective method of producing economic benefit for society at large. The competitive regime minimizes those forms of economic oppression that arise from monopoly privilege or conspiracy. Although Smith advocated this system, and drew

[1] C. S. Montesquieu, *The Spirit of the Laws*, p. 317.
[2] *TMS* II.ii.3.2.

97

attention to ways in which it was powerful enough to overcome the effects of legislative infringement, it is also well known that he was not very optimistic about the chances for its thorough implementation.

To expect, indeed, that the freedom of trade should ever be entirely restored in Great Britain, is as absurd as to expect that an Oceana or Utopia should ever be established in it. Not only the prejudices of the publick, but what is much more unconquerable, the private interests of many individuals, irresistibly oppose it.[1]

There were cases where Smith acknowledged that the interests of state should be given priority over the system of natural liberty, the best-known one being the Navigation Acts, on the grounds that defence is more important than opulence. But the fear that runs like a constant refrain through the *Wealth of Nations* is that the merchant interest will always be successful in exerting pressure on the legislature to obtain or retain its special, and hence unjust, privileges. One of the main reasons given in the *Theory of Moral Sentiments* for the divergence between positive and natural law in otherwise well-governed states was that: 'Sometimes what is called the constitution of the state, that is, the interest of the government; sometimes the interest of particular orders of men who tyrannize the government, warp the positive laws of the country from what natural justice would prescribe.'[2] Precisely the same concern over 'the interest of government', of course, lies behind Smith's endorsement of the separation of the judicial and executive powers.

The moral and philosophical basis of Smith's theory of justice can be found in the *Theory of Moral Sentiments*, yet in view of the compatible relationship of this book with the *Wealth of Nations*, any adequate interpretation of this theory cannot afford to ignore his views on economic justice. From a narrow philosophical point of view, and bearing in mind the complacent remarks in the *Theory of Moral Sentiments* on inequality and the invisible hand which were cited earlier, it may be true to say that 'Smith was no more sensitive than Hume to an

[1] *WN* iv.ii.43.
[2] *TMS* vii.iv.36.

egalitarian conception of justice'.[1] While this statement allows room for Smith's interest in equity, considered as fairness or equality of opportunity and access, it does not prepare the reader of the *Wealth of Nations* for the pervasive concern with injustice and oppression. The difficulty here may arise out of Smith's decision in the *Theory of Moral Sentiments* to adopt a manageably restricted concept of commutative justice, where rules could be established which 'are accurate in the highest degree, and admit of no exceptions or modifications, but such as may be ascertained as accurately as the rules themselves'.[2] As Thomas Campbell has pointed out, this view only retains plausibility when confined to cases where injury can be precisely assessed.[3] This is not the case with infringements of economic liberty, especially where justice may require conscious acts of wisdom by legislators. Hence Smith's pessimism on this score, when joined to a negative concept of justice, creates an impression that economic injustice, though a significant feature of life even in well-ordered commercial societies, is not easily remedied – which, of course, does not mean that it ought not to be remedied.

There is one final matter which is of relevance to an understanding of Smith's account of the advantages and disadvantages of commercial society, namely the role accorded to the 'middling ranks'. On this question Smith's position has to be handled, for the most part, inferentially – always a risky business where intentions are concerned.

It was noted earlier that Hume regarded the increase in size and importance of the 'middling rank' as 'the best and firmest basis of public liberty'. Hume's usage of the term 'middling rank' in the essays cited earlier covers the large group which exists somewhere between the feudal nobility and a dependent peasantry; it certainly seems to include the gentry as well as the merchant classes, and cannot be equated with what later became known as the 'middle classes'. Forbes has argued that

[1] See D. D. Raphael, 'Hume and Adam Smith on Justice and Utility', *Proceedings of the Aristotelian Society*, LXXII (1972–3), 101.
[2] *TMS* III.6.10.
[3] T. Campbell, *Adam Smith's Science of Morals*, p. 190.

Smith probably conveys his own, as well as Hume's, meaning best when he speaks of 'the natural aristocracy of every country', which still leaves open the question of its precise composition and mode of recruitment.[1]

It is also possible to make use of John Millar's more explicit analysis of the effect of commerce and the emergence of the 'middling rank' on liberty as a means of inferring Smith's position. In his *Origin of the Distinction of Ranks*, a work published in 1771, but clearly bearing the imprint of his teacher's lectures, Millar counterposed the influences produced by commercial opulence which favour the sovereign against those which are 'manifestly conducive to a popular form of government'. As far as the latter is concerned, commerce and manufactures gradually eliminate feudal dependence and servile habits; 'and as the lower people, in general, become thereby more independent in their circumstances, they begin to exert those sentiments of liberty which are natural to the mind of man'. The pursuit of luxury undermines hereditary wealth and allows estates to fall into the hands of 'the frugal and industrious merchant', who then adopts the profligate habits of the landed gentry and is in turn succeeded. Such 'fluctuation of property' limits the influence of established wealth and therefore has 'a tendency to introduce democratical government'. In small states, where the people are able to unite against encroachments on their liberty, such forces are likely to prevail. In large commercial kingdoms, however, where the sovereign is able to raise large revenues and hence employ a standing mercenary army and command the support of a large body of dependants, the outcome is more likely to be despotism.[2] The contest between those forces likely to favour popular liberty, and those likely to strengthen royal 'influence' provided one of the main themes of Millar's posthumously published *Historical View of the English Government*.

Some knowledgeable commentators have suggested that

[1] For Forbes's discussion of 'middling rank' see D. Forbes, *Hume's Philosophical Politics*, especially pp. 176–9; and 'Sceptical Whiggism, Commerce, and Liberty', in *EAS*, p. 196.
[2] See J. Millar, *Origin of the Distinction of Ranks*, especially chapter 5.

Millar's line of argument can be taken as representative of Smith's position as well.[1] There is clearly a good deal to be said for this view. The effect of commerce in diffusing the power of the feudal nobility can be amply supported from Smith's writings. But it is more difficult to find references to the 'middling rank' which have the *political* significance attributed to them by Hume, or to find any support for Millar's extension of the argument to the people at large. Cropsey speculated that since Smith regarded each of the three main economic orders – landowners, merchants, and labourers – as suspect or crippled in their capacity to rule or take part in government, his 'political preference, so far as it is expressed, favours the "men who were educated in the middle and inferior ranks of life, who have been carried forward by their own industry and abilities"'.[2] The reference here is to a section of the *Theory of Moral Sentiments* in which Smith considers the virtues which the man of inferior rank should cultivate if he is to achieve respect and attention in society. 'Patience, industry, fortitude, and application of thought' are his chief resources; and since these virtues are not to be found among those born in high stations, Smith gives this as the reason why 'even in monarchies, the highest offices are generally possessed, and the whole detail of the administration conducted, by men who are educated in the middle and inferior ranks of life'.[3] Cropsey's qualifying 'so far as it is expressed' needs emphasis. The section in the *Theory of Moral Sentiments* carries no specifically political message, and even the references in the *Wealth of Nations* to 'natural aristocracy' could be taken to encompass merit *and* high station, especially if we take seriously, as we must, Smith's views on the importance of, and sympathy accorded to, *established* wealth and authority.[4]

Biographical evidence alone – or rather perhaps, the lack of it – suggests that it is very unlikely Smith would have adopted the militant Whig position espoused by Millar. This seems all

---

[1] See A. S. Skinner, 'Adam Smith: An Economic Interpretation of History', *EAS*, p. 178; and D. Forbes, 'Sceptical Whiggism, Commerce, and Liberty', *EAS*, p. 200.

[2] J. Cropsey, *Polity and Economy*, pp. 68–9.   [3] *TMS* I.iii.2.5.

[4] See pp. 109, 155–7, 162, 168 below for further discussion of 'natural aristocracy'.

the more likely when it is borne in mind that Smith did not endorse that part of Millar's argument which centred on the growth of royal 'influence'.[1] There is also no evidence to suggest that Smith would have been at all sympathetic to Millar's apparent acceptance of 'the clamour and tumultuary proceedings of the populace in the great towns' as one of the most effective means of preserving the spirit of liberty.[2] Quite the contrary, for as his opposition to the merchant interest reveals, he was highly critical of extra-parliamentary pressures on the legislature – an attitude he shared with Hume.[3] But if 'not proven' seems the best verdict on the subject of the 'middling rank', a firmer judgement can be recorded against any hasty reduction of 'natural aristocracy' to the merchant order for the purposes of moving on to the nineteenth-century concept of a 'middle class', thereby yielding the impression that Smith placed great reliance on 'the countervailing power of the new middle classes'.[4]

In summary, what has been shown so far is the relationship between the natural jurisprudential ground-plan of Smith's politics and his attempt to give this plan historical or 'experimental' substance by 'an account of the general principles of law and government, and of the different revolutions they have undergone in the different ages and periods of society'. Further insight into Smith's method and style of political analysis can be gained from an examination of his treatment of three important eighteenth-century political topics, namely standing armies versus militias, and the related question of education; the problem posed by the growth of the public debt; and finally, the most significant political problem to arise during the composition of the *Wealth of Nations*, the revolt of the thirteen American colonies.

[1] See the passage from *LJ*(A) cited on p. 62 above.
[2] For Millar's argument see the posthumous essay reprinted in W. C. Lehman, *John Millar of Glasgow* (1960), pp. 336–9.
[3] See pp. 140, 144–5, 153 below for further discussion of this issue.
[4] This is the sequence followed by D. A. Reisman in *Adam Smith's Sociological Economics* (1976); see pp. 93, 100, 194, 199.

5

Martial spirit and mental mutilation

By deciding to include a separate section in his *Lectures on Jurisprudence* on 'arms', and in expanding the treatment given to this subject in Book v of the *Wealth of Nations*, Smith was, of course, addressing himself to what he described as 'the first duty of the sovereign'.[1] His aim in dealing with this subject remained that given in the introduction to the *Lectures*.

Though the peace within-doors be never so firmly established, yet if there be no security from injuries from without, the property of individuals cannot be secure. The danger to them on this head is no less to be feared than from those of their own society; and not only is the security of private persons in danger, but the very being of the state. It is therefore requisite that an armed force should be maintained, as well to defend the state against external injuries as to obtain satisfaction for any that have been committed! In treating of this subject we shall consider the various species of armed forces that have been in use in ancient and modern states, the different sorts of militias and trained bands, and observe how far they were suited to the different natures of governments.[2]

In practice the issue resolved itself into an examination of the merits of various kinds of citizen's armies or militias when compared with those associated with mercenary or professional armies at different stages in the development of society and of the military arts. In dealing with militias versus standing armies, however, Smith was not addressing himself to a mere historical *curiosum*; he was concerning himself with a standard, but at times highly sensitive, issue in eighteenth-century politics, while at the same time responding to an important theme in the more philosophical literature comparing ancient and

[1] *WN* v.i.a.1.   [2] *LJ*(A), volume I, pp. 4–6.

modern conceptions of virtue and citizenship. When Smith was first giving shape to his lectures in the 1750s and 1760s, the militia question was an especially lively one in Scotland, particularly among his close friends and acquaintances. The dangers of an unarmed and unprepared citizenry had been underlined by the comparative ease with which the Pretender's army had advanced in Scotland during the 1745 rebellion, and by the invasion scare aroused by Thurot's landing in 1759. In the following year the first of several unsuccessful attempts was made to introduce a bill which would extend to Scotland the provisions of the English Militia Act of 1757.[1] Smith was one of the founder-members of the Edinburgh Poker Club formed in 1762, one of the main objects of the club being agitation for the establishment of a Scottish militia. Among the many friends belonging to the club were Hume, Kames, and Ferguson, the last two of whom at least can properly be described as zealots in the cause.[2] Smith remained a member of the club until 1774, during which period the issue was intermittently active; it was revived in 1776 as a result of military set-backs in the war with the American colonies, when yet another bill introduced by a member of the club, Lord Mountstuart, was defeated.

Although Smith's endorsement of the Navigation Acts on the grounds that defence was more important than opulence has received a good deal of notice, the same cannot be said of the other, more significant, military themes that run through his writings. This could be the result of these themes becoming obscured by the nineteenth-century association of economic liberalism with pacific sympathies. Those who have dealt with Smith's position on defence have tended to treat it as an extension of the mercantilist debate on power versus plenty, thereby overlooking the importance which Smith attached to the martial virtues as human or moral qualities,

[1] For an exhaustive study of the whole subject see J. R. Western, *The English Militia in the Eighteenth Century; The Story of a Political Issue, 1660–1802* (1965).
[2] Other members of the club were: the Duke of Buccleuch (Smith's pupil), Dundas, Blair, William Robertson, William Johnstone (later Sir William Pulteney), and Sir Gilbert Elliot, the last of whom, together with James Oswald, introduced the 1760 Bill into Parliament. See A. Carlyle, *Autobiography* (1861), p. 324; and J. Rae, *Life of Adam Smith*, pp. 134–140.

and his belief that the capacity to wage effective war was a significant indicator of the state of 'refinement'. We have noted the pervasive attention given to military considerations in Smith's account of political and economic progress in his *Lectures*. This wider background needs to be borne in mind when reading the abbreviated version of the history of arms given in Book v of the *Wealth of Nations*. Indeed, there is some evidence to suggest that military considerations assumed increased importance to Smith as he grew older. Defence was promoted above justice in the list of sovereign's duties in the *Wealth of Nations*, and while it seems that Smith always regarded the art of war as the noblest of arts, the section added to the *Theory of Moral Sentiments* in 1790 reemphasises this view by portraying the patriotic and heroic military virtues in glowing terms.[1]

The contemporary significance of Smith's treatment of defence in the *Wealth of Nations* lay in the strong support which he gave to the view that in modern commercial states the establishment of a standing army was the proper response to the logic of events. Moreover, since the creation of a standing or professional army required a conscious 'act of wisdom' on the part of the state, Smith's support for the idea could only be interpreted as straightforward advocacy or endorsement, implying, in the circumstances of the day, denigration of the militia alternative. Both Rae and Halévy concluded that Smith underwent a change of heart on the militia question on the grounds that his support for standing armies ran counter to his membership of the Poker Club.[2] Indeed, Smith's attitude on this matter has been taken as conclusive proof of his rejection of the radical Whig and standard oppositional position. This was part of Halévy's case against regarding Smith as a Whig, for here Smith decided 'to defy the prejudices dear to the party to which he was held to belong'.[3] Halévy's view derives considerable support from contemporary evidence

---

[1] Justice appeared before defence in *LJ*(A), volume 1, p. 1; see also *WN* v.i.a.14 and *TMS* vi.ii.2.13; vi.ii.3.4; and vi.iii.7.

[2] J. Rae, *Life of Adam Smith*, pp. 137–8; and E. Halévy, *La Formation du radicalisme philosophique*, volume 1, fn. to p. 75.

[3] E. Halévy, *La Formation du radicalisme philosophique*, p. 75 (p. 142 of English translation).

which shows that this was how Smith's apostasy on militias struck some of his Scottish friends. Thus Ferguson said that it was the one question on which he disagreed with the book, adding that: 'The gentlemen and peasants of this country do not need the authority of philosophers to make them supine and negligent of every resource they might have in themselves in the case of certain extremities, of which the pressure God knows, may be at no great distance. But of this more at Philippi.'[1] Another acquaintance and fellow-member of the Poker Club, Alexander Carlyle, went as far as writing a pamphlet attacking Smith on this subject.[2]

Smith's position has been misunderstood. In spite of his remarks on the superiority of standing armies, he continued to support militias; hence his views do not appear to have undergone a change between the *Lectures* and the *Wealth of Nations*. The evidence leading to this conclusion is reviewed below, but the conclusion is less important to my purpose than the premises of Smith's argument and the setting within which he chose to pose the problem, namely within the context of education and a discussion of the moral and social consequences of the division of labour in modern societies.

Before reexamining what Smith has to say on this subject, it may be helpful to take a bearing from an earlier version of the 'Commonwealth' position by considering Hutcheson's views on militias. Hutcheson does not devote a special chapter or section to 'arms'; he deals with militias as part of his discussion of the duty of the legislator, following ancient practice, 'to promote, by all just and effectual methods, true principles of virtue' among the people. This 'virtue' has a Christian dimension in that 'education, instruction, and discipline' are required to restrain the unsocial passions, and, within the limits set by religious toleration, to cultivate 'pious dispositions toward God, a firm persuasion of his goodness, and of his providence governing the world'.[3] Education also

---

[1] *Corr.*, Letter 154, 18 April 1776.
[2] The London edition of Carlyle's anonymous attack was entitled *A Letter to His Grace the Duke of Buccleuch on National Defence with Some Remarks on Dr. Smith's Chapter on that Subject, in Book entitled 'An Inquiry into the Nature and Causes of the Wealth of Nations'* (1778).
[3] F. Hutcheson, *System of Moral Philosophy*, volume II, pp. 310–11.

has a secular and a civic purpose to fulfil: it should be provided to discourage idleness, and to inculcate sobriety, prudence, and industry, especially in states where the virtues of justice and fortitude have been undermined by excessive luxury and wealth. In addition to a regular system of civil and criminal laws, public participation in elections has an educative role to play: 'Elections either popular, or partly such, to temporary dignities and offices, promote a general humanity and justice in the deportment of such as hope to rise in the state... Virtue ever was an will be popular, where men can vote freely.'[1]

It was within this context that Hutcheson advocated the use of militias to make 'fortitude and military discipline' as universal as possible: 'As war is a thing accidental, and designs of conquest are almost always injurious, military service should not be a constant profession to any; but the whole people should be trained to it to be ready whenever just occasions may require it; and during peace be kept in mind of their discipline.'[2] His plan for the militia required rotation of the offices of command, partly so as not to be reliant on too few men, and partly to provide a reserve 'to oppose them if they turned their arms against their country'. A standing army, particularly if composed of mercenaries, constitutes more of a drain on the productive resources of the community than a rotating army of virtuous citizens devoting a few years to military service before 'returning joyfully to peaceful industry'. It might also be possible to employ the militia on various public works so as to 'strengthen both their bodies and minds'. Hutcheson clearly felt that the scheme was a practicable one, though he ended his account of it with a darker hint that 'other views than those of defending a country have recommended the use of mercenaries'.[3]

The sections explicitly devoted to militias, discipline, and standing armies in Smith's *Lectures* are highly compressed, at least according to the notes that have survived. Nevertheless, taken in conjunction with the earlier remarks on these subjects, they give an adequate foretaste of the equivalent sections in *Wealth of Nations*. Thus, in explaining how the ancient

---

[1] *Ibid.*, p. 317.   [2] *Ibid.*, pp. 323-4.
[3] *Ibid.*, p. 325.

republics lost their liberty, Smith speaks of a time 'when the arts arrive at a certain degree of improvement, the number of people increase, yet that of fighting men becomes less'. Instead of the whole nation going to war, only a few are willing to give up more refined, peaceful, and productive avocations. Slaves, mercenaries, and 'the dregs of the people' have to be recruited, though large states, notwithstanding 'politeness and refinement', continue to gain at the expense of small.[1] He returns to the question under 'Police' when discussing the effect of commerce and the division of labour in sinking the courage of mankind and extinguishing the martial virtues. War becomes a trade like any other: 'The defence of the country is therefore committed to a certain set of men who have nothing else ado, and among the bulk of the people military courage diminishes. By having their minds constantly employed on the arts of luxury, they grow effeminate and dastardly.'[2] And it is perhaps worth noting that Smith's first example of this decline is the '45 rebellion, when 'four or five thousand naked unarmed Highlanders took possession of the improved parts of this country without any opposition from the unwarlike inhabitants'.

With this as background, the section dealing explicitly with arms hardly comes as a surprise. After repeating the historical analysis and stating that Britain has arrived at the advanced state of commerce when 'it falls to the meanest to defend the state', Smith shows how fear has to replace honour as the means of disciplining standing armies; these are treated as an inevitable product of social progress, however much 'they may be exclaimed against'. Nevertheless, he recognizes that 'they should be raised in the most convenient way, and with as little hurt as possible to the country'. The potential danger to civil liberty is accepted, but a compromise proposed in order to minimise the risk:

A militia commanded by landed gentlemen in possession of the public offices of the nation can never have any prospect of sacrificing the liberties of the country for any person whatever. Such a militia would no doubt be the best security against the standing army of another nation.[3]

[1] *LJ*(B), pp. 27–9, 32.　　　　[2] *LJ*(B), pp. 257–8.
[3] *LJ*(B), p. 263.

Although the earlier set of lecture notes stop short of the section on arms, this statement is fully in accord with the view cited from them earlier (see p. 62) to the effect that a standing army commanded by 'persons of chief rank and station' poses no threat to British liberties. This is the group to which Smith refers, on other occasions, as the 'natural aristocracy'.

On the basis of this evidence it would seem that none of Smith's ex-students, if not the members of the Poker Club, could have been surprised by the content of the chapter on defence in the *Wealth of Nations*. There is, however, one potential source of misunderstanding which arises out of Smith's tendency in the *Lectures* (as just illustrated) to use 'standing army' and 'militia' interchangeably – the important consideration being how they are commanded. This ambivalence was carried over into the *Wealth of Nations*, where the identical argument used to defend properly-commanded militias in the *Lectures* is employed in favour of standing armies as part of his answer to the fears expressed by 'men of republican principles'. Having accepted that the examples of Caesar and Cromwell confirm these fears, Smith goes on to say:

But where the sovereign is himself the general, and the principal nobility and gentry of the country the chief officers of the army; where the military force is placed under the command of those who have the greatest interest in the support of the civil authority, because they have themselves the greatest share of that authority, a standing army can never be dangerous to liberty.[1]

If Smith had offended the susceptibilities of 'men of republican principles' by making this point, his proof of the final proposition concerning the *favourable* effect on liberty of standing armies must have added a further insult.

That degree of liberty which approaches to licentiousness can be tolerated only in countries where the sovereign is secured by a well-regulated standing army. It is in such countries only, that the public safety does not require, that the sovereign should be trusted with any discretionary power, for suppressing even the impertinent wantonness of this licentious liberty.[2]

In terms of Pocock's Court versus Country spectrum, Smith

[1] *WN* v.i.a.41.   [2] *WN* v.i.a.41.

was not only adopting a Court stance but inverting the logic of the Country position to strengthen his case. The novel character of Smith's argument on this occasion is brought home by the fact that, as Forbes has indicated, he was disagreeing with Hume, who not only favoured a Scottish militia, but came to accept the 'melancholy truth' that the supreme magistrate might have to possess discretionary powers if he was to be able 'to execute the laws and support his own authority'.[1]

As was pointed out earlier, the term 'republican' was a rather elastic one by this period. Moreover, as the dramatic example of Bolingbroke showed, the adoption of an oppositional position towards standing armies and other potential sources of executive tyranny cut across any of the imprecise party dividing lines. It is not clear whether Smith had the members of the Poker Club in mind when he referred to 'men of republican principles', though fortunately some idea of their position can be gained from Carlyle's attack on Smith's chapter on defence, which he treated as a 'sally' or excursion into 'general politicks'. The immediate background to Carlyle's pamphlet was the rejection of the Mountstuart Bill for establishing a Scottish militia and the fears aroused by the defeats in America. In other words the pamphlet was not directly concerned to rehearse any of the older fears of imminent executive tyranny. Carlyle agreed with Smith that standing armies were generally superior, but maintained that the supporters of a militia 'only proposed to subjoin it to the regular force, as useful at all times to preserve the warlike spirit among the people, and as necessary often for national defence'. The two together would 'unite a wise economy to constant preparation for war'. Contrary to Smith's opinion, 'the habits of the husbandman or manufacturer do not in the least incapacitate him for the trade of a soldier', even under modern conditions; and the acquisition of military skills would not render the populace less fit to carry on their normal occupations. After all, had not Smith himself acknowledged

[1] See D. Forbes, 'Sceptical Whiggism, Commerce, and Liberty', *EAS*, pp. 183–4. For Hume's views on the Scottish militia see D. Hume, *Letters*, ed. J. T. Y. Greig, volume I, pp. 325, 341–2; volume II, p. 212.

that the American militia had become the match for Britain's standing army? Yet elsewhere he had been guilty of 'such a predilection for a standing army, that he ascribes bravery to the magic of that name, and not to the manhood, with which all men are inspired, when not debased by oppressive governments'. Surely this was still the case in Britain? The militia would be a powerful supplement to the army, 'and the whole nation being not only free, but warlike, the spirit of our standing army could not fail to rise to the utmost height'.[1]

Carlyle's attack has something of a sham passage of arms about it, as Smith recognised when he commented on it in a letter to Andreas Holt written in 1780.

When he wrote this book, he had not read mine to the end. He fancies that because I insist that a Militia is in all cases inferior to a well-regulated and well-disciplined standing Army, I disapprove of Militias altogether. With regard to that subject, he and I happened to be precisely of the same opinion.[2]

Smith was drawing attention to a later chapter in Book v where he returns to the subject when dealing with the education of youth. The passages which appear there are the exact counterpart of the section in the *Lectures,* considered earlier, in which Smith outlined the drawbacks of the effects of division of labour on society. It also seems worth noting that they correspond precisely with the parts of Hutcheson's *System* which deal with 'fortitude and military discipline' under the educational duties of the legislator. The relevant passage in the *Wealth of Nations* is as follows:

That in the progress of improvement the practice of military exercises, unless government takes proper pains to support it, goes gradually to decay, and, together with it, the martial spirit of the great body of the people, the example of modern Europe sufficiently demonstrates. But the security of every society must always depend, more or less, on the martial spirit of the great body of the people. In the present times, indeed, that martial spirit alone, and unsup-

---

[1] See [A. Carlyle], *A Letter to his Grace the Duke of Buccleuch on National Defence,* especially pp. 23–53.

[2] *Corr.,* Letter 208, 26 October 1780. Smith was wrong in his guess as to the authorship of the pamphlet; he thought it had been written by an acquaintance named Douglas and 'was a little surprised at his attack upon me, and still more at the mode of it'.

ported by a well-disciplined standing army, would not, perhaps, be sufficient for the defence and security of any society. But where every citizen had the spirit of a soldier, a smaller standing army would surely be requisite. That spirit, besides, would necessarily diminish very much the dangers to liberty, whether real or imaginary, which are commonly apprehended from a standing army. As it would very much facilitate the operations of that army against a foreign invader, so it would obstruct them as much if unfortunately they should ever be directed against the constitution of the state.[1]

There was in fact a double sham involved in the Smith–Carlyle 'exchange'. Contrary to Smith's assertion, Carlyle not only noticed this passage, but made considerable play with Smith's apparent inconsistency. As he very wisely said, 'we must understand this respectable author, you see, my lord, as we do Scripture, by comparing one passage with another, and taking the general scope of the whole'.[2]

In common with Carlyle, we are faced with a problem of interpreting a characteristic Smithian ambivalence. The burden of his historical account of the changes in methods of conducting war associated with the progress of society, from its earlier stages up to the modern commercial state, was that the growing complexity of economic life together with improvements in the art of war had made recourse to a standing army both inevitable and desirable. It was easier in agricultural societies for men to leave their work and yet continue to be supported while under arms. This was not the case where 'a great part of the inhabitants are artificers and manufacturers'; their work stops entirely, and they have to be maintained at public expense. The sheer expense of modern war means that the opportunity cost to society of withdrawing men from productive activities grows. At the same time, the populace of civilised nations lose their capacity to undertake war-like ventures, while the wealth of such nations produces envy and hence greater likelihood of attack from poorer nations. Of the two expedients available for defence in these circumstances, a 'well-disciplined and well-exercised standing army' is always superior to a militia, except where the militia

[1] *WN* v.i.f.59.
[2] [A. Carlyle], *A Letter to his Grace the Duke of Buccleuch on National Defence*, p. 48.

has acquired the necessary qualities as a result of experience in the field. The long history of warfare could be adduced to show that: 'It is only by means of a standing army...that the civilization of any country can be perpetuated, or even preserved for any considerable time.'[1]

Not only were professional armies inevitable, but they need not – as we have seen – be dangerous to liberty; they might even confer some unintended benefits on this score. Nevertheless, Smith does not dismiss the long-standing fears expressed in the oppositional literature; they must be respected and the army kept to a minimum by raising a militia and providing some kind of military training for the populace at large. But the clinching point comes at the end, and like its counterpart in the discussion of the narrowing effect on men's intellects of the division of labour, it is based on an explicitly non-utilitarian position which can only be fully appreciated by reference to a perspective capable of recognising Smith's concern with the preconditions for effective citizenship.

Even though the martial spirit of the people were of no use towards the defence of the society, yet to prevent that sort of mental mutilation, deformity and wretchedness which cowardice necessarily involves in it, from spreading themselves through the great body of the people, would still deserve the most serious attention of government; in the same manner as it would deserve its most serious attention to prevent a leprosy or any other loathsome and offensive disease, though neither mortal nor dangerous, from spreading among them; though, perhaps no other publick good might result from such attention besides the prevention of so great a publick evil.[2]

The significance of Smith's discussion of this subject within the context of the duties of the state with respect to education has frequently been overlooked or even distorted in much of the interpretative literature. As was hinted in the previous chapter, this is particularly the case in the large body of work recently devoted to the 'alienation' theme, where it is assumed that what has to be explained is whether or not, and in what respects, Smith anticipated Marx's vision of the dehumanising character of factory labour under modern capitalism. The

[1] *WN* v.i.a. *passim.*   [2] *WN* v.i.f.6o.

more specialised literature on the economics of education by historians of economic thought provides little antidote to this kind of speculative scholarship, mainly because it is interested in establishing Smith's place within a separate 'professional' genealogy – by examining, for example, his contribution to the modern theory of human capital, or by portraying him as an early cost–benefit analyst, concerned to examine cases of non-coincidence between private and social benefits where 'externalities' might dictate that market provision should give way to state intervention or regulation.[1] In both cases, though for different reasons, the shadow of the nineteenth century hangs heavily over the discussion. Indeed, both among Smith's detractors and defenders, Marx's contemptuous description of Smith's educational remedies as mere 'homeopathetic doses' has set the tone for much of the comment on his solution to the problems created by the division of labour in commercial societies.[2] His proposals have been described as inadequate, and the educational aims behind them have been characterised as merely 'vocational' or 'strictly practical'.[3] Where wider aims are recognised, these are spoken of as 'propaganda', and at least one bold spirit has actually deduced that any wider political aim is impossible within Smith's scheme of things.[4]

In what follows I shall not be concerned with the adequacy (by what standard?) of Smith's remedy so much as with its character and context. This requires that due attention should be paid to the moral and civic purposes Smith had in mind when discussing education. In writing 'Of the Expence of the Institutions for the Education of Youth', Smith called upon

[1] For a survey of this literature see M. Blaug, 'The Economics of Education in English Classical Political Economy: A Re-Examination', in *EAS*, pp. 568–99.

[2] See K. Marx, *Capital*, Moscow edition, volume I, p. 362.

[3] See e.g., J. Cropsey, *Polity and Economy*, p. 90; and D. A. Reisman, *Adam Smith's Sociological Economics* (1976), pp. 156–7.

[4] See D. A. Reisman, *Adam Smith's Sociological Economics*, p. 158. The bold spirit is R. L. Heilbroner who states: 'It follows, rather, from what I believe is both implicit and explicit in the *Wealth of Nations* – that the advocacy of a genuine *political* education as a necessary condition of freedom or liberty would have been not only uncongenial to, but even incompatible with, Smith's conception of the social order itself.' See R. L. Heilbroner, 'The Paradox of Progress...', in *EAS*, p. 536.

his broad knowledge of modern universities and the development of their curricula in advancing certain well-known
criticisms of their antiquarian and ecclesiastical biases and
consequent general inattention to the needs of students. Much
of his discussion under this heading was directed at the problem of finding the best system for financing education, and
for ensuring that educational institutions were responsive to
the needs of students and society at large. For the most part,
Smith recorded negative answers to the questions which he
posed at the outset, and an especially negative answer to the
question whether modern institutions had 'directed the course
of education towards objects more useful, both to the individual and the public, than those to which it would naturally
have gone of its own accord'.[1]

While this may sound a suitable *laissez-faire* way of posing
the problem, part of Smith's answer to it entailed a comparison
between ancient and modern educational institutions, with the
former being exemplified by Rome and the Greek republics,
where 'every free citizen was instructed, under the direction
of the publick magistrate, in gymnastick exercises and in
musick'. The object of these exercises was to prepare citizens
for military service and 'to humanize the mind, to soften the
temper, and to dispose it for performing all the social and
moral duties both of publick and private life'.[2] While Smith
was not entirely uncritical of ancient practice, his account of
it was obviously designed to serve as a useful model. For as
Smith asserted: 'The abilities, both civil and military, of the
Greeks and Romans, will readily be allowed to have been, at
least equal to those of any modern nation.'[3] It was certainly
in the light of deficiencies revealed by the comparison with the
ancient model that Smith proceeded to consider whether the
public interest requires state intervention, or whether, as was
usually the case in the ancient republics, with the exception
of military training, educational provision could be left to the
forces of demand and supply.

To answer this question Smith contrasted those states of
society which place 'the greater part of individuals in such

[1] *WN* v.i.f.3. [2] *WN* v.i.f.39.
[3] *WN* v.i.f.45.

situations as naturally form in them, without any attention of government, almost all the abilities and virtues which the state requires, or perhaps can admit of', and those which do not, where consequently 'some attention of government is necessary in order to prevent the almost entire corruption and degeneracy of the great body of the people'.[1] It should be noted that this is exactly the same problem to which Hutcheson addressed himself when dealing with education. The famous passages on the corrupting and enfeebling influence of the progress of the division of labour follow immediately, with an explicit contrast being drawn between civilised and barbarous states of society. The conclusion is that whereas in civilised states a few men acquire an 'improved and refined understanding', the bulk of the 'labouring poor', whose attention is confined to a narrower range of tasks, suffer extinction of 'all the nobler parts of the human character'. Their understanding is confined; their imagination and capacity for invention is restricted; and they become incapable of forming a judgement on 'the great and extensive interests of [their] country'.[2]

In view of the emphasis given in the secondary literature to 'the factory system', it seems worth pointing out that although an unfavourable contrast is made earlier between the morals of independent workmen and those employed in 'large manufactories', Smith's main contrast is between the urban and rural occupations of the common people; his illustrations mention 'the mechanic who lives in a town', a cabinet-maker, and a worker in the 'very trifling manufacture' of pins, the contrast being with rural or agricultural pursuits where the division of labour is not so extensive and hence leaves greater scope for variety in the tasks undertaken.[3]

Smith's problem of 'corruption' is posed with reference to ideas on the spectator of social opinion, the distinction of ranks, and the principle of authority expounded in the *Theory of Moral Sentiments*. Men of 'some rank and fortune' do not

---

[1] *WN* v.i.f.49. [2] *WN* v.i.f.50.

[3] The earlier reference to 'large manufactories' can be found in *WN* I.viii. 48. The rural/urban contrast can be found in *LJ*(B), pp. 255–6; *WN* I.x.c.23–4 and v.i.f.50–53.

enter a business or profession until they have reached an age at which it is possible to have acquired 'every accomplishment which can recommend them to the public esteem, or render them worthy of it'. Their occupations are not 'simple or uniform'; they leave them with the leisure to improve on the foundation of knowledge furnished by their earlier education. The common people, on the other hand, have few opportunities to acquire education; their children are set to earn their keep at an early age, parental authority is thrown off, and when arrived at maturity the child has no foundation for the constructive use of what little leisure is available after work.[1]

The 'man of low condition' who leaves the country to take up employment in an anonymous urban setting suffers from a further disadvantage. Unlike the man of rank, he is 'far from being a distinguished member of any great society'.

While he remains in a country village his conduct may be attended to, and he may be obliged to attend to it himself. In this situation, and in this situation only, he may have what is called a character to lose. But as soon as he comes into a great city, he is sunk in obscurity and darkness. His conduct is observed by nobody, and he is therefore very likely to neglect it himself, and abandon himself to every sort of low profligacy and vice.[2]

Not only is an important moral regulator and source of social cohesion being undermined, but civilised society is no longer capable of providing opportunities for the majority of its members to exercise those active qualities essential to them as moral beings. The very purposes for which societies exist are being defeated. And if such language seems exaggerated, it can only be said that Smith's is more so. Given the nature of the problem, and leaving aside other compensating elements in the balance sheet of progress, it is hard to see how any solution could be regarded as adequate. That is what is meant by 'historical pessimism', though the fact that a heavy price must be paid for progress does not imply, of course, that pessimism should be equated with nostalgia.

Smith's remedies may not strike the twentieth-century reader as particularly far-reaching; they turn on the necessity

[1] See *LJ*(B), pp. 256–7; *WN* v.i.f.53–4.   [2] *WN* v.i.g.12.

for compulsory education for the common people at the public expense along the lines of the Scottish parish schools, where the pupils' families made some contribution to the cost. The curriculum should be adapted to the needs of the poor, and apart from the three Rs they should be 'instructed in the elementary parts of geometry and mechanics'. These subjects are readily applicable in most common trades, and would therefore 'gradually exercise and improve the common people in those principles, the necessary introduction to the most sublime as well as to the most useful sciences'.[1] Those who wish to stress the vocational bias of this modest proposal concentrate on the word 'useful' to the neglect of 'sublime', and sometimes underline their case by demoting the Scottish parish establishments to mere 'trade schools'.[2]

As we have seen, Smith's 'homeopathic dose' goes beyond this to include some kind of military training along ancient lines. It also includes an unusual remedy for the a-social condition of the urban labourer which arises naturally out of Smith's hostile account of the way in which religious establishments, like their endowed educational counterparts, have neglected their pastoral duties, and how they had become embroiled in politics. Even 'if politics had never been called in the aid of religion', however, Smith favoured a policy of 'independency', and of allowing a multitude of sects to proliferate and compete for followers – a policy which he correctly described as one of 'no ecclesiastical government'.[3] Not only would such a solution diffuse zeal and encourage 'good temper and moderation in all', it would answer the needs of the urban labourer by providing him with an opportunity to join the 'respectable society' of a small religious sect, within which his conduct could be observed and judged by his fellows. Smith conceded that the morals of such sects tended to be 'rather disagreeably rigorous and unsocial', but felt that this could be ameliorated, first, by encouraging the study of 'the more difficult sciences' among the 'middling' and

[1] WN v.i.f.55.
[2] This is the tactic employed by R. L. Heilbroner in 'The Paradox of Progress...', in *EAS*, p.536.
[3] WN v.i.g.8.

'superior ranks', and allowing its qualities as an 'antidote to the poison of enthusiasm and superstition' to filter downwards; and secondly, by 'the frequency and gaiety of publick diversions' – that is through state encouragement to the arts so as to dissipate the fanaticism and 'melancholy and gloomy humour' of the little sects.[1]

Whether or not this solution strikes the modern reader as quirky and inadequate is of secondary interest compared to the fact that, taken in conjunction with the militia idea, it is clearly an attempt to match the aims served by the ancient provision for gymnastic exercises and music, which were – to repeat – 'to humanize the mind, to soften the temper, and to dispose it for performing all the social and moral duties both of publick and private life'. Such parallels with an older conception of education, however, should not be necessary to make the point when Smith provided us with an explicit statement of the political or civic purposes he had in mind.

A man, without the proper use of the intellectual faculties of a man, is, if possible, more contemptible than even a coward, and seems to be mutilated and deformed in a still more essential part of the character of human nature. Though the state was to derive no advantage from the instruction of the inferior ranks of people, it would still deserve its attention that they should not be altogether uninstructed. The state, however, derives no inconsiderable advantage from their instruction. The more they are instructed, the less liable they are to the delusions of enthusiasm and superstition, which, among ignorant nations, frequently occasion the most dreadful disorders. An instructed and intelligent people besides are always more decent and orderly than an ignorant and stupid one. They feel themselves, each individually, more respectable, and more likely to obtain the respect of their lawful superiors, and they are therefore more disposed to respect those superiors. They are more disposed to examine, and more capable of seeing through, the interested complaints of faction and sedition, and they are, upon that account, less apt to be misled into any wanton or unnecessary opposition to the measures of government. In free countries, where the safety of government depends very much upon the favourable judgement which the people may form of its conduct, it must surely be of the highest importance that they should not be disposed to judge rashly or capriciously concerning it.[2]

[1] *WN* v.i.g.10–15.   [2] *WN* v.i.f.61.

This is the passage that has been described as 'propaganda'. More politely and accurately, it can be characterised as a political argument for strengthening the mechanisms of social control within a society of ranks in which 'opinion' plays an important part in determining the smooth functioning and stability of the polity. It certainly conveys something that is central to an understanding of Smith's brand of political analysis.

6

A ruinous expedient

The growth of the public debt in Britain during the first half of the eighteenth century was one of the most remarkable economic developments in the period following the Whig Settlement. More perhaps than any other institutional innovation, the new system of public borrowing was responsible for the interconnected growth of Britain's commercial and military strength during this period. Together with the creation of the Bank of England, the spread of paper money, and the rise to prominence in the capital market of the joint stock companies, the public debt provided a basis for what has justly been called a 'financial revolution'.[1] The political and economic implications of this revolution gave rise to a debate which was, in its own way, as profound as that aroused by the more familiar revolution associated with industry during the early decades of the nineteenth century.[2] Most of the opposition to the new financial institutions was concentrated on the political implications of the growth in size and influence of the moneyed interest associated with the debt. During the first half of the century the most determined and vocal opposition came from Bolingbroke, Pulteney, and other spokesmen for 'Country' interests, for whom public borrowing represented one of the main pillars of 'Robinocracy' – Walpole's sinister network of influence. The two main points of attack centred on the corrupting relationship which had grown up between the executive and the stockholders; and on the additional burden of taxation borne by landowners as a result of having

---

[1] See the comprehensive study by P. G. M. Dickson, *The Financial Revolution in England: A Study in the Development of Public Credit, 1688–1756* (1967).
[2] For a brief account of the debate see *ibid.*, chapter 2.

to service a debt which grew steadily during frequent wars.

One of the important byproducts of the revisionist literature referred to in Chapter 2 has been a renewed interest in the ideological character of this oppositional literature, largely dismissed by many earlier historians as party clap-trap generated by ritual exchanges between 'ins' and 'outs'. Once Pocock had broadened the radical Whig or Commonwealth canon to include Bolingbroke, the civic humanist dimensions of the attack on the connections between Walpole's ministry and the moneyed interest could be further explored.[1] Thus Isaac Kramnick's study of the ideas and tactics employed by Bolingbroke and his supporters places considerable emphasis on the appeal to an old order within which an independent class of landowners acted as the chief protectors of English liberties against the encroachments of the executive. Kramnick describes this appeal as a 'nostalgic flight from the political and economic innovations of the day', and as the 'political philosophy of the declining gentry'.[2] Quentin Skinner has gone beyond the simpler notion that Bolingbroke was a Tory engaged in the process of out-Whigging Walpole's Whigs by showing the close connections between Bolingbroke's case against Walpole and the radical Whig tradition, thereby demonstrating the polemical rationality of stressing these connections at a time when opposition and lack of patriotism were considered dangerously close to one another.[3]

For the purposes of this essay much of this work will be taken for granted; it will be adopted as evidence of a profound concern with the challenge posed to the existing political order – or rather, an idealised version of it – by the new moneyed interest and forms of property which appeared to

---

[1] See J. G. A. Pocock, *Politics, Language, and Time*, p. 134. In his latest book, *The Machiavellian Moment*, Pocock has developed the original idea at great length, particularly in chapter 13 on 'Neo-Machiavellian Political Economy; The Augustan Debate over Land, Trade and Credit'.

[2] I. Kramnick, *Bolingbroke and his Circle; The Politics of Nostalgia in the Age of Walpole* (1968). The most recent biography of Bolingbroke (1970) by H. T. Dickinson also makes use of the civic humanist perspective in giving an account of Bolingbroke's tactics.

[3] See Q. Skinner, 'The Principles and Practices of Opposition: The Case of Bolingbroke versus Walpole' in N. McKendrick (ed.), *Historical Perspectives, Studies in English Thought and Society* (1974).

have none of the citizenly or virtuous qualities possessed by visible or landed property. The essential idea was expressed in Bolingbroke's maxim that 'landed men are the true owners of our political vessel; the moneyed men, as such are but passengers in it'.[1] What was at stake was not simply a shift of power and initiative from the landowner to the City, but the delicate balance between the elements making up England's mixed constitution, and hence maintaining its stability and liberties. Commerce was capable of posing a challenge to the political order, though the burden of the 'modern' case, as argued by Montesquieu, Hume, and later by Smith, was that fears on this score had either been exaggerated or were misplaced. Indeed, one reading of the eighteenth-century English literature on trade – normally considered under the heading of mercantilism, liberal or otherwise – would be to describe it in terms of an increasing recognition of the dispensability of many of those earlier regulations thought necessary to reconcile commerce with political stability and power. But the debate aroused by public credit was largely focussed on novel features of a more rootless, perhaps evanescent, form of property connected with a separate moneyed interest. Trade had long been recognised and domesticated; it was obviously essential to England's wealth and power. Moreover, considerable agreement had been reached on those general forms of mercantile regulation most likely to prevent disruption of national interests. It was certainly one of the features of Bolingbroke's campaign that he attempted to unite landed and mercantile interests against the new moneyed interest.[2] If not the owners of the political vessel, or even its officers, merchants and manufacturers were treated as being a good

[1] Bolingbroke, *Works*, volume III, p. 174. A Whig version of the same idea was expressed by Robert Molesworth as follows: 'An old Whig is for choosing such sort of representatives to serve in Parliament, as have estates in the kingdom; and those not fleeting ones, which may be sent beyond sea by bills of exchange by every packet-boat, but fixed and permanent. To which end, every merchant, banker, or other moneyed man, who is ambitious of serving his country as a senator, should have also a competent, visible land estate, as a pledge to his electors that he intends to abide by them, and has the same interest in the public taxes, gains and losses.' Preface to second edition of his translation of *Francis Hotman, Franco–Gallia* (1721), p. xx.

[2] See H. T. Dickinson, *Bolingbroke*, chapter 11.

deal more essential to its capacity for motion than the idle passengers.

The purpose of the remainder of this chapter will be to consider what light the Augustan debate on land and public debt, as recently reinterpreted, sheds on Smith's treatment of similar issues.

Smith is frequently bracketed with Hume on the subject of public debt, if only as an illustration of how two of the most penetrating intelligences of the day could be wrong on one of the period's major economic developments.[1] An initial consideration of Hume's position certainly helps to establish a valuable perspective on Smith's political and economic priorities. Hume's 'Of Public Credit' is the only essay in his collection of economic essays that can legitimately be described as alarmist: he does not appear to have even aimed at the balance and philosophic stance that is such a marked feature of the other essays in this group.[2] 'Poverty, impotence, and subjection to foreign powers' were held out as the prospect facing all modern states that continued to finance themselves, particularly during periods of war, by means of the practice of mortgaging future revenue. Here was a case where ancient practice – the use of accumulated treasure to finance war – was more prudent. Hume proceeded to examine the case for public debt, recently embraced 'by great ministers, and by a whole party among us', under two headings: the effect on commerce and industry, and the effect on 'wars and negotiations'. On the credit side of the account, he acknowledged the benefits conferred by the new liquid asset arising out of the debt: it was capable of performing the functions of money while yielding an income to its users, thereby facilitating trade, reducing the general level of trading profit, and diffusing industry throughout the community. Heavier on the debit side, however, lay the disadvantages of the growth in size of London at the expense of the provinces, the inflationary effect

[1] See, for example, J. R. McCulloch's preface to *A Select Collection of Scarce and Valuable Tracts and Other Publications on the National Debt and the Sinking Fund* (1857), p. x.
[2] By 'economic' essays I mean those collected by E. Rotwein in his edition entitled *David Hume; Writings on Economics* (1955).

of expansion in a form of paper money, the onerous taxes required to service the debt, the transfer problems created by foreign ownership, and the encouragement given to an idle *rentier* class. Hume does not pause to weigh the advantages and disadvantages in any detail, or to resolve the apparent conflict between such arguments as the stimulus to trade and the increase in a class that lead a 'useless and inactive life'. He moves directly to the nub of the problem, namely 'the prejudice that result to the state considered as a body politic', where the bad effects are 'pure and unmixed'.

In arguing this position Hume first disposes of the view that debt is harmless because it merely entails 'transferring money from the right hand to the left'. Debt service adds to the burden already borne by the poor through taxes on commodities, and by landowners through the land tax. Such exactions contain the 'seeds of ruin' and must, therefore, have a natural limit. Hume then depicts a situation in which the stockholders are able to engross the revenue of the nation; they are described as men 'who have no connexions with the state'. By virtue of the mobility of their wealth, they are able to avoid taxes and 'enjoy their revenue in any part of the globe in which they choose to reside'. The following disruptive political consequences are predicted as the possible outcome of this state of affairs:

Adieu to all ideas of nobility, gentry, and family. The stocks can be transferred in an instant, and being in such a fluctuating state, will seldom be transmitted during three generations from father to son. Or were they to remain ever so long in one family, they convey no hereditary authority or credit to the possessor; and by this means, the several ranks of men, which form a kind of independent magistracy in a state, instituted by the hand of nature, are entirely lost; and every man in authority derives his influence from the commission alone of the sovereign. No expedient remains for preventing or suppressing insurrections, but mercenary armies: No expedient at all remains for resisting tyranny: Elections are swayed by bribery and corruption alone: And the middle power between king and people being totally removed, a grievous despotism must infallibly prevail. The landholders, despised for their poverty, and hated for their oppressions, will be utterly unable to make any opposition to it.[1]

[1] See *ibid.*, pp. 98–9.

125

While this takes the form of a speculative flight of fancy, there is good reason to believe that Hume intended it as a serious warning. Hence the insight which it provides into his fears and views on the process of decline into despotism and 'a state of languor, inactivity, and impotence' must be taken seriously. Indeed, considerable use has been made of this passage, and of Hume's views on the national debt in general, to support a 'Tory' interpretation of his political sympathies.[1] It will be obvious how well the passage suits Kramnick's portrait of an ideology founded on nostalgia and Augustan despair.[2] Forbes's devastating critique of attempts to apply conventional labels to Hume was mentioned earlier and is again relevant at this juncture.[3] We should be suspicious of a nostalgic reading of any writer of Hume's calibre, especially when we know that he attacked the habit of appealing to ancient constitutions and magnifying 'the virtue of remote ancestors'.[4] If Hume must be situated on a contemporary party spectrum, it may do less harm to employ the 'Country' and 'Court' alternatives which he regarded as the only 'natural' parties of principle within the British mixed constitution.[5] The enthusiastic qualities of his account of the connections between commerce and progress, his acceptance of paper money, and his realistic analysis of both influence and parties place him at the 'Court' end of the spectrum. The fact that he took up a 'Country' position on the national debt can be taken as an illustration of Pocock's idea that the spectrum was a genuine one, allowing freedom of movement, rather than a sharp divide.[6]

Hume's predictions concerning the likely results of mounting public debt have a definite air of calamity about them; he maintains that 'either the nation must destroy public credit,

[1] See G. Giarrizzo, *David Hume politico e storico* (1962), pp. 50, 60, 69–71, 94–5.
[2] Kramnick cites the passage on pp. 82–3 of *Bolingbroke and his Circle* and refers to Hume's views as belonging to 'his late pessimistic Tory period', basing this on Giarrizzo's authority.
[3] See D. Forbes's review article on Giarrizzo's book in the *Historical Journal*, VI (1963) 280–95; and *Hume's Philosophical Politics*, especially pp. 126–7, 173–5.
[4] See D. Hume, *Essays*, eds. T. H. Green and T. H. Grose, volume I, pp. 307, 467–8.   [5] See *ibid.*, pp. 134–43.
[6] See J. G. A. Pocock, *The Machiavellian Moment*, pp. 493–7.

or public credit must destroy the nation'. This will come about in one of three ways. First, an attempt might be made to eliminate the debt by means of a levy on property; secondly, the nation could become so oppressed by taxation that it will raid the sinking fund and repudiate its debts, most likely during a war; thirdly, and more calamitously, it could fail to grasp the nettle and hence succumb to its foreign enemies. Since he felt that a levy would fall exclusively on 'visible property in lands and houses', Hume considered the first solution as unlikely to be adopted. In any event, since the attempt to implement visionary schemes for the discharge of debt would cause the whole credit structure to collapse, he described this as dying of the doctor. The third solution was 'violent death'; it would arise if a policy of voluntary bankruptcy was not adopted in time by a Parliament dominated by the landed interest, but more sensitive to the claims of stockholders than prudence would dictate. It is clear then that the second solution, depicted as a 'natural death', was the one favoured by Hume. Unfortunately, voluntary bankruptcy was the policy least likely to be accepted by 'free governments', as opposed to monarchies like that of France, in spite of the fact that Hume regarded it as a policy which would have no lasting effects on the nation's credit. Under free governments, therefore, public debt was the main 'source of degeneracy'; they were least prepared to take effective action before taxes had become intolerable and 'all the property of the state be brought into the hands of the public'.[1] Consequently, Hume hoped for an 'open struggle' between landowners and stockholders, with the well-established representatives of millions emerging victorious over the mere thousands of stockholders. His main fear was that the struggle would not take place, simply because 'these two Orders of Men are so involved with each other by Connexions and Interest, that the public Force will be allowed to go to total Decay, before the violent Remedy, which is the only one, will be ventur'd on'.[2]

Hume's priorities, if not his precise fears, were shared by

[1] See 'Of Civil Liberty' in D. Hume, *Essays*, eds. T. H. Green and T. H. Grose, pp. 162–3.
[2] See the letter to Strahan in 1771 in D. Hume, *Letters*, ed. J. T. Y. Greig, volume II, p. 248, see also pp. 210, 237, 242, 245.

Montesquieu, who had said that the English passion for liberty was such that heavy taxes were accepted as the price of its defence. By means of public credit it had become possible for England 'to undertake things above its natural strength, and employ against its enemies immense sums of fictitious riches, which the credit and nature of the government may render real'.[1] Montesquieu did not accept the arguments of apologists for the debt who claimed that it conferred direct economic benefits on the nation; his list of disadvantages – he saw no advantages – is similar to that given by Hume. Of the four classes which he recognised as paying the debts of the state – landed proprietors, merchants, labourers, and the annuitants – the last could, in case of emergency, be sacrificed to the rest. This was simply a matter of choosing between a passive or 'indolent' class and the other three active classes. Montesquieu noted, however, that it was impossible to tax the annuitant or creditor class without destroying public confidence. Moreover, since this class was always in the eye of Ministers, it obtained special protection.[2]

The conflict foreseen by Hume was more dramatic, but it seems important to stress that he was speaking of conflict between the landed and *moneyed* interests, rather than between the landed and *merchant* interests. On the latter question his view was that these 'are not really distinct and never will be so, till our public debts increase to such a degree, as to become altogether oppressive and intolerable'.[3] Hume gives little indication of his reasons for thinking that a division between landed and merchant interests will emerge at this point, but there are no grounds for equating the merchant and moneyed interests. The burden of Hume's attack is on stockholders; he considered that the merchant interest would suffer along with others if the system of public borrowing continued; and he never retracted his opinion that merchants were 'one of the most useful races of men'.[4]

[1] See C. S. Montesquieu, *The Spirit of the Laws*, p. 310.
[2] *Ibid.*, pp. 395–6.
[3] See D. Hume, *Essays*, eds. T. H. Green and T. H. Grose, p. 130. Rotwein's notes on the 'middle class', and his query about Hume's consistency (*David Hume: Writings on Economics*, pp. 99, 106), suggest that he has conflated the merchant and moneyed interests.
[4] See E. Rotwein (ed.), *David Hume: Writings on Economics*, p. 52.

The earliest evidence of Smith's attitude to the same range of questions can be found in the *Lectures on Jurisprudence*, where there are two sections on stocks and stock-jobbing under 'Of Revenue'. In view of the pejorative overtones which still clung to 'stock-jobbery', it may be significant that the account of perpetual funding, of the meaning of 'bull' and 'bear', and the explanation for day-to-day market fluctuations in the funds given in these sections is straightforwardly factual.[1] Elsewhere in the *Lectures*, however, there are comments of a broader nature. Under domestic expenditure, for example, Smith joins Hume in rejecting the idea that public debt entails harmless transfer payments on the grounds that taxes have to be increased to service the debt; and there is a further echo of Hume and Montesquieu in the remark that 'industry is taxed to support idleness'.[2] But when Smith deals with the redistributional effect of taxes falling on the landowner, the tone returns to one that is studiously neutral.

The landlord who pays his annual land tax pays also a great part of the taxes on consumptions. On this account the landed interest complains first of a war, thinking the burden of it falls upon them, while on the other hand the monied men are gainers, and therefore oppose them. This perhaps occasions the continuance of what is called the Tory interest.[3]

There is a hint of larger disagreement with Hume over the sinking fund, though it must be remembered that Smith is mainly concerned with the part played by the institution in the history of the English Parliament. Whereas Hume had argued that no great harm would result from a scheme of calculated repudiation, Smith praised the sinking fund in 'vulgar' Whiggish terms as one of the marks of English liberty and constitutional stability. The funds mortgaged to service the debt were not available to the king; they were paid to an independent court of exchequer which operated according to rules laid down by Parliament.

---

[1] *LJ*(B), pp. 247–52.
[2] *Ibid.*, pp. 210–11. Walpole is criticised for having endorsed the view that 'the public debt was no inconvenience, though it is to be supposed that a man of his abilities saw the contrary himself'.
[3] *Ibid.*, p. 241.

The surplus of the mortgages goes into what is called the sinking fund for paying the public debt, which secures the government in the present family, because if a revolution were to happen, the public creditors, who are men of interest, would lose both principal and interest. Thus the nation is quite secure in the management of the public revenue, and in this manner a rational system of liberty has been introduced into Britain.[1]

Towards the end of his life Hume made a similar concession, based perhaps on his increasing concern for the maintenance of public order. In a passage added to the essay on public credit in 1770, he observed that the support of the stockholders would strengthen the hand of government in dealing with 'Jacobitical violence and democratical frenzy'. The precariousness of property held in stocks would increase the sensitivity of stockholders to any threat to public peace posed by the 'factious, mutinous, seditious, and even perhaps rebellious' London mob.[2] It is noticeable, however, that Hume made no attempt to reconcile this concession with his critical remarks about the ability of stockholders to shift their property to any part of the globe. But the very fact that both Hume and Smith recognized the potential contribution to public order made by the diffusion of debt ownership marks a departure in the 'Court' direction from the oppositional literature of the earlier part of the century, where the growth of the moneyed interest was treated largely as a threat to liberty by virtue of its close connection with the executive. The identical observation was being used to support divergent concerns.

In the *Wealth of Nations*, of course, Smith greatly expanded the treatment given to such topics as the public debt, government expenditure, and taxation, assimilating them into the economic design of the whole edifice. Thus his views on public debt in Book v must be taken in conjunction with the theory of capital accumulation, and the related distinction between productive and unproductive labour, expounded in Book ii. This book is one of the new parts of the *Wealth of Nations*, and is generally considered to reveal the influence of Smith's contacts with the Physiocrats in 1765–6. Its significance to

[1] *Ibid.*, p. 45; and *LJ*(A), volume iv, pp. 86–7.
[2] E. Rotwein (ed.), *David Hume: Writings on Economics*, p. 95.

the question of public debt lies in the contrast which it makes possible between public and private prodigality, where government expenditure was defined as 'unproductive'.

> Great nations are never impoverished by private, though they some-times are by publick prodigality and misconduct. The whole, or almost the whole public revenue, is in most countries employed in maintaining unproductive hands. Such are the people who compose a numerous and splendid court, a great ecclesiastical establishment, great fleets and armies, who in time of peace produce nothing,... such people...are all maintained by the produce of other men's labour.[1]

Fortunately, owing to the operation of 'the uniform, constant, and uninterrupted effort of every man to better his condition', private frugality was generally powerful enough to offset the effects of public prodigality on economic progress. The testimony to this was furnished by England's growth in the years since the Revolution, in spite of a succession of expensive wars and the fact that the country had 'never been blessed with a very parsimonious government'.[2]

The distinction between productive and unproductive labour has given rise to many problems of interpretation for students of economic thought, but the point to note about the introduction of the new terminology is that it does not seem to have been essential as a basis for Smith's observations on public prodigality. The same idea is implicit in the earliest known statement of his general position cited earlier, and it is also prefigured in certain passages in the *Lectures*, which were given before Smith adopted Physiocratic terminology.[3] Neverthe-less, the additional force and pejorative application of the term 'unproductive' to most forms of government expenditure provided a basis for orthodox treatments of the same theme by later political economists, as well as for the kinds of popular nineteenth-century maxims epitomised in the Gladstonian idea of allowing money to fructify in the pockets of the people.[4]

---

[1] *WN* II.iii.30. [2] *WN* II.iii.36.

[3] See the citation on p. 4 above and Smith's criticisms of Mandeville's view that 'no expense at home can be hurtful' in *LJ*(B), pp. 207–11; *LJ*(A), volume VI, pp. 78–80.

[4] For post-Smithian developments of the view that government expenditure was unproductive see B. A. Corry, *Money, Saving and Investment in English Economics, 1800–1850* (1961), chapter 9.

These premonitions must be mentioned here because they have contributed powerfully to Smith's *laissez-faire* image – an image which does not prepare the reader for the fairly tolerant attitude towards the expenses of the sovereign adopted in Book v of the *Wealth of Nations*.

In addition to the ordinary costs involved in carrying out the normal sovereign's duties with respect to defence, justice, public works, and education, Smith considered that 'a certain expence is requisite for the support of his dignity'; and he added that the costs of defence and 'dignity' are 'both laid out for the general benefit of the whole society'.[1] In the *Lectures* he committed himself to a slightly more affirmative position.

We may observe that the government in a civilized country is much more expensive than in a barbarous one; and when we say that one government is more expensive than another, it is the same as if we said that the one country is farther advanced in improvement than another. To say that the government is expensive and the people not oppressed is to say that the people are rich. There are many expenses necessary in a civilized country for which there is no occasion in one that is barbarous. Armies, fleets, fortified palaces, and public buildings, judges, and officers of the revenue must be supported, and if they be neglected, disorder will ensue.[2]

The same idea runs through most of the discussion of government expenditure in Book v. Although 'we naturally expect more splendor in the court of a king, than in the mansion-house of a doge or burgomaster', the general expense of government rises in all civilised states. Republics as well as monarchies have acquired 'the taste for some sort of pageantry, for splendid buildings...and other public ornaments'.[3] Rising expenditure on necessary services, *as well as* 'want of parsimony', is responsible for the practice of contracting debt to meet the extraordinary needs of war in all modern states.

Before considering the relationship between wars and public debt more closely, it may be helpful to return to the treatment of prodigality given in Book ii. We have already noted Smith's belief that the individual pursuit of happiness

[1] *WN* v.i.h.1.   [2] *LJ*(B), p. 239.
[3] *WN* v.i.h.3.

through material goods was in large measure illusory, though genuine public benefits of an unforeseen variety accrue from the ambition to satisfy vanity.[1] In dealing with the effects of frugality and prodigality Smith introduced a similar idea based on the distinction between individual motives and social results. This occurs towards the end of his account of productive and unproductive labour, where he acknowledges that 'some modes of expence...seem to contribute more to the growth of public opulence than others'. This was true of durable goods which could be accumulated, used over time, and either passed on to successive generations or down the social scale. The distinction is between expenditure on immediate services and expenditure on goods which yield a flow of services throughout their effective life, whether in the hands of the original purchaser or not. Durable goods are also capable of maintaining productive labourers; the consumption of immediate services merely supports unproductive labour, and therefore does not increase 'the exchangeable value of the annual produce of the land and labour of the country'.

For all the references to the importance of private frugality, therefore, Smith also recognised that: 'Noble palaces, magnificent villas, great collections of books, statues, pictures, and other curiosities, are frequently both an ornament and an honour, not only to the neighbourhood, but to the whole country to which they belong. Versailles is an ornament and an honour to France, Stowe and Wilton to England'.[2] He appends an interesting argument derived from the *Theory of Moral Sentiments* to show that durable magnificence may actually be conducive to frugality. The man who finds it necessary to reduce his expenditure on such goods is not exposed 'to the censure of the public'; he is merely thought to have 'satisfied his fancy'. Retrenchment in the number of servants or in the lavishness of hospitality, however, implies 'some acknowledgement of preceding bad conduct'. Typically though, Smith does not endorse the former as the superior

[1] See pp. 91–2 above.
[2] *WN* II.iii.39. For further comment on the importance of durables to Smith see N. Rosenberg, 'Adam Smith, Consumer Tastes, and Economic Growth', *Journal of Political Economy*, LXXVI (1968) 361–74.

morality when compared with that of the man who by means of hospitality shares his prodigality with others.[1] The entire argument, from the denigration of the satisfactions derived from individual wealth, to the laudatory references to aggregate wealth, particularly when it assumes the form of durable magnificence of the kind that is a credit to the genius and achievements of a collectivity, such as a city or nation, conforms – as Jacob Viner indicated – to a classical–renaissance view of communal enrichment.[2] The standard portrait of Smith as the upholder of a business ethic of acquisitive individualism is unable to deal with such matters, and so ignores them.

The doctrine of productive and unproductive labour reappears in the chapter on public debt in Book v. But since Smith is dealing with an important institution, he provides a historical account of its origins. As in the *Lectures*, prior to the introduction of commerce and civilisation, the expenses of government, including those of war, could be met from public treasure or from the revenue derived from the sovereign's estates. Standing armies were unnecessary, and the 'bounty and hospitality' of primitive rulers, unlike the 'vanity' associated with commerce in modern times, did not encroach on treasure troves.[3] There is no equivalent in the *Wealth of Nations* to the Whiggish political story of the alienation of Crown lands and the rise of the Commons in England, but Smith maintains that the lands that remain in royal hands are no longer adequate to meet even part of the costs of government. He estimated that they yielded less than a quarter of the rents they would fetch under private, and hence more effective, management; and recommended that, if national advantage were to be consulted, it would be better to sell all Crown lands and use the revenue to pay off public debt. By placing the land in numerous private hands the nation would gain more through increased efficiency and prosperity than it would have to replace in the form of more direct methods of meeting the

[1] *WN* ii.iii.40–2; see editorial notes for cross-references to *TMS*.
[2] See Viner's article on 'Adam Smith' in *International Encyclopaedia of the Social Sciences* (1968), p. 325.
[3] *WN* v.iii.1–2.

sovereign's expenses. An exception should be made in the case of land which could be used 'for the purposes of pleasure and magnificence, parks, gardens, publick walks etc. possessions which are every where considered as causes of expence, not as sources of revenue' in 'a great and civilized monarchy'.[1] This underlines the classical–renaissance view of communal 'magnificence', and provides a more natural interpretation than any derived from an attempt to foster back onto Smith such modern doctrines as those surrounding the concept of 'public goods'.

Like Hume's essay on public credit, therefore, though with greater historical elaboration, Smith's account of public debts begins by contrasting ancient and modern practice in the light of the revolution associated with commerce. Modern sovereigns are obliged to contract debt in order to fight wars, but Smith stresses the fact that facility of borrowing is increased with the need to do so. Commercial nations abound with merchants and manufacturers who have both the means to lend to government, and the willingness to do so which accompanies confidence and security. Why then should this sympathetic process lead him to the conclusion that the burden of debt 'will in the long-run probably ruin, all the great nations of Europe'?[2] Though calmly stated, this conclusion seems to bring us back to Hume's alarmist references to the 'seeds of ruin'. But while critical of a 'ruinous expedient', and of the 'improvident spendthrift' habits of modern governments who anticipate revenue by borrowing on an increasing scale, there is no air of imminent political cataclysm to Smith's discussion of the problem. In contrast to Hume, he points out that the ease of borrowing money to finance war enables governments to avoid the necessity of raising taxes sharply, with the result that: 'In great empires the people who live in the capital, and in the provinces remote from the scene of action, feel many of them, scarce any inconveniency from the war; but enjoy, at their ease, the amusement of reading in the newspapers the exploits of their own fleets and armies'.[3] Smith maintains a nice balance between serious concern and complacent contem-

---

[1] *WN* v.ii.a.20.   [2] *WN* v.iii.10.
[3] *WN* v.iii.37.

135

plation of ruin by concentrating on the best method of reducing the burden of debt, though like his attitude to the
corruption of the morals of the common people, it cannot be
said that he reaches optimistic conclusions.

Sinking funds are easily raided, and are usually inadequate
to retire debt; it would be chimerical to expect the debt to be
discharged out of the ordinary revenue from taxation. While
subscribers to the public funds merely exchange one form of
capital for another, this was not the case for the nation as a
whole – a subtraction from productive funds in order to
support an unproductive activity was involved. On the one
hand, the taxes required to service the debt hindered further
capital accumulation, while on the other, the effect of funding
was to postpone increases in taxation, but only by destroying
capital already accumulated. The latter expedient was justifiable during war, though it had the effect of reducing public
opposition to wars 'wantonly undertaken'. In the long run,
of course, funding also increased the tax burden on agriculture
and manufacturing. While the public creditor had a general
interest in national prosperity, he had no means of ensuring
that means sufficient to this end would be adopted – a very
mild version of the idle *rentier* argument, with no redistributional overtones. Since funding had 'gradually enfeebled
every state which had adopted it', was there any reason why
Britain should escape the same fate? The fact that as a result
of economic growth the country was able to bear a greater
burden of debt than had once been thought conceivable was
no guarantee that she was 'capable of supporting any burden'.
Wisely, and once more in company with Hume, Smith re-
frained from stating what level of debt would be insupportable, and from predicting when ruin and bankruptcy was likely
to occur; but he agreed with Hume in thinking that 'avowed
bankruptcy' was preferable to the pernicious process of allowing inflation to reduce the effective claims against the state.

Smith did have one further proposal to make, namely his
speculative scheme for an empire union, which would, in
return for fair and equal representation in 'the estates-general
of the British empire', enable the tax revenue paid by all the
provinces of the empire to be applied to the reduction of

Britain's debt. The political significance of this proposal will be considered in the next chapter.

The question of public debt was linked with taxation. The unfair tax burden falling on visible property, especially land, was one of Hume's main criticisms of the debt. Yet while Smith's first general maxim on taxation was that 'the subjects of every state ought to contribute towards the support of the government, as nearly as possible, in proportion to their respective abilities', he explicitly stated that he was not concerned with inequality of treatment as between the three main sources of revenue – rent, profits and wages – and hence between the associated classes of income recipient.[1] This not only sets him apart from the later interest in class distribution associated with the name of David Ricardo, but distances him from much of the earlier oppositional literature concentrating on conflicts between landowning and moneyed interests. In consonance with the neutrality towards the 'Tory interest' shown in the *Lectures*, Smith does not criticise the English land tax on grounds of equity: he clearly felt that it was a good tax, and one that agricultural prosperity had made easier to bear. He was not averse to the use of differential taxation to encourage or discourage particular economic activities; and there is a mildly redistributive flavour about some of his proposals for taxing luxuries consumed by the rich as well as profits made out of monopoly positions. It was reasonable to ask the rich to pay more than proportionately towards the expenses of the sovereign; and it was equally reasonable for those rents which owed their existence to the security provided by good government to bear a special tax.

Throughout his discussion of taxation there are two main concerns, namely the 'ease, comfort and security of the inferior ranks', and the minimisation of the 'odious visits and examination of the tax-gatherer'. The latter concern was one based on considerations of liberty and public opinion, but the impression left by Smith's long chapter on this subject is one of modified complacency. Though not perfect, the English system 'is as good or better than that of most of our neighbours'.[2] It was superior, for example, to that of France, and

[1] *WN* v.ii.g.3.   [2] *WN* v.ii.k.66; see also v.iii.58.

all things considered, a tribute to 'the mild government of England'.

Neither on public debts nor on taxation, therefore, is it possible to detect any fundamental disquiet on Smith's part concerning the political strains created by the public debt. There are, however, at least two places in the *Wealth of Nations* where Smith uses phrases which are redolent of the earlier oppositional literature on the special import which attaches to landed property as the key to civic personality.

> The capital...that is acquired to any country by commerce and manufactures, is all a very precarious and uncertain possession, till some part of it has been secured and realised in the cultivation and improvement of its lands. A merchant, it has been said very properly, is not necessarily the citizen of any particular country. It is in a great measure indifferent to him from what place he carries on his trade; and a very trifling disgust will make him remove his capital, and together with it all the industry which it supports, from one country to another. No part of it can be said to belong to any particular country, till it has been spread as it were over the face of that country, either in buildings, or in the lasting improvement of lands.[1]

> The proprietor of land is necessarily a citizen of the particular country in which his estate lies. The proprietor of stock is properly a citizen of the world, and is not necessarily attached to any particular country. He would be apt to abandon the country in which he was exposed to a vexatious inquisition...and would remove his stock to some other country where he could either carry on his business, or enjoy his fortune more at his ease.[2]

It is interesting to note that Smith attaches no political significance to these observations. The first passage largely serves to underline the economic argument mentioned above concerning the role of 'durability', while the second is meant to emphasise the risks of heavy taxation. It is also significant that in the first passage he is speaking about merchants *and* stockholders; he is not attempting, as Bolingbroke, Montesquieu, and Hume did, to separate an idle moneyed interest from the legitimate productive activities of the landowner and merchant. Of course, Smith was not formulating a political

---

[1] *WN* III.iv.24.   [2] *WN* v.ii.f.6.

platform, as Bolingbroke was, though attempts have been made on other grounds to show that a definite agrarian bias runs through his work. The evidence for this can be found in passages like the first one just cited, which state that agricultural improvements constitute a more stable and lasting basis for a nation's wealth than commerce and manufacturing. Agriculture is also given 'natural' priority in Smith's scheme of economic development, and investment in agriculture occupies the top position in his pecking order of employments for capital.[1] There are even passages in the *Wealth of Nations*, like the following one, which have a pastoral quality.

The beauty of the country besides, the pleasures of a country life, the tranquillity of mind which it promises, and wherever the injustice of human laws does not disturb it, the independency which it really affords, have charms that more or less attract every body; and as to cultivate the ground was the original destination of man, so in every stage of his existence he seems to retain a predilection for this primitive employment.[2]

Political significance can be attached to this agrarian bias by emphasising the closing parts of Book 1 of the *Wealth of Nations*, where Smith discusses the effect of economic progress on 'the three great, original and constituent orders of every civilized society', namely those receiving rents, wages, and profits.[3] Since rents rise with progress, the landowners' interest is 'strictly and inseparably connected with the general interest of society'. It follows that 'when the public deliberates concerning any regulation of commerce or police, the proprietors of land can never mislead it'. Those who lived by wages also stood to gain from progressive conditions, that is when capital accumulation was taking place. For reasons mentioned earlier, however, although the wage-earner's interest, like that of the landowner, was connected with that of society, he is 'incapable either of comprehending that interest, or of understanding its connexion with his own'. In consequence, 'his voice is little heard and less regarded' in public debate, except when, for

---

[1] See *WN* I.xi.c.8; II.v.19–37; III.vi.18–24; IV.ix.38. For the best and most recent analysis of the economic significance of Smith's imputed agrarian bias see S. Hollander, *The Economics of Adam Smith*, pp. 286–97.
[2] *WN* III.i.3.   [3] *WN* I.xi.

interested reasons of their own, his case is supported by employers.

Smith's agrarian bias can only be accorded political meaning by contrasting his views on the landowning interest with that of the profit-receivers, the merchants and manufacturers. Smith's consistent antagonism towards organised mercantile interest groups is so well known that it needs only to be mentioned. Since profits fall with the progress of society, the interest of merchants and manufacturers does not coincide with that of society at large. Any legislative or administrative proposal made by this order should be examined with suspicion, because it comes from a group 'who have generally an interest to deceive and even to oppress the public'.[1] It was their 'sneaking arts' and 'mean rapacity' that prevented commerce from being a 'bond of union' among nations and between individuals; and the same 'monopolising spirit' convinced Smith that merchants and manufacturers 'neither are, nor ought to be, the rulers of mankind'.[2] Trade might not endanger a man's soul, but its organised protagonists suffered from grave civic defects, and should not be entrusted with powers of government or even influence on government. This was the burden of Smith's case against the East India Company as rulers and traders; and it was the source of his contemptuous dismissal of the idea of founding a great empire according to mercantile principles with the remark that it was a project 'fit for a nation whose government is influenced by shopkeepers'.[3]

Such outspoken hostility clearly requires explanation, but it is first necessary to show why agrarian bias cannot be regarded as having great political significance. Landowners suffer from their own species of defect in Smith's eyes: 'That indolence, which is the natural effect of the ease and security of their situation, renders them too often, not only ignorant, but incapable of that application of mind which is necessary in order to foresee and understand the consequence of any publick regulation.' In common with high profits, rents from large landholdings have a debilitating effect on their recipi-

---

[1] *WN* I.xi. p. 10.   [2] *WN* IV.iii.c.9.
[3] *WN* IV.vii.c.63.

ents. The difference between merchants and landowners was that since the former spent their life making 'plans and projects', they had only too clear a sense of their own interests; hence 'they have frequently more acuteness of understanding than the greater part of country gentlemen'.[1] Smith shared with Hume an assumption that landowners tended to be spenders rather than savers.[2] Moreover, the ignorance of the landowner might, on occasion, be accompanied by 'liberality'.[3] But Smith's criticism of large landholdings, and his antagonism to such feudal relics as the laws of primogeniture and entail, show that he took an impartial view of the distribution of greed and love of dominion among the different orders of society: 'Entails are thought necessary for maintaining this exclusive privilege of the nobility to the great offices and honours of their country; and that order having usurped one unjust advantage over the rest of their fellow-citizens, lest their poverty should render it ridiculous, it is thought reasonable that they should have another.'[4]

On the basis of this evidence alone it ought to be as difficult to force Smith into the category of nostalgic Tory as it is to fit him into the portrait of 'an unconscious mercenary in the service of a rising capitalist class', or for that matter into the role of pioneer theorist of labour exploitation along Marxian lines.[5] Nevertheless, determined efforts continue to be made to thrust Smith into one or other of these categories, chiefly by means of the open-ended expedient of seeking 'anticipations' at the expense of what is actually presented in the texts. The adoption of the liberal capitalist perspective by most economists and historians of economic thought has taken the

[1] *WN* I.xi. p. 10.
[2] Hume's view is most clearly expressed in his essay 'Of Interest' as reprinted in E. Rotwein (ed.), *David Hume: Writings on Economics*, pp. 47–59.
[3] *WN* I.xi.a.1. But notice that Smith had said earlier that: 'As soon as the land of any country has all become private property, the landlords, like all other men, love to reap where they never sowed, and demand a rent even for its natural produce.' (*WN* I.vi.7.)
[4] *WN* III.ii.6; see also *LJ*(B), pp. 118–20, 224, 228.
[5] We owe the first of these descriptions to Max Lerner, whose introduction to the Modern Library version of the Cannan edition of *WN*(1937) is a useful compendium of such *clichés*. The literature on exploitation theories is given in the note on p. 90 above.

form of supplying nineteenth-century meanings to the less familiar eighteenth-century concepts which comprise Smith's system. The first step in this process has become so common-place that it is hardly noticed; it consists in the rapid trans-lation of Smith's 'commercial society' into 'capitalism' *tout court*. The simple fact that 'capitalism' was not available to Smith, and that he did not find it necessary to coin the term, passes without comment. The same is true of his failure to employ the term 'industry' in anything but its eighteenth-century sense of a human quality or a general attribute of all economic activity, including, of course, the 'industry of the country' as opposed to that of the town. It is a rare ex-ception to find anyone who makes the translation offering an argument for doing so, unless some remarks about the early state of the industrial revolution in 1776 are accepted as all that is required.[1] There *may* be a case for substituting our terminology for the one Smith chose to employ, in the full knowledge that it would be understood by his audience, but it should not go by default: the onus should be on those making the substitution to show not merely that a gain in understanding is achieved but that there are no losses in the process. Thus in the case of the substitution of 'capitalism' for 'commercial society' it ought to be demonstrated that Smith's aim, both as historian of civil society and economic analyst, is so closely focussed on a specific type of relationship between capital and wage-labour as the clue to the nature of commercial society, that only 'capitalism' will adequately capture his mean-ing. If, on the other hand, it is not possible to demonstrate the centrality of this relationship, perhaps because it is merely one aspect of the whole range of market relationships which exist in a society in which 'everyone becomes in some measure, a merchant', then it seems that the losses in understanding are likely to exceed the gains.

Another popular strategy has been to 'Ricardianise' Smith's political economy. In one of the most recent and

[1] For an interesting exchange on this see C. P. Kindleberger, 'The Historical Background: Adam Smith on the Industrial Revolution' and the comments by Asa Briggs and R. M. Hartwell in T. Wilson and A. S. Skinner (eds.), *The Market and the State* (1976), pp. 1–41.

dogged attempts along these lines Smith has been attributed with a complete vision of decline into 'general poverty', and with pessimistic ideas of a miserable stationary state, of an improbable, not to mention anachronistic, Ricardo–Malthus provenance.[1] Although Smith recognised elements of monopoly return in the income of landowners, he drew none of the political and economic conclusions which Ricardo was later to draw from his version of the rent doctrine. Diminishing returns in agriculture do not play the key role in Smith's system that they were to play in the work of Ricardo and later orthodox classical writers. While Smith speaks of the possibility of a country attaining 'that full complement of riches which the nature of its soil and climate, and its situation with respect to other countries, allowed it to acquire', he immediately points out that 'no country has ever yet arrived at this degree of opulence'.[2] China's stationary state was due to its 'laws and institutions' rather than to any inherent economic limitations. Like Ricardo, though for quite different reasons, Smith believed that profits would decline with progress. Unlike Ricardo, however, he did not consider high profits to be necessary to protect the motive for, and sources of, further capital accumulation.[3] He was, in fact, more concerned about high rather than low profits, partly because they could be a sign of a successful attempt to suppress competition, and partly because he believed they would be accompanied by inefficiency and poor management. Finally, although Smith was aware of the basic Malthusian population mechanism, he made no effort to give it a crucial role in his vision of the prospects for the future living standards of the mass of society. Indeed, since aggregate wealth, beyond certain minimum standards, was more important than *per capita* wealth, he endorsed increasing population

[1] See R. L. Heilbroner, 'The Paradox of Progress...', in *EAS*, pp. 524–539.
[2] *WN* I.ix.15.
[3] To be precise, it should be said that Smith's theory of savings does not depend on the rate of profit except when net savings are zero, namely at the stationary state. The special characteristics of Smith's theory of profit and savings have long been recognized in the scholarly literature; for a good statement of Smith's position see G. S. L. Tucker, *Progress and Profits in British Economic Thought, 1650–1850* (1960), chapter 5. Smith's antagonism to high profits is examined in N. Rosenberg, 'Adam Smith on Profits – Paradox Lost and Regained', in *EAS*, pp. 377–89.

both as a sign and as a potential cause of the increase in aggregate wealth.[1] In the light of this evidence it should not be surprising that Smith does not express fears or explain the mechanisms *à la* Ricardo which bring the decline into a state of 'general poverty'. And since this does not form any part of his conclusions, it is purely adventitious to proceed to accuse him of 'ambivalence', and of purveying a 'social dynamic from which any possibility of a fundamental change in socio-economic change has been removed', simply because he did not produce remedies for a world he did not envisage. Such failures and 'limitations that seem to our age so patent and so crippling' may be regrettable from the safety of hindsight, but they certainly cannot be described as placing 'Smith's masterpiece in its proper historical perspective', or as proof that his work is 'a dismaying failure, *in its own* terms'.[2]

Rightly or wrongly, Smith's fears for contemporary society – and even 'fears' seems exaggerated when applied to such a master of the art of equipoise – were concentrated on such matters as the 'corruption' considered in the previous chapter. While the middling and upper ranks of society possessed the means to exercise their civic personalities, in excess the same means could also prevent them from exercising their civic functions properly. The lower ranks were incapacitated by lack of these means, and might undergo a further deterioration in this respect with the advance of commercial society if special measures were not adopted.

To a lesser extent, the 'ruinous expedient' considered in this chapter was also of concern to Smith, though it remains true that if a single worry has to be selected then the motive and capacity of the mercantile interest to combine against the public interest seems to have been the most important one. The 'overgrown standing army' which Smith feared was a figurative one composed of merchants banding together to 'intimidate the legislature'.[3] It should not be necessary to point out that in choosing to use this expression Smith was well aware

---

[1] See Viner's article 'Adam Smith' in the *International Encyclopaedia of the Social Sciences*, p. 325.

[2] All the statements quoted can be found in R. L. Heilbroner, *The Paradox of Progress*, pp. 532, 536, 538; emphasis supplied.

[3] *WN* IV.ii.43.

of its contemporary resonances; it implied the existence of a dangerous extra-parliamentary pressure group or faction. It is also well known that one of the expressions that Smith *did* find it useful to coin – 'the mercantile system' – was specifically designed to cover the specious arguments employed by merchants and governments to justify restrictive measures on trade, particularly with colonies. Smith's views on both factions and colonies are considered in the following chapter.

7

The present disturbances

In spite of the fact that Smith consistently chose to refer to the American Revolution simply as the 'present' or 'recent disturbances', we have good reason to believe that it meant much more to him than this flat description implies. During the three years which he spent in London prior to the publication of the *Wealth of Nations* we know that he was 'very zealous in American affairs'.[1] Indeed, he may even have delayed publication in order to complete those parts of his general treatment of colonies which contained his views on the causes of American revolt and his remedies for dealing with its consequences. We also know that Smith chose not to follow the advice of his friend, Hugh Blair, to omit the passages dealing with American affairs from future editions 'when public measures come to be settled'. Smith clearly did not accept Blair's view that they made the book seem 'too much like a publication for the present moment'.[2] And yet in the light of the curious fact that Smith was fairly unusual among his contemporaries, certainly among the more purely economic writers, in not writing a single topical pamphlet at any stage of his career, it is unlikely that he was simply responding to an opportunity to incorporate his views on an urgent matter of public concern. Hence, while the sections dealing with American affairs clearly owe a good deal to the circumstances ruling in 1773–6, it is consonant with what we know of Smith's attitude to the role of the philosopher in public affairs to suspect that he had a didactic (but non-polemical) purpose in

[1] The phrase appears in a letter from Hume to Smith; see *Corr.*, Letter 149, 8 February 1776.
[2] *Corr.*, Letter 151, 3 February 1776.

mind. As Andrew Skinner has convincingly argued, Smith was making use of a major, though passing, event to illustrate wider principles, and to 'strike a telling blow where, at the time and from his point of view, it was most needed'.[1] The other general point to notice is that Smith's treatment of this subject provides a striking exception to Dugald Stewart's general verdict that Smith did not indulge in speculations concerning 'plans of new constitutions'.

Smith's interest and involvement in colonial affairs was of long standing; he could legitimately be regarded as one of the leading experts of the day on such matters. He had advised Townshend on taxation of the American colonies in 1766–7 when the first fiscal difficulties with the colonies began to make their appearance, thereby, in the eyes of some historians at least, becoming implicated in the decision to impose import duties which sparked off the revolt.[2] In 1778, after the British defeat at Saratoga, Smith was consulted by his friend, Alexander Wedderburn, then Lord North's Solicitor-General, on the alternatives open to the government: the memorandum which he wrote on that occasion has become one of the major pieces of evidence on his views.[3] His advice continued to be sought after the war, when the first attempts were made to come to terms with the economic problems caused by the loss of the American colonies.

The two main solutions propounded by Smith as remedies for the American problem were voluntary separation and an imperial or consolidating union. The fact that these solutions were diametrically opposed has given rise to a sizeable body of literature offering competing assessments of his priorities and sympathies.[4] The ambiguity becomes acute when it is

[1] A. S. Skinner, 'Adam Smith and the American Economic Community', *Journal of the History of Ideas*, XXXVII (1976), 59–78.
[2] See for example C. R. Fay's claim that 'it was professorial advice which lost us the first empire'; *Adam Smith and the Scotland of his Day* (1956), p. 116.
[3] See 'Smith's Thoughts on the State of the Contest with America, February 1778' as reprinted in *Corr.*, appendix B, pp. 377–85. In subsequent notes this will be referred to simply as 'Thoughts on America'.
[4] See, for example, J. S. Nicholson, *A Project of Empire* (1909); E. A. Benians, 'Adam Smith's Project of an Empire', *Cambridge Historical Journal*, I (1925), 249–83; R. Koebner, *Empire* (1961), 226–37, 357–8; D. N. Winch, *Classical Political Economy and Colonies* (1965), chapter 2; D. Stevens, 'Adam Smith

considered necessary to decide which of the two alternatives Smith actually favoured. Only in the context of a search for 'anticipations' does such a choice have relevance – by which criteria it has been possible to claim that Smith was either an enlightened anti-imperialist or a far-sighted proponent of imperial federation.[1] Freed from such Whiggish obligations, however, it may be possible to see why he should have bothered to rehearse and retain the case for these opposed alternatives, neither of which was entirely novel; neither of which commanded public support in 1776; and both of which were a matter of history when later editions of the book appeared. It is not possible to cite such points as evidence of political naievety on Smith's part because he went out of his way to emphasise the lack of public support for his remedies to his readers. He regarded separation as the most likely outcome of events in 1776, but claimed that only a 'visionary enthusiast' would expect it to be embraced as a political solution. Similarly with his scheme of imperial union, he merely stated that it was not inappropriate to 'a speculative work of this kind', adding that 'such speculation can at worst be regarded as a new Utopia, less amusing certainly, but not more useless and chimerical than the old one'.[2] Since none of this accords with a rational strategy for immediate persuasion, we are free to concentrate on the underlying didactic purpose of the analysis.

There is no mystery surrounding the economic lessons of the analysis; they are part and parcel of Smith's attack on the 'monopolising spirit' of the mercantile system, and his general case for free trade between nations. Moreover, given the nature of the *Wealth of Nations*, it is hardly surprising that economic considerations were stressed in both the diagnosis and remedies for the American problem. Nevertheless, I would like to suggest that the parallel treatment accorded to political issues can be given separate consideration, provided

and the Colonial Disturbances', in *EAS*, pp. 202–17; and the article by A. S. Skinner cited in n. 1, p. 147 of this chapter.
[1] Smith occupied the former position in liberal free-trading circles for much of the nineteenth century, but was accorded the latter status by the end of the century; see, for example, J. S. Nicholson, *A Project of Empire* (1909).
[2] *WN* v.iii.68.

only that the main economic conclusion is borne in mind, namely that Britain's national interest, as opposed to that of the merchants engaged in the colony trade, was not served by the existing system; that the loss of monopoly privileges consequent upon separation, voluntary or otherwise, would constitute no long-term loss to the nation. The legitimacy of this partial separation may become more obvious as the argument proceeds, but it is worth remembering that Smith himself saw no problem in concentrating on the political lessons in his memorandum on the subject to Wedderburn.

Smith's main economic conclusion on the American dispute was anticipated by Hume in the letter he wrote to Smith while waiting anxiously for the appearance of the *Wealth of Nations*.

My Notion is, that the Matter is not so important as is commonly imagind. If I be mistaken, I shall probably correct my Error, when I see or read you. Our Navigation and general commerce may suffer more than our Manufactures. Should London fall as much in its size, as I have done, it will be better. It is nothing but a hulk of bad and unclean humours.[1]

Since Hume was writing from what he knew to be his death-bed, it is hardly surprising perhaps that medical analogies were uppermost in his mind. But it is interesting to note that Smith employed similar language to describe current public apprehensions of the effects of loss of the colony trade.

A small stop in that great blood-vessel, which has been artificially swelled beyond its natural dimensions, and through which an unnatural proportion of the industry and commerce of the country has been forced to circulate, is very likely to bring on the most dangerous disorders upon the whole body politick. The expectation of a rupture with the colonies, accordingly, has struck the people of Great Britain with more terror than they ever felt for a Spanish armada, or a French invasion. It was this terror, whether well or ill grounded, which rendered the repeal of the stamp act, among the merchants at least, a popular measure. In the total exclusion from the colony market, was it to last only for a few years, the greater part of our merchants used to fancy that they foresaw an entire stop to their trade; the greater part of our master manufacturers, the entire ruin

---

[1] *Corr.*, Letter 149, 8 February 1776. For a similar expression of view by Hume see Letters to W. Strahan in *Letters of David Hume*, ed. J. T. Y. Greig, volume II, pp. 300–1, 304–5.

of their business; and the greater part of our workmen, an end of their employment. A rupture with any of our neighbours upon the continent, though likely too to occasion some stop or interruption in the employment of some or all these different orders of people, is foreseen, however, without any such general emotion. The blood, of which the circulation is stopt in any of the smaller vessels, easily disgorges itself into the greater, without occasioning any dangerous disorder; but, when it is stopt in any of the greater vessels, convulsions, apoplexy, or death, are the immediate and unavoidable consequences.[1]

In this passage Smith is making a plea for moderation, while at the same time using current fears to reinforce his case for 'the natural system of perfect liberty and justice'. A man who has ruined his health by a lifetime of dissipation cannot expect to be cured without some loss of comfort, but the 'terror' relates to a disease rather than to loss of real vigour.

A related 'terror' concerned the effect of the loss of the American colonies on Britain's prestige and power in other parts of the world. Such considerations, as we shall see, were not entirely absent from Smith's mind; but in view of the overuse of the famous quotation about defence being more important than opulence, it is worth pointing out that Smith did not regard the maintenance of the colony trade as being necessary from this point of view. On the contrary, he believed that British naval strength rested on the trade with Europe, and one of the many drawbacks of the trade with colonies was that it diverted trade from Europe. Moreover, since under the existing system the colonies contributed nothing to the defence of empire, they were more a source of weakness than strength. Once more, therefore, the economic arguments served to dismiss or minimise a popular fear concerning the effect of loss or separation.

Although in principle Smith considered the colonial system to be 'a manifest violation of the most sacred rights of mankind', in practice the relative liberality of the British system, together with the stage of development attained by her American colonies, had ensured that the effects had not so far been very harmful to the colonies. He recognised, however, that

[1] *WN* IV.vii.c.43.

what were at present merely 'impertinent badges of slavery' could in time become 'really oppressive and insupportable'.[1] It does not follow that Smith can be counted as sympathetic to the American cause; there is plenty of evidence to the contrary. But the main point to make again is that for Smith, like Hume, the question of sympathy or otherwise is irrelevant to an understanding of the purposes of the analysis.

It is obvious that Smith was no Cartwright or Price, anxious to press the parallels between the cause of the colonists and English liberties. Nor, less obviously, is it clear that Smith shared the anxieties of some of his Scottish friends in thinking that:

> ...if this rebellion in America proves successful, it will be in consequence of republican principles of the most levelling kind; and the victors will no doubt aim, with the assistance of their restless friends in England, to overturn that happy limited monarchy, which experience has taught us is best suited to a realm so extensive as ours, and which has been long the glory of Britain and the envy of all the world.[2]

Smith did, however, take seriously the view that the main threat posed by the American revolt was – in Hume's words – to the 'Credit and Reputation of government, which has already but too little Authority'.[3] This emerges clearly in his acknowledgement of the political barriers to acceptance of voluntary separation as a solution. In spite of the enormous difficulties Britain was experiencing in subduing her colonies, and the continuing expense of governing them under the old arrangements, Smith accepted that it was a policy no nation would consciously adopt. But his reasons for making this concession are perhaps more revealing than the conclusion itself.

> Such sacrifices, though they might frequently be agreeable to the interest, are always mortifying to the pride of every nation, and what is perhaps of still greater consequence, they are always contrary to the private interest of the governing part of it, who would thereby be deprived of the disposal of many places of trust and profit, of many

---

[1] *WN* IV.vii.b.44.
[2] The quotation is from Alexander Carlyle's anonymous pamphlet *A Letter to the Duke of Buccleuch on National Defence* (1778), p. 23.
[3] See D. Hume, *Letters*, ed. J. T. Y. Greig, volume II, pp. 304–5.

opportunities of acquiring wealth and distinction, which the posses-sion of the most turbulent, and, to the great body of the people, the most unprofitable province seldom fails to afford.[1]

When taken in conjunction with the passage that follows, where Smith summarises his view that separation, succeeded by a treaty of commerce, would bring with it a chain of fortunate consequences to both sides, these remarks might seem to contain an ironic criticism of the role played by curruption in the British system of government. Irony is never entirely absent in Smith's writings, but on this occasion it seems best to take the statement at face value. In the memorandum to Wedderburn written two years later, the equivalent passage dealing with unilateral termination of the war reads as follows:

But tho' this termination of the war might be really advantageous, it would not, in the eyes of Europe appear honourable to Great Britain; and when her empire was so much curtailled, her power and dignity would be supposed to be proportionably diminished. What is of still greater importance, it could scarce fail to discredit the Government in the eyes of our own people, who would probably impute to mal-administration what might, perhaps, be no more than the unavoidable effect of the natural and necessary course of things. A government which, in times of the most profound peace, of the highest public prosperity, when the people had scarce even the pretext of a single grievance to complain of, has not always been able to make itself respected by them; would have every thing to fear from their rage and indignation at the public disgrace and calamity, for such they would suppose it to be, of thus dismembering the empire.[2]

The last two passages cited provide an important clue to Smith's method of dealing with political subjects. If the first is read as a straightforward factual proposition, implying neither approval nor disapproval, it gives us a clear idea of Smith's views on the sensitive question of 'influence' or 'corruption'. His failure to endorse the standard oppositional view of this matter in his lectures was noted earlier, but here Smith – if not being ironic – could be adopting a more definite Humean stance on 'influence'. Contrary to the 'Country' position, Hume argued that influence was necessary to the

[1] *WN* IV.vii.c.66. [2] See 'Thoughts on America', *Corr.*, p. 383.

maintenance of balance between the elements making up Britain's mixed constitution.

> The crown has so many offices at its disposal, that, when assisted by the honest and disinterested part of the house, it will always command the resolutions of the whole so far, at least, as to preserve the antient constitution from danger. We may, therefore, give to this influence what name we please; we may call it by the invidious appellations of *corruption* and *dependence*; but some degree and some kind of it are inseparable from the very nature of the constitution, and necessary to the preservation of our mixed government.[1]

Viewed in this light, the passages mark a noticeable contrast between Smith's attitude to the mercantile interests which supported the colonial system and anticipated disaster from the loss of their special privileges, and his attitude to the privileges enjoyed by the 'governing part' of the nation. In both cases he was, according to his own diagnosis, dealing with a situation in which there was a conflict between special interests and those of the nation. Smith rejected the expectations, claims, and fears of the mercantile interest, but appears to have adopted a more sympathetic attitude towards those sacrifices of interest considered necessary to the preservation of the prestige and stability of established government. This could tell us something about Smith's priorities when faced with a conflict between 'interest' and 'opinion', and it may also say something about the much larger issues involved in the relationship between 'polity' and 'economy'. But in case this seems to be running ahead of the evidence, let me turn to the political arguments used by Smith in proposing his alternative scheme of imperial union.

An empire in which relations between the mother-country and its progeny were regulated by mercantile principles was dismissed as a project suited only 'for a nation whose government is influenced by shopkeepers'; and it was made doubly unacceptable by the impossibility of making the shopkeepers pay for the privileges they received. The cost of the civil establishment and defence of empire under the existing system fell mainly on tax-payers in the mother-country in the

[1] See 'Of the Independency of Parliament', *Essays Moral, Political, and Literary*, eds. T. H. Green and T. H. Grose, volume I, pp. 120–1.

form of mounting debt, additional taxes, and borrowings from the sinking fund. This explains why Smith's most elaborate discussion of the fiscal aspect of his scheme of imperial union appears in the final chapter on debt and taxation. Indeed, the closing words of the *Wealth of Nations* consist of a warning that unless some way could be found of making colonies contribute to the costs of the present civil and military establishment, much of which had been created in order to administer and defend them, it would be better for Britain to give up her mere 'project of an empire', and 'to accommodate her future views and designs to the real mediocrity of her circumstances'.[1] This return to a subject considered at length earlier in the book can hardly be described as accidental; it suggests a desire to give the message special emphasis. Nor does it seem frivolous to point out that two of Hume's most outspoken letters on his hopes and fears for the nation link 'public Bankruptcy' with 'the total Revolt of America' in a way that leaves no doubt that both events were to be expected and welcomed.[2]

As an alternative to separation, any scheme for making empire more than 'a sort of splendid and showy equipage' would have to meet Smith's objections to monopoly and the current apportionment of fiscal burdens. Expressed in modern jargon, it would have to be a free trade zone with complete fiscal harmonisation and proportionate sharing of burdens among the different provinces of empire. Again though, while Smith devoted a good deal of effort to showing just how this ambitious economic scheme might be implemented, the exercise can be interpreted as one of marking out the economic boundaries for an acceptable solution rather than as a piece of straightforward advocacy. In other words, he was setting out the stringent conditions that would have to be met if empire was to be made tolerable, without necessarily endorsing imperial union as a practicable solution.

For the present, however, I am mainly concerned with the arguments deployed in support of the political machinery which Smith proposed as a means of sealing the imperial

[1] *WN* v.iii.92.
[2] See D. Hume, *Letters*, ed. J. T. Y. Greig, volume II, pp. 210, 237.

bargain and making it acceptable to all parties. In essence the proposal entailed turning Parliament into 'the states-general of the British Empire' by allowing each province to be directly represented in numbers determined by its contribution to the general revenue, with provision for the seat of empire to be shifted across the Atlantic once the proceeds of American taxation exceeded that of Britain. Smith arrived at this radical solution by showing that the colonial assemblies could not be relied upon to vote the necessary funds. Nor were they competent to assess the needs of empire as a whole. Taxation by requisition was equally unworkable, since it was unlikely that Parliament would have either the authority or inclination to levy a full and fair assessment on the colonies. More to the point, however, taxation by requisition would undermine the currently-enhanced status and power of the colonial assemblies. And it was at this juncture that Smith introduced the colonial equivalent of his reason for believing that the 'governing part' of the British nation would never accept voluntary separation.

Men desire to have some share in the management of publick affairs chiefly on account of the importance which it gives them. Upon the power which the greater part of the leading men, the natural aristocracy of every country, have of preserving or defending their respective importance, depends the stability and duration of every system of free government. In the attacks which those leading men are continually making upon the importance of one another, and in the defence of their own, consists the whole play of domestick faction and ambition. The leading men of America, like those of all other countries, desire to preserve their own importance. They feel, or imagine, that if their assemblies, which they are fond of calling parliaments, and of considering as equal in authority to the parliament of Great Britain, should be so far degraded as to become the humble ministers and executive officers of that parliament, the greater part of their own importance would be at an end. They have rejected, therefore, the proposal of being taxed by parliamentary requisition, and like other ambitious and high-spirited men, have rather chosen to draw the sword in defence of their own importance.[1]

It followed from this diagnosis that any imperial solution would have to cater to the ambitions, new dignity, and sense

[1] *WN* IV.vii.c.74.

of importance of the 'natural aristocracy' in America. Hence the offer of seats at Westminster. The use of the term 'natural aristocracy' is an immediate reminder of Smith's argument that standing armies commanded by those who have a substantial stake in the country are least likely to pose a threat to liberty and stability. In the memorandum to Wedderburn the identity between the two arguments becomes manifest.

The principal security of every government arises always from the support of those whose dignity, authority and interest, depend upon its being supported. But the leading men of America, being either members of the general legislature of the empire, or electors of those members, would have the same interest to support the general government of the empire which the Members of the British legislature and their electors have at present to support the particular government of Great Britain.[1]

The cynical way in which this is expressed in the *Wealth of Nations* may raise, once more, suspicions of irony.

Instead of piddling for the little prizes which are to be found in what may be called the paltry raffle of colony faction; they might then hope, from the presumption which men naturally have in their own ability and good fortune, to draw some of the great prizes which sometimes comes from the wheel of the great state lottery of British politicks.[2]

As before though, the alternative to irony is a Humean acceptance that 'influence' or 'corruption' was essential to the preservation of balance within the British constitution. This is amply confirmed by Smith's account of the problems of 'managing' the legislative branch of government.

It was a long time before even the parliament of England, though placed immediately under the eye of the sovereign, could be brought under such a system of management, or could be rendered sufficiently liberal in their grants for supporting the civil and military establishments even of their own country. It was only by distributing among the particular members of parliament, a great part either of the offices, or of the disposal of the offices arising from this civil and military establishment, that such a system of management could be established even with regard to the parliament of England.[3]

[1] See 'Thoughts on America', *Corr.*, p. 381.   [2] *WN* iv.vii.c.75.
[3] *WN* iv.vii.c.69. See also the approval given to 'management and persuasion' of Parliament and ecclesiastical establishments in v.i.g.19.

The implied contrast here is with the colonial assemblies. When discussing these earlier Smith had drawn attention to the absence of hereditary nobility, the greater equality, and hence prevalence of republican manners and forms of government – all of which had made it difficult for the executive to manage or 'corrupt' the assemblies.[1] Management was also very much in Smith's mind when he countered fears that the admission of American representatives would disturb the balance between the monarchical and democratic elements in the British constitution by maintaining that since representation would be in proportion to tax revenues, 'the number of people to be managed would increase exactly in proportion to the means of managing them'.[2]

At the heart of Smith's diagnosis and remedy for the American problem lay certain propositions designed to achieve balance by curbing mere faction, while at the same time providing scope for healthy ambition and contest. The underlying rationale for these propositions can be found in several places, but Smith provided the clearest statement of his general position in the section added to the *Theory of Moral Sentiments* in 1790, where he speaks of the character and stability of any state being determined by the balance struck between its various constituent 'orders and societies', and by 'the ability of each particular order or society to maintain its powers, privileges, and immunities, against the encroachments of every other'.[3] Each of these orders derive security from and are subordinate to the state, though partiality towards one's own order may lead to unjustified opposition to changes that affect established privileges adversely. Nevertheless, by a characteristic Smithian twist, it is acknowledged that this defect of partiality may serve a useful purpose in checking 'the spirit of innovation', especially those 'alterations of government which may be fashionable and popular at the time'.[4] It is to this group of ideas that Smith is referring in the *Wealth of Nations* when he speaks of 'the whole play of domestick faction and ambition', where he may have been echoing Montesquieu's recognition

---

[1] *WN* IV.vii.b.51. [2] *WN* IV.vii.c.78.
[3] *TMS* VI.ii.2.8–9. [4] *TMS* VI.ii.2.10.

of the importance of restless party ferment to the stability of the English constitution.[1] It is more likely, however, that he was following Hume's related demonstration that parties were a necessary, if regrettable, feature of all systems of government, but especially those, like Britain, which were both 'mixed' and 'free'.

The treatment of 'faction' is obviously related to the larger question of rights of resistance. Attention was drawn to Smith's cautious approach to this question in Chapter 3.[2] Striking an appropriate philosophical balance between 'respect and reverence for that constitution or form of government which is actually established', and the 'earnest desire to render the condition of our fellow-citizens as safe, respectable, and happy as we can' remained a problem for Smith throughout his life. In a section added to the sixth edition of the *Theory of Moral Sentiments* in 1790, which may reflect his reaction to the French Revolution, he contrasted the normal situation in which these principles were in harmony, with periods in which they might point in different directions.

...in times of public discontent, faction, and disorder, those two principles may draw different ways, and even a wise man may be disposed to think some alteration necessary in that constitution or form of government which, in its actual condition, appears plainly unable to maintain the public tranquillity. In such cases, however, it often requires, perhaps, the highest effort of political wisdom to determine when a real patriot ought to support and endeavour to re-establish the authority of the old system, and when he ought to give way to the more daring, but often dangerous spirit of innovation.[3]

While the emphasis on 'public tranquillity' accords with

---

[1] For Montesquieu's views see C. S. Montesquieu, *The Spirit of the Laws*, pp. 307–12. The key passage is as follows: 'All the passions being unrestrained, hatred, envy, jealousy, and an ambitious desire of riches and honours, appear in their extent; were it otherwise, the state would be in the condition of a man weakened by sickness, who is without passions because he is without strength' (p. 308). For a recent account of Montesquieu's treatment of the relationship between liberty, stability, and conflict, which stresses the debt to Machiavelli, see N. Wood, 'The Value of Asocial Sociability: Contributions of Machiavelli, Sidney, and Montesquieu' in M. Fleisher (ed.), *Machiavelli and the Nature of Political Thought* (1972), pp. 282–307.
[2] See pp. 54–5 above.   [3] *TMS* VI.ii.2.12.

better-known features of Smith's politics, the point to notice
about this passage is that it serves as a prelude to the appearance of a neglected figure in Smith's view of political activity
– the 'legislator'. Some years ago Jacob Viner drew the attention of those who stress the *laissez-faire* implications of Smith's
dislike of the 'insidious and crafty animal, vulgarly called a
statesman or politician' to the contrasting picture presented
of the 'legislator'.[1] During periods of civil faction and disorder
the leader of a successful party can display public spirit and
render patriotic service by acting with moderation. By re-
establishing order and improving a constitution which has
lost its capacity to command the support of public opinion, he
may be transformed 'from the very doubtful and ambiguous
character of the leader of a party' into 'the greatest and
noblest of all characters, that of the reformer and legislator of
a great state'.[2]

Neither Montesquieu nor Hume was willing to dispense with
the idea of the legislator and great founder of states, and Smith
remained closer to them on this matter than is normally
thought to be the case.[3] As historian of civil society Smith may
not have laid great emphasis on the creative role of individual
law-givers, but he regarded law and government as 'the highest effort of human prudence and wisdom'.[4] As a sceptical
observer of the contemporary scene, he was certainly not
impressed by the ordinary character of politicians. But this
should not blind us to the fact that he asked us to admire 'the
solid virtues of a warrior, a statesman, a philosopher, or a
legislator'; and that he was capable of speaking – in terms that
Machiavelli himself might have approved of the value of
prudence in a legislator.

We talk of the prudence of the great general, of the great statesman,
of the great legislator. Prudence is, in all these cases, combined with
many greater and more splendid virtues, with valour, with extensive
and strong benevolence, and all these supported by a proper degree
of self-command... It is the best head joined to the best heart.[5]

[1] See J. Viner's *Guide to John Rae's Life of Adam Smith*, pp. 30–1.
[2] *TMS* VI.ii.2.14.
[3] On Hume see D. Forbes, *Hume's Philosophical Politics*, pp. 316–19.
[4] *LJ*(B), pp. 160–1.   [5] *TMS* VI.i.15.

And later, when Smith introduces 'the man whose public spirit is prompted altogether by humanity and benevolence', the comparison is with one of the leading figures in the republican 'myth': 'When he cannot establish the right, he will not disdain to ameliorate the wrong; but like Solon, when he cannot establish the best system of laws, he will endeavour to establish the best that people can bear.'[1]

Having recognised the role of the legislator it is possible to return to the question of faction and dissent. The problem for any prudent man or legislator was one of deciding how to distinguish between healthy opposition and mere faction. Smith called attention to the dangers of civil and religious faction on many occasions in the *Theory of Moral Sentiments*. It was held responsible for the difficulty experienced in achieving the necessary stance of the impartial spectator, and for giving rise to dissimulation in public behaviour; it corrupted 'the natural principles of religion'; and it encouraged the 'spirit of system' to take charge over its virtuous equivalent, namely 'public spirit'.[2] On the other hand, the prudent man who shuns ambition and is averse to party disputes practises none of the 'ennobling virtues' and hence only 'commands a cold esteem'; he also forsakes one of the best opportunities for schooling himself to the virtues of self-command.[3] But perhaps one of Smith's clearest statements appears in a casual remark in a letter to Shelburne: 'I hear there is no faction in parliament, in which I am glad of. For tho' a little faction now and then gives spirit to the nation the continuance of it obstructs all public business and puts it out of the power of the best Minister to do much good.'[4]

This provides the clue to Smith's view of the colonial assemblies in America. Like the 'troublesome jealousy' of some of the small European republics, they had departed from the golden mean in becoming prey to 'rancorous and virulent factions'. One of the main advantages held out to the colonies in Smith's scheme of union was deliverance from an excessive 'spirit of party'. This had occurred in Scotland since the Act of Union, and similar benefits would be conferred on Ireland

[1] *TMS* VI.ii.2.16. [2] *TMS* III.3.43; III.5.13; VI.ii.2.15; VI.iii.12.
[3] *TMS* VI.i.13–14; VI.iii.19–20. [4] *Corr.*, Letter 28, 21 February 1759.

if she were to be united with England – greater in fact, because in Ireland the contest between oppressors and oppressed took the particularly odious form of a religious divide. Smith also felt that union would curb the eagerness of the colonists 'to become excessively rich', and dampen 'the vivacity and ardour of their excessive enterprize in the improvement of land'.[1] Under some circumstances, it seems, the pursuit of wealth was not a substitute for virtue – even to the author of the most authoritative work on the subject.

Smith agreed with those who prophesied that with the succession of hostilities, and after the common enemy had been removed, the colonists would 'compare the mildness of their old government with the violence of that which they have established in its stead'; they could not 'fail both to remember the one with regret and to view the other with detestation'. The English had experienced similar feelings after they had 'rashly overturned' the monarchy, but had been fortunate in having 'regal Government' restored 'by such a concurrence of accidental circumstances as may not, upon a similar occasion, ever happen again'.[2] The expression of such sentiments in a semi-private communication would not necessarily be significant, except perhaps as an indication of a personal belief in the virtues of Britain's mixed constitution. They acquire significance when seen against the background of similar views expressed in the *Lectures on Jurisprudence* and in the mature published writings, where Smith expounds them as part of a self-conscious system of moral and political analysis.

It is also interesting to consider Smith's opinion in the light of some of the fears expressed by the founding fathers of the American republic in *The Federalist Papers*, when, indeed, the unity achieved during the Revolutionary War had dissolved, and when it had become necessary to construct a constitutional alternative to the political system that had been overthrown. The extensive work that has been done in recent years on the political ideas of the American founding fathers makes it unnecessary to do much more than direct the reader's attention to this remarkable body of literature, and more espe-

[1] *WN* v.iii.87–90.
[2] See 'Thoughts on America', *Corr.*, p. 384.

cially to those parts of it which show how Madison and Hamilton attempted to apply the eighteenth-century science of politics to the circumstances of the new republic.[1] Nevertheless, it seems worth drawing attention to the important parallels which exist between, for example, Smith and Hamilton's interest in 'natural aristocracy', and between Smith's arguments in favour of imperial union and the case advanced by Madison for an extended union of confederated republics in *The Federalist Papers*, Number 10. The parallelism in the latter case is quite striking when one bears in mind the common concern with ways of controlling and harnessing the more destructive effects of the natural tendency to form factions in all forms of free government. The similarities are less surprising when the results of Douglas Adair's pioneering research on *Federalist* Number 10 are brought into the picture: Adair demonstrated Madison's heavy reliance on Hume's essays on parties and on his 'Idea of a Perfect Commonwealth' as an answer to the general eighteenth-century view associated with Montesquieu, namely that republican forms of government were only suitable to small states.[2] For as Hume said: 'Though it is more difficult to form a republican government in an extensive country than in a city; there is more facility, when once it is formed, of preserving it steady and uniform, without tumult and faction.'[3] Smith's scheme of imperial union employs the same pattern of ideas; and in view of the other affinities between Hume and Smith which have been noted earlier, the indirect link between Smith and Madison which runs through Hume's political essay should not be regarded as one involving casual juxtaposition.[4] The three men are

[1] See the references to the revisionist literature on the American Revolution and on the formation of the constitution cited in chapter 2, p. 31, but see especially G. Stourzh, *Alexander Hamilton and the Idea of Republican Government* (1970).

[2] See D. Adair, '"That Politics May be Reduced to a Science": David Hume, James Madison, and the Tenth *Federalist*', *Huntington Library Quarterly*, XX (1956–7), 343–60.

[3] See D. Hume, 'Idea of a Perfect Commonwealth' in *Essays*, eds. T. H. Green and T. H. Grose, volume I, p. 492.

[4] For further discussion of this linkage see pp. 178–80 below. Apart from Adair's pioneering work, I have also benefited from reading two papers given at the Fourth International Congress on the Enlightenment, Yale

united by the common preoccupations of the eighteenth-century science of politics – a science founded by Montesquieu, but significantly developed by Hume, Smith, and other Scottish historians of civil society in their attempts to understand and assess the effect of commerce on the political arrangement of society.

University, 1975 by R. Branson, 'James Madison and the Scottish Enlightenment' and C. Walton, 'Political Economy and Republican Virtue; The Tragedy of the American Constitution'.

8

Conclusion

Since this essay purports to be a study in intention rather than premonition, and has attempted to show how pursuit of the latter without regard for the former frequently leads to historically meaningless interpretations being advanced, it would run counter to the spirit of the enterprise to close by suggesting latent implications of the reading given here which go well beyond the issues and range of textual evidence already considered. It seems desirable, however, to underline a few points by way of conclusion.

I hope the reader will by now have a clear idea of what is being claimed in speaking of the need for a historical approach to Adam Smith's politics. In attempting to concentrate attention on what Smith appears to have been doing when he wrote on such matters, I have approached the problem in much the same temper as other recent historical studies of Hobbes, Locke, Rousseau, and Hume, even if I cannot lay claim to equivalent scope and depth.[1] Moreover, although I have not mounted a self-contained case for the criteria and methods of interpretation employed here, I would align myself with others who have expounded the historiographic problems involved in establishing necessary conditions for the recovery of meaning from texts considered within historical and linguistic contexts.[2]

---

[1] See, for example, Quentin Skinner, 'The Ideological Context of Hobbes's Political Thought', *Historical Journal*, IX (1966), 286–317; K. V. Thomas, 'The Social Origins of Hobbes's Political Thought', in K. C. Brown (ed.), *Hobbes Studies* (1965); J. Dunn, *The Political Thought of John Locke* (1969); J. Shklar, *Men and Citizens; A Study of Rousseau's Social Theory* (1969); and D. Forbes, *Hume's Philosophical Politics* (1976).

[2] Again, see, for example, J. Dunn, 'The Identity of the History of Ideas', *Philosophy*, XLIII (1968), 85–116; Quentin Skinner, 'Meaning and Under-

This essay has had two related objectives, one positive, the other negative. First, to maintain that Smith does in fact have a 'politics' which is neither trivial nor vestigial. Secondly, to show that the main obstacle in any effort to recapture the eighteenth-century context of Smith's politics is what I have described as the liberal capitalist perspective. Though perhaps overly-capacious for some purposes, this categorisation displays certain common features in what might otherwise be regarded as discordant schools of thought. For example, it reveals why those who come to bury capitalism as well as those who come to praise it, why those who wish to argue for a smaller or larger role for the state in economic affairs, are so much in agreement in regarding the propositions which Smith might or might not have maintained on these matters as central to their purpose. My object has been to show how the application of what are basically nineteenth-century perspectives to what is quintessentially a work of the eighteenth century not only introduces various artificialities and anachronisms, but obscures important features of Smith's project.

The failure to identify or give due recognition to the integrity of Smith's politics has provided a standing invitation to take short cuts through unmapped territory. An interesting illustration of this tendency can be found in the case put forward by George Stigler, a Chicago economist, who is also one of Smith's most knowledgeable admirers.[1] Whereas some historians of political theory have been content to suggest that 'economy' was on the point of subsuming 'polity' in the *Wealth of Nations*, or that a form of materialist history embodying economic determinism was eclipsing an autonomous political realm, Stigler takes the bolder line of criticising Smith for failing to carry through the project of creating a thorough-going economic theory of political behaviour. He notes a number of cases where Smith appears to give 'a larger role to emotion, prejudice, and ignorance in political affairs than he ever allowed in economic affairs'; and he regrets Smith's apparent

standing in the History of Ideas', *History and Theory*, VIII (1967), 3–53, and 'Some Problems in the Analysis of Political Thought and Action', *Political Theory*, II (1974), 277–303; and J. G. A. Pocock, *Politics, Language and Time* (1973), chapter 1.

[1] G. S. Stigler, 'Smith's Travels on the Ship of State' in *EAS*, pp. 237–46.

unwillingness to unite *homo oeconomicus* with *homo politicus* by applying 'the organon of self-interest to political behaviour'. According to Stigler, this failure consigned Smith, as it has most economists since, to the role of mere preacher in political matters, where the 'only remedy for erroneous polity is sound analysis, and that remedy is appropriate only to a minority of objectionable policies'.

Stigler's counter-factual approach – considering why Smith did not do something Stigler feels he ought to have done – rests on two assumptions which are common to most economic theories of politics: first, that economic man and political man are basically the same animal pursuing the same ends by different means, the one through the market place, the other through pressure to obtain legislation favourable to his interests; secondly, that politics can be essentially described as a process whereby the state mediates between competing interest-groups, where the interests involved are either directly economic or capable of being expressed in economic terms. I am not concerned here with the general validity of counter-factual reasoning in intellectual history, still less with that of economic theories of politics. Clearly neither approach can be ruled out on *a priori* grounds. Given the pervasive role in economic affairs accorded by Smith to mechanisms based on self-interest, it is legitimate to ask why he does not extend their operation consistently to a wider realm of social and political behaviour, especially when we notice how alive he was to the fact that certain interest-groups were both active and alarmingly effective in procuring legislation favourable to their commercial interests.

Nevertheless, if our object is to understand *Smith's* politics, it is by no means obvious why we should expect him to make use of a narrower, more mechanical, and more rationalistic version of the self-interest principle than the one he upheld when discussing behaviour in economic, let alone political, settings. Hence it seems gratuitous to foist on to him the following (tautologous?) interpretation of what constitutes 'failure' of the self-interest principle: 'Every failure of a person to make decisions which serve his self-interest may be interpreted as an error in logic: means have been chosen which are inappropriate to the person's ends.' That is the kind of statement that later brought Macaulay's scorn down on James Mill's head, and it cuts across the grain of Smith's approach to such matters.[1] Stigler's counter-factual strategy might be more convincing if he had shown willingness to explore the alternatives that Smith considered to be available – if, for example, Stigler had even entertained the possibility that the *Theory of Moral Sentiments*, as well as the *Wealth of Nations*, might be relevant, and if he had thought it necessary to consider Smith's own opinion on the role of the philosopher in public affairs before condemning him for confining himself to 'moral suasion'.

This is not the place to reopen the debate surrounding the nature of the conciliation between sympathy and self-interest in Smith's writings, but certain basic propositions will be accepted by all those who recognise the need to consider his two major works as related enterprises, especially where questions of psychology or motivation are involved. In summary form these are that sub-rational instincts play a crucial part in both works; that in consequence a low priority is accorded to calculating forms of rationality; and that the adjustment of means to ends in society at large is frequently explained, therefore, in terms of unintended consequences. Men act on what they *perceive* to be their interests and have a great capacity for self-deceit both as to the worth of the ends and the appropriateness of the means of achieving those ends. Since considerable emphasis is placed on the social setting within which these perceptions are formed, there are problems of interdependence between individuals and groups which cannot be encompassed by any of the simpler economistic models of interaction. Smith does not make use of the construct known as 'economic man'. Self-interest is not directed solely by pecuniary motives towards economic ends: honour, vanity, social esteem, love of ease, and love of domination figure alongside the more usual considerations of commercial gain as motives in economic as well as other pursuits. Although by the second half of the eighteenth century the concept of

[1] See T. B. Macaulay's attack on James Mill's *Essay on Government* in the *Edinburgh Review*, March, June, and October, 1829.

'interest' increasingly connoted in large measure *economic* interest, this was compatible with Smith's employment of the term to cover men's aspirations or ambitions in general; he certainly made no attempt to distinguish narrow and broad interpretations of the term.[1]

An illustration of the difference between the approach adopted here and Stigler's method of interpretation can be found in the passage from the *Wealth of Nations* cited on page 155 above, where Smith is discussing the 'leading men of America'. To Stigler this passage is evidence of Smith's occasional capacity to view political behaviour 'in perfectly cold-blooded, rational terms'; and the related passage on the rewards to be obtained from 'the great state lottery of British politics' seems to be taken as a sign of Smith's shrewdness in placing a pecuniary valuation on political interests. On Stigler's reading it is tempting to suggest that Smith would have been even more effectively cold-blooded and rational if he had suggested buying off the American 'natural aristocracy' by offering them a capital sum based on their average life expectation of gain from the lottery. In fact, of course, he recommended offering them seats in the British House of Commons as a means of assuaging their 'ambition', 'sense of importance', and 'dignity', thereby linking their 'interests' with the 'stability and duration' of the suggested form of government. When every allowance is made for cynicism, this amounts to more than the offer of a free lottery ticket.[2]

But if a broad interpretation of the concept of interest is called for – one that takes into consideration both of Smith's major works – it is equally important to recognise the pervasive role played by 'opinion' in Smith's politics. There certainly seems little reason to share Stigler's impatience with Smith's attentiveness to 'emotion, prejudice, and ignorance in political life', and not simply on the grounds that such qualities are more likely to manifest themselves in the political arena than in the market place. This concedes too much to an

---

[1] On the general development of the concept of 'interest' in relation to the 'passions' see A. O. Hirschman, *The Passions and the Interests* (1977).

[2] It also conforms with every other statement made by Smith on the wisdom of harnessing the interest of the 'natural aristocracy', see pp. 62, 109, 155–7 above.

economistic approach from the outset by implicitly accepting that politics can be described as a more complex process of articulating and adjudicating between the interests of individuals, and that modern economic theories of politics furnish a relevant standard by which to interpret and judge Smith's politics.[1] Emotion and prejudice are dimensions of 'opinion'; they take their place alongside such other terms as 'pride', 'ambition', 'resentment', 'fear', 'terror', 'enthusiasm' and 'rage', which appear frequently in Smith's discussion of social and political affairs. Taken together, they provide an important clue to the nature of his politics.

Here again Hume furnishes a natural point of entry with his statement that 'it is. . .on opinion only that government is founded'.[2] This is a corollary of the psychological basis given to deference and authority, and of the fact that for both Hume and Smith the significant connections between property and power rest on beliefs and opinions formed in society, rather than on objective material forces alone. That is why Hume rejected Harrington's thesis that the balance of power was determined by the balance of property, and why Smith treated the Harringtonian proposal for an 'agrarian law' as outmoded. One of the benefits which modern societies derived from the decline of feudalism was that power and property were no longer necessarily connected.[3] This was true of all forms of government but it was especially true of 'free countries', where, as Smith said, 'the safety of government depends very much upon the favourable judgement which the people may form of its conduct'. Opinion in this sense cannot be equated with anything so abstract and formal as Locke's doctrine of consent – as Smith's remarkable criticisms of this doctrine make clear – still less with mechanisms of democratic

---

[1] Hence my reservations about A. W. Coats's comments on Stigler's article, in spite of agreement with its general tendency; see A. W. Coats, 'Adam Smith's Conception of Self-Interest in Economic Affairs', *History of Political Economy*, VII (1975), 132–6. For similar reasons I do not find useful to my purpose E. G. West's recent attempt to rebut Stigler by drawing on conjectures concerning Smith's relationship to various alternative modern economic theories of politics in E. G. West, 'Adam Smith's Economics of Politics', *History of Political Economy*, VIII (1976), 515–39.

[2] D. Hume, 'Of the First Principles of Government' in *Essays*, eds. T. H. Green and T. H. Grose, volume I, p. 110.

[3] For Hume's views see *ibid.*, pp. 110–13, 122; for Smith's see pp. 67, 78–9, 91 above.

representation.[1] Opinion was the fluid and sometimes volatile medium within which governments operated; it acted as a constant constraint on their actions, though never as a creative influence.[2] Opinion could be synonymous with mere prejudice and ignorance; it could also be swayed by more pathological conditions of 'terror', 'rage', and 'enthusiasm'. That is why education of the people at large was so important to Smith, and why he recommended 'publick diversions' and the proliferation of religious sects.

Whereas the politician was defined as someone 'whose councils are directed by the momentary fluctuations of affairs', or by an excessive sensitivity to vociferous interests and clamorous opinion, the 'man of system' suffered from the opposite defect – an unwillingness to recognize the constraints posed by existing powers and the state of opinion. Between these two extremes lay the course of the legislator or wise statesman, accommodating legitimate interest and opinion to one another, respecting certain fears while tempering those arising out of mere 'terror'.

The man whose public spirit is prompted altogether by humanity and benevolence, will respect the established powers and privileges even of individuals, and still more those of the great orders and societies, into which the state is divided. Though he should consider some of them as in some measure abusive, he will content himself with moderating, what he often cannot annihilate without great violence. When he cannot conquer the rooted prejudices of the people by reason and persuasion, he will not attempt to subdue them by force...He will accommodate, as well as he can, his public arrangement to the confirmed habits and prejudices of the people; and will remedy as well as he can, the inconveniencies which may flow from the want of those regulations which the people are averse to submit to. When he cannot establish the right, he will not disdain to ameliorate the wrong; but like Solon, when he cannot establish the best system of laws, he will endeavour to establish the best that the people can bear.[3]

This is Smith firmly occupying the moderate or centrist

[1] For Smith's criticisms of Locke see pp. 52–4 above.
[2] On this see D. Forbes, *Hume's Philosophical Politics*, pp. 91–2, 320.
[3] *TMS* VI.ii.2.16. Those who continue to doubt the priority of Smith's concern with 'orders and societies' over that of individuals might consider the force of 'even of individuals' in the first sentence.

position – a position which some have described as 'Burkean'.[1]
As the following quotation from Hume strikingly reveals, if
labels of this kind are required, it would be more accurate to
substitute 'Humean'.

To tamper...or try experiments merely upon the credit of supposed
argument and philosophy, can never be the part of a wise magistrate,
who will bear a reverence to what carries the marks of age; and though
he may attempt some improvements for the public good, yet he will
adjust his innovations, as much as possible, to the ancient fabric, and
preserve entire the chief pillars and supports of the constitution.[2]

Smith's moderation, like that of Hume, is the result of an
analysis derived from a philosophical position rather than a
mere attitude of conservatism or even of mandarin scepticism.[3] The role of moderate is a political as well as a philosophical one, and it is particularly important during 'times
of public discontent, faction, and disorder'. The American
dispute was such a period, and Smith's advice on that and other
occasions can, I think, be construed as seeking to encourage
the legislator at the expense of the politician. Rhetorical and
didactic aims become difficult to separate.

Stigler's regret that 'Smith's only remedy for erroneous
policy is sound analysis' actually conforms to Smith's own view
of the responsibilities of the philosopher or scientific observer
in public life. Hence, for example, his disregard for the
utopian qualities of his scheme of imperial union; they suited
his notion that public spirit was best aroused by an aesthetic
appeal to a sense of design or system, rather than to any
specifically utilitarian features of the improved arrangements
alone.

...if you would implant public virtue in the breast of him who seems
heedless of the interest of his country, it will often be to no purpose
to tell him, what superior advantages the subjects of a well-governed

---

[1] For example, by T. D. Campbell in his *Adam Smith's Science of Morals*,
pp. 215–16.
[2] D. Hume, 'Idea of a Perfect Commonwealth', *Essays*, eds. T. H. Green and
T. H. Grose, volume I, p. 480. Those who are inclined to think that Hume
and Burke can be lumped together as 'conservatives' should consult S.
Wolin, 'Hume and Conservatism', *American Political Science Review*, XLVIII
(1954), 999–1016.
[3] On the qualities of Hume's moderation see D. Forbes, *Hume's Philosophical
Politics*, pp. 137, 194, 219–23, 285, 309.

state will enjoy; that they are better lodged, that they are better clothed, that they are better fed. These considerations will commonly make no great impression. You will be more likely to persuade, if you describe the great system of public police which procures these advantages, if you explain the connexions and dependencies of its several parts, their mutual subordination to one another, and their general subserviency to the happiness of the society; if you show how this system might be introduced into his own country, what it is that hinders it from taking place there at present, how these obstructions might be removed, and all the several wheels of the machine of government be made to move with more harmony and smoothness, without grating upon one another, or mutually retarding one another's motions.[1]

In drawing attention once more to the relatively neglected figure of the legislator, the man 'whose deliberations ought to be governed by general principles', I do not wish to suggest that Smith offers him an unlimited range of circumstances in which to operate with surety or even hope of success. That would simply be to meet caricature with caricature. Smith is too much the sceptic and believer in Mandevillian indirection and unintended consequences to endow the legislator with an active or innovatory role in human affairs; his main task was to accommodate laws to the habits of men and their existing social condition. But in so doing he should be guided by a knowledge of what was 'right'.

As far as the private economic affairs of individuals are concerned, the system of natural liberty functioning under rules of justice provided the best general guide to action. In carrying out his duties of 'promoting the prosperity of the commonwealth', the civil magistrate or sovereign did best to confine himself to the main categories of external defence, justice, and public works. It can be shown that these categories, and the principles put forward by Smith to guide intervention within them, allowed wider scope for the state than the nineteenth-century *laissez-faire* image suggests.[2] Considered as a treatise on natural jurisprudence, and particularly when

[1] *TMS* iv.i.11.
[2] See J. Viner's 'Adam Smith and *Laissez-Faire*' in his *Long View and the Short* (1958), and A. S. Skinner's 'Adam Smith on the Origins, Nature and Functions of Government', mimeographed paper given at the International Political Science Association meetings, Edinburgh, 1976.

compared with the earlier models for such treatises, the *Wealth of Nations* reveals how extensive the realm of justice must become in modern commercial societies – even starting from a negative concept of commutative rather than distributive justice. Nevertheless, it remains true that in moving beyond this realm the sovereign was 'always exposed to innumerable delusions'; that it required 'the greatest delicacy and reserve to execute with propriety and judgement', largely because 'no human wisdom or knowledge could ever be sufficient'.[1]

In addition to the constraints imposed by lack of knowledge there were others connected with the state of ordinary opinion, whether this took the form of 'the prejudices of the public' in general, or the oppressive form of the 'insolent outrage' of private interests.[2] The 'wise and virtuous man' was always willing to see his private interest, or that of 'his own order or society' sacrificed to the public interest, but partiality towards one's own interest was the general rule, and had some beneficial side-effects in curbing political innovation.[3] More to the point, however, the legislator would sacrifice his own claims to wisdom if he acted on an assumption of the predominance of wisdom and virtue in the populace at large. Such considerations account for Smith's well-known pessimism concerning the possibilities of implementing the system of natural liberty – a pessimism counterbalanced by his belief that much of the effect of unwise and unjust action by the sovereign or politician was capable of being nullified by the more powerful and steady operations of human nature. Finally, Smith's science of politics, or of the legislator, recognised that there were limits to its application which went beyond knowledge and opinion; that there were circumstances in which it would be wrong to expect solutions to be arrived at on anything other than a basis of pure expediency or 'interest of government'. National defence provided an example of this, as well as retaliatory trade restrictions.[4]

If the legislator as opposed to the politician has been neglected, the recurrent classical–renaissance echoes of Augustan humanism have been almost completely overlooked or even

---

[1] See *WN* iv.ix.51 and *TMS* ii.i.8.   [2] *WN* iv.ii.43.
[3] *TMS* vi.ii.2.10.   [4] *WN* iv.ii.39 and *TMS* vii.iv.36.

denied existence. *Homo civicus*, it might be said, has been up-staged by a rampantly acquisitive *homo oeconomicus* on the one side, and by his more generous, other-directed, *Theory of Moral Sentiments* counterpart, *homo socius*, on the other. Joseph Cropsey gives what is perhaps the most authoritative statement of this point of view when he states that although the *Theory of Moral Sentiments* established the natural sociality of man, it does not prove that man is a political animal: 'Man is tied to humanity by the bonds of immediate sense and feeling, but he is tied to his fellow citizens as such by weaker, superinduced, bonds of calculation or reason, derivative from considerations of utility.' It follows that political society rests only on rules of justice of a circumscribed and negative kind.[1] Although this is a distinct advance on the idea that political society is simply the market place writ large, I hope that earlier chapters have shown that what might be colourlessly called a civic dimension has to be brought into the picture. Economic circumstances exercise a profound influence on men's capacity to act as citizens, but it is precisely the threat of men becoming no more than economic agents operating in anonymous settings that is part of Smith's assessment of the gains and losses incurred in the historical process of economic and social change. By the same token, civic capacities cannot be acquired in men's more private social dealings, where considerations of sympathy and benevolence have their greatest chance to display themselves.

It may be that a proper appreciation of Smith's interest in corruption and civic virtue requires one to go beyond the eighteenth-century political sources which have been the main focus of this essay. As was mentioned earlier, a fuller study of the eighteenth-century context would have to consider Smith's affinities with the earlier debate carried out by the Augustan literati on the relationship between commerce, luxury, urbanity, tolerance, and civility – all those qualities for which it became necessary to coin the word 'civilisation'.[2] It

[1] J. Cropsey, 'Adam Smith and Political Philosophy' in *EAS*, pp. 136–7.
[2] For an interesting discussion of the background to the introduction of the new term see S. Rothblatt, *Tradition and Change in English Liberal Education* (1976), chapter 2.

certainly does not seem fanciful to suggest that Smith's pre-occupation with propriety in the *Theory of Moral Sentiments* could well be regarded as a philosophical examination of the social foundations of modern civility – a scientific extension of the eighteenth-century courtesy book and more essayistic Augustan attempts to comprehend the modernity of English society. The classical roots of Augustan humanism have been explored in several recent studies, and it might be fruitful to extend similar perspectives to Smith, particularly in the light of our enhanced understanding of his *Lectures on Rhetoric and Belles Lettres* and the Stoic emphases in the *Theory of Moral Sentiments*.[1] But even without such an extension it is still possible to appreciate the insight into Smith's position contained in John Pocock's view that the interest of the Scottish historians of civil society in progress, and their recognition of the enlarged role played by economic factors in modern commercial society, did not lead to a complete abandonment of the humanist criteria provided by the concepts of virtue and corruption for judging the point at which progress worked to the disadvantage of man as citizen or political animal.[2]

Having registered this insight, however, it is important not to exaggerate its significance for an understanding of Smith's politics. Smith does not share the passionate concern for the decline of active citizenship that can be found, for example, in Ferguson, even if Smith's diagnosis of the factors contributing to this decline is equally far-reaching. Nor does Smith share Ferguson's desire to infuse the aristocracy with renewed political zeal as an antidote to the economic specialisation of commercial society. Although Hume did not even recognise the problem diagnosed by Smith and Ferguson, Smith's general stance is still closer to Hume's than it is to Ferguson's. Indeed, as David Kettler has recently demonstrated, much of Ferguson's position can only be appreciated by an understanding of his desire to counter what he regarded as the

---

[1] On the *Lectures* see the penetrating essay by W. S. Howell, 'Adam Smith's Lectures on Rhetoric: An Historical Assessment' in *EAS*, pp. 11–43. The Stoic influence is well brought out in the editorial introduction to the bicentennial edition of *TMS*; see especially pp. 5–10.

[2] See J. G. A. Pocock, *Politics, Language and Time*, pp. 101–3, 146; and *The Machiavellian Moment*, pp. 498–504.

fatalistic implications of the more contemplative position adopted by Hume and Smith.[1]

A similar point can be made by stressing the connections between Hume and Smith on the subject of public institutions and constitutional machinery. It was a fundamental tenet of Hume's politics that 'in contriving any system of government, and fixing the several checks and controls of the constitution, every man ought to be supposed a knave, and to have no other end, in all his actions, than private interest'.[2] It should not now be necessary to add that interest covers all aspects of men's ambition, though Hume assumes that in political settings, where party contest is the order of the day, honour will act as a less effective check on the ambitions of the majority than it does in men's private dealings. Smith's version of the same idea comes as a warning that 'though management and persuasion are always the easiest and safest instruments of government, as force and violence are the worst and most dangerous, yet such, it seems, is the natural insolence of man, that he almost always disdains to use the good instrument, except when he cannot or dare not use the bad one'.[3] The complexity of human motivation together with Smith's consistently low estimate of human nature in public settings explains why 'spontaneous harmony' and 'sunny optimism' are such a travesty of his position, and why, as Nathan Rosenberg has shown, Smith devotes so much attention to proposing institutional devices, besides the rules of justice, that would either frustrate certain anti-social impulses or make use of them to serve the public interest.[4] It also helps to explain why realism sometimes gives way to world-weariness: 'The violence and injustice of the rulers of mankind is an ancient evil, for which, I am afraid, the nature of human affairs can scarce admit of a remedy.'[5]

[1] See 'History and Theory in the Politics of Adam Ferguson: A Reconsideration' in *The Year 1776 in the History of Political Thought*, ed. J. G. A. Pocock (mimeographed, Conference for the Study of Political Thought, Chicago, 1976).

[2] 'Of the Independency of Parliament' in *Essays*, eds. T. H. Green and T. H. Grose, volume I, pp. 117–18.

[3] *WN* v.i.g.19.

[4] See N. Rosenberg, 'Some Institutional Aspects of the *Wealth of Nations*', *Journal of Political Economy*, LXVIII (1960), 537–70.

[5] *WN* IV.iii.c.9.

For Smith then, in company with Hume, politics is far more a matter of legal and constitutional machinery than of men or any specifically political qualities which they may be called upon to display in public settings. According to Hume, it was this very dissociation between the regular effects of forms of government and variability of 'the humours and tempers of men', their manners and morals, which made a science of politics possible.[1] This belief, and the approach to politics which it sanctions, is one of the reasons why the Hume–Smith position must be distinguished from that strand of 'vulgar Whiggism' described as 'Machiavellian moralism', which so many of the standard spokesmen for a 'Country' party view of English politics upheld. While, as Kettler has argued, it may be misleading to regard Ferguson as a Machiavellian moralist, he differs from Hume and Smith in giving much greater priority to active political qualities in the citizenry, and more especially in its leaders; he is much more concerned to bridge the gap between public and private virtue that Hume's and Smith's views opened up.

I imagine that it will be abundantly clear by now that I regard the political affinities between Hume and Smith as more significant than the issues on which they adopted different positions. Smith may not have written penetrating, self-contained essays which can be neatly labelled 'political', but the underlying spirit of his politics is much the same. I am not suggesting, however, that there are no important differences of outlook between the two men when their work is considered as a whole. Here I would follow others in believing that Smith's enterprise is more consistently 'sociological', where this implies a pervasive interest in relating institutions to an underlying pattern of historical change.[2] Nevertheless, for reasons given earlier, I would not equate 'sociological' with anything as strong as the notion suggested by economic determinism.

---

[1] 'That Politics May be Reduced to a Science', in *Essay*, eds. T. H. Green and T. H. Grose, volume I, p. 99. See D. Forbes, *Hume's Philosophical Politics*, especially chapter 7; and J. Moore, 'Hume's Political Science and the Classical Republican Tradition' in *The Year 1776 in the History of Political Thought*, ed., J. G. A. Pocock (mimeographed, Conference for the Study of Political Thought, 1976).

[2] See D. Forbes, *Hume's Philosophical Politics*, chapter 9; and J. Moore, 'Hume's Political Science and the Classical Republican Tradition'.

It may further help to situate Smith's politics, as well as highlight weaknesses in more economistic interpretations, to revert to the parallels mentioned in the previous chapter between Smith's scheme of imperial union and James Madison's case for an extended republic as put forward in *The Federalist Papers*, Number 10. Both entailed suggestions for constitutional machinery which would curb and harness the spirit of faction by encompassing a wide variety of interests, and by extending the arena in which those interests competed and counterbalanced one another. The similarities no longer seem fortuitous when Hume is recognised as the major influence on Madison's position on the theory of extended republics and factions. Indeed, it has been rightly claimed that 'the most direct beneficiaries of Hume's political science were the authors of *The Federalist Papers*'.[1]

Madison's *Federalist*, Number 10, continues to occupy a pivotal situation in the debate on the American constitution. It was, of course, this essay that provided the centreprice of Charles Beard's highly influential, but now discredited work, *An Economic Interpretation of the Constitution of the United States* published in 1913. Under Beard's influence, Madison's contribution to the federalist position was accepted as 'a masterly statement of the theory of economic determinism in politics', even though, from another point of view, the burden of Beard's unmasking operation was to show that the constitution was the work of practical men who were anti-democratic in their sympathies and anxious to protect the specific types of property which they held. Subsequent dissection of Beard's case has revealed just how one-sided was the construction he placed on Madison's views on the subject of interest. Beard concentrated on the interests attached to horizontal divisions in society based on wealth and creditor/debtor status, thereby ignoring Madison's vertical divisions of society into 'a landed interest, a manufacturing interest, a mercantile interest, a moneyed interest, and many lesser interests'.[2] More to the

---

[1] J. Moore, 'Hume's Political Science and the Classical Republican Tradition'.

[2] *The Federalist Papers*, Sesquicentennial edition (1937), p. 56. See especially D. Adair's analysis of Beard's interpretation in 'The Tenth Federalist Revisited', *William & Mary Quarterly*, VII (1951), 48–67. For a blow-by-blow

point, perhaps, Beard completely overlooked that part of
Madison's borrowing from Hume which dealt with non-
economic factions based on personal loyalties and animosities,
and on 'principle', where the latter included 'opinions' concerning religion and government. Only by such a narrowing
process, apparently, could Madison be made to serve Beard's
preeminently early twentieth-century purposes of revealing
the property-serving and anti-democratic inspiration which
informed the constitution from its inception. It has required
a full appreciation of the eighteenth-century sources of Madison's position, the revisionist scholarship on the ideological
underpinnings of the Revolution and on the political cross-
currents of the post-Revolutionary period, to appreciate the
real source of modernity in Madison's federalism in 1787, and
the departure which it made from the predominant radical
Whig or Country ideologies which had done so much to fire
the Revolution itself.

Madison's innovation has been described as giving birth to
'a kinetic theory of politics' and as marking the end of classical
politics.[1] By a further extension the Madisonian legacy can be
held responsible for providing a foundation for what is now
described as interest-group liberalism or pluralism. Like
Beard's interpretation earlier, however, this view owes more
to current preoccupations with defects in the American constitution, nostalgia for a more participatory ethic, and dis-
illusionment with the impoverished view of politics which
interest-group liberalism appears to embody, than anything
a more strictly historical interpretation will permit.[2] For as
Adair pointed out in criticising Beard's anachronisms, 'Madison's Tenth *Federalist* is eighteenth-century political theory
directed to an eighteenth-century problem.' It was certainly

refutation of Beard's case, see Robert E. Brown, *Charles Beard and the Constitution* (1956).
[1] See G. S. Wood, *The Creation of the American Republic, 1776–1787* (1969), pp. 605–16. For J. G. A. Pocock's qualifications to this judgement see *The Machiavellian Moment*, pp. 520–45.
[2] For two recent scholarly treatments of this question see R. Morgan, 'Mad-ison's Theory of Representation in the Tenth Federalist', *Journal of Politics*, XXXVI (1974), 852–85; and P. F. Bourke, 'The Pluralist Reading of James Madison's Tenth Federalist', *Perspectives in American History*, XI (1975), 271–95.

7   179   WAS

an innovation which was thoroughly grounded on inferences drawn from the contemporary science of politics, the result of a search, in Madison's words, for 'a republican remedy for the diseases most incident to republican government', particularly a government required to operate in a commercial society of wide extent. It would require a firm application of present-minded perspectives to make the Hume–Smith–Madison nexus on the politics of interest as opposed to virtue seem like a step towards something recognisably 'liberal' in the nineteenth-century sense – a liberalism, it should be noted, that has somehow lost its Lockean pedigree. One simple antidote to such extrapolative or teleological forms of interpretation is to point out that 'was becoming' does not tell us 'what was' – and might be taken as a sign of evading that question.

Smith may have intended many things when writing on politics, some of which may be inconsistent with one another, confused, and just plain wrong. I have certainly not claimed privileged access to his intentions, and am only too aware of the problems posed by a writer who operated with ease on a series of interconnected levels of generality; who was not merely a practitioner of a variety of different modes of discourse, but held sophisticated theories about those modes; who employed stylistic devices which involved rhetoric and irony; and who was, above all, infuriatingly balanced. But if there is one intention he was incapable of forming it was that of anticipating what later generations, with or without warrant, would make of his views.

It may help perhaps to bring the anti-teleological implications of my reading to the fore if I state in short order what Smith's politics is not. It is not an episode – however crucial – that occurred some way along a road which runs from Locke to Marx. Smith was not in the grip of some hidden historical force which destined him to work out in more detail or more frankly the ramifications of a set of problems posed by Locke, the true and sinister import of which was only discerned by Marx. Smith did not advocate the establishment of a particular economic order called capitalism; nor did he prize what he set out to analyse, namely commercial society, for the sake of its benefits in the form of democratic freedoms. He was even less of a nineteenth-century liberal or social democrat in the making than he was a standard eighteenth-century Whig. Indeed, even the Earl of Buchan's mistaken description of him as a 'republican' would come closer to the truth. Nor was Smith setting up in business as the spokesman or apologist for an emerging middle class, any more than he was attempting to provide a foundation for 'a psychology basic to the radical bourgeois vision of man'.[1] If every single one of Smith's criticisms of the landed aristocracy were assembled, they would still not add up to an endorsement of acquisitive 'middle-class' values – except, of course, to those who are vouchsafed knowledge of how the 'progressive' forces in society must be, or came to be, aligned. In terms of these preemptive categories, Smith's values were pre-capitalist and pre-industrial as well as pre-democratic; they were not even noticeably pro-mercantile. They were also both post- and pre-individualist in the sense defined, say, by Hobbes on the one side, and redefined by Bentham and James Mill on the other. When the most is made of Smith's negative and contemplative utilitarianism, and when his concept of self-interest is reduced to its narrowest form, it is still not possible to bridge the gap between his politics and the radical individualism of nineteenth-century utilitarianism: his science of the legislator is not the Benthamite science of legislation.[2]

While negative statements can, of course, have truth-values assigned to them, the most elaborate demonstration of who

[1] This view is taken by I. Kramnick in 'Sophisters, Economists and Calculators: Bourgeois Radicalism in the Age of Burke' in *The Year 1776 in the History of Political Thought*, ed. J. G. A. Pocock (mimeographed, Conference for the Study of Political Thought, 1976).

[2] Consider whether it is conceivable for Smith to have made the following claims on behalf of a science of legislation: 'I have no doubt about removing all your difficulties; and showing you that instead of being a science, the practical results of which must always be uncertain, rendering it always prudent to try to remain in the state we are in, rather than venture the unknown effects of a change, legislation is essentially a science the effects of which may be computed with an extraordinary degree of certainty; and the friends of human nature cannot proceed with too much energy in beating down every obstacle which opposes the progress of human welfare.' Letter by James Mill to David Ricardo, 3 December 1817, D. Ricardo, *Works & Correspondence*, ed. P. Sraffa, volume VII, pp. 210–11.

Adam Smith was *not* adds nothing to our knowledge of Adam Smith. In earlier chapters I have tried to show what shape Smith's politics took, and how it worked when applied in a non-*ad hoc* fashion to a number of contemporary issues. I hope this excuses me from supplying a lengthy abstract description at this late stage, but as an alternative to some of the negative labels I have rejected, here are a few positive ones.

Judged by its view of the motives, ambitions, and pretensions of political actors, Smith's politics was sceptical, pessimistic, or realistic, according to the reader's taste. By the same token, it was neither nostalgic in its appeal to the values of a past or passing order, nor utopian in its reliance on an intellectualist vision of the future, according to which men would exercise increasing dominion over Nature, including their own, in order to remodel society. And what men's reason and humanity was unlikely to accomplish, the impersonal forces of history were unlikely to deliver according to plan. Change there would be, and change might bring improvement in the future as it had done in the recent past. But the gains might be only *net* gains; they might be achieved at severe cost to older virtues. While there were strong principles that bound men together in society and through their economic activities, polities were more fragile entities. There was no permanent reason why the classical cycle of rise and fall should be in abeyance. Accident and local circumstances had played a part in creating present establishments, and though there were persistent forces working for cohesion and stability, history contained enough examples of breakdown, stagnation, and downright folly and injustice to warn against complacency – and to leave scope for the exercise of wisdom.

The role of the philosopher in such a world was to preserve a cool head, to observe human conduct and assign the proper causes and consequences, which meant that manners and customs had to be related to psychological propensities and circumstances, social institutions to historical location. Empty moralising and wishful thinking ought to be avoided; the balance sheet of progress should be recorded with as much clinical detachment as was humanly possible. This did not mean that the philosopher should be bloodless or abstracted from society. The useful implications of his experimental knowledge should be proclaimed, warnings should be issued, and judgements of worth passed. And while partisan engagement should be avoided, it was always necessary to defend such fundamental and instrumental values as liberty, humanity, tolerance, and moderation in order to protect the benefits of civilised society from such characteristic disorders as faction, enthusiasm, and superstition. It was also necessary on occasion to fortify didactic conclusions with rhetoric, but it would be an act of enthusiasm in itself to believe that 'the most sublime speculations of the contemplative philosopher' could 'compensate the neglect of the smallest active duty';[1] that such speculations supported gifts of prophecy; and that the philosopher was capable of moulding outcomes except by a large measure of indirection. For its day, Smith's politics was modern, moderate, and centrist. It is difficult, and strictly unnecessary, to imagine what its direct normative or scientific significance could be to the twentieth century, though presumably it will appeal to all those who like these qualities, and incur the dislike of all those who do not.

While I would acknowledge a desire to bypass some of the more well-trodden access routes, it is perhaps worth repeating that the kind of historical approach adopted here does not entail a denial of Smith's claims to originality or significance. The counter-charge that such an approach is at least a necessary preliminary to establishing such claims would be closer to the truth. There may, however, appear to be a stronger case for the related objection that the result of attending to historicity must be to reduce the claims to present-day 'relevance' frequently made on Smith's behalf, replacing them with a dusty antiquarianism.[2] A full answer to this objection would require consideration of the larger questions surrounding the value of studying intellectual history, but a start can be made

---

[1] *TMS* vi.ii.36.
[2] This has certainly been one reaction to Quentin Skinner's defence of the historical approach; see C. D. Tarlton, 'Historicity, Meaning, and Revisionism in the Study of Political Thought', *History & Theory*, xii (1973), 307–28; and M. Leslie, 'In Defence of Anachronism', *Political Studies*, xviii (1970), 433–47.

by distinguishing between the trivial and more serious consequences of entertaining the objection. For those to whom Smith is chiefly important either as a cultural emblem or as a convenient method of bolstering a present-minded polemic, it can do little harm to propose that they reformulate their position on firmer grounds than those furnished by a historical stereotype. It is also possible to go one step further to suggest that the cultivation of pasts for their supposed value in shedding light on our present discontents frequently results in a reduced capacity to learn from the past: we merely construct a mirror in which we see our own reflection, and lose a genuine source of indirect illumination in the process.

There may, however, be more serious revisionist implications of turning Smith's back on the present, or rather of detaching him from some of the established nineteenth-century readings. If this essay has any merit, it may be necessary to accept that the gulf between Smith's intellectual enterprise and those that are often regarded as its successors runs deeper than has been suspected. That this is clearly the case with Benthamite utilitarianism has already been touched upon, and will be fairly readily conceded by all those who are not too dogmatically committed to the *idée de convenance* of an unbroken tradition of liberalism, or bourgeois ideology, stretching from Locke through Smith and Hume to John Stuart Mill. Indeed, any history of the social sciences which fails to confront the discontinuity marked by the transition from Scottish moral philosophy and its associated histories of civil society on the one side, to Benthamism on the other, would be guilty of sidestepping one of the most intriguing problems in that history.[1]

Even within the more restricted confines of the history of classical political economy – the science 'founded' by Smith – the discontinuity between Smith and both his orthodox and unorthodox successors is more remarkable than is sometimes imagined. We are used to the idea that in the hands of such figures as Malthus and Ricardo, political economy emerged or

[1] The fullest attempt to tackle this problem within the context of the history of the social sciences is that by J. W. Burrow, *Evolution and Society: A Study in Victorian Social Theory* (1965), chapters 1–3.

escaped from its Scottish moral philosophy integument to become a separate, more narrowly deductive, discipline in its own right. But the nature and extent of the divergence may have been underestimated or become overlaid in the process of professional assimilation that set in once political economy had gained a measure of autonomy. Most commentators, whether critical or not, would recognise Ricardo to be more of an economists' economist than Smith, and some attempts have been made to characterise and explain the rise of an 'English' science of political economy at the expense of its 'Scottish' original counterpart.[1] But perhaps the question should be pursued a little further by inquiring whether there are *any* obvious candidates – Scottish, English, or French for that matter – for the role of successor to the author of the *Wealth of Nations*.[2] For one reason or another, Say, Sismondi, and Lauderdale do not seem capable of filling the bill, while Millar and Dugald Stewart have some of the qualifications, but only if one is prepared to overlook their lack of any sustained interest in political economy. James Mill and J. R. McCulloch have some of the qualifications, but must be ruled out on other grounds.[3]

A similar point can be made by reminding economists just how little Smith himself did to aid the process of 'escape' during the fourteen years that remained of his life after the publication of the first edition of the *Wealth of Nations*. Apart from his additions and corrections to subsequent editions, he published no further work on political economy. On the other hand, he did return to the *Theory of Moral Sentiments*, and made rather important additions to that work in the last year of his life. We also know that, given time, his next task was to make good his promise to give an 'account of the general principles of law and government'.

[1] See, for example, A. L. Macfie, 'The Scottish Tradition in Economic Thought' in his *The Individual and Society* (1967), pp. 19–44.

[2] This and the next three paragraphs are drawn from my comment on a paper by R. D. C. Black which appears in T. Wilson and A. S. Skinner (eds.), *The Market and the State* (1976), pp. 67–72.

[3] McCulloch's claims to affinity with Smith are fully rehearsed in D. P. O'Brien, *J. R. McCulloch; A Study in Classical Economics* (1970), especially pp. 121–5.

It is still true to say that the period in the history of classical political economy that is most in need of illumination is that marked out by the *Wealth of Nations* on one side and Ricardo's *Principles* published in 1817 on the other. Without pretending to provide that illumination here, it seems necessary to avoid minimising the extent of the changes which took place not long after Smith passed from the scene. This could, for example, explain why Dugald Stewart found it necessary only three years after Smith's death to answer a sneer published in *The Times* to the effect that Smith had 'converted the Chair of Moral Philosophy into a professorship of trade and finance'. Stewart did so by stressing the connections between Smith's 'system of commercial politics, and those speculations of his earlier years, in which he aimed more professedly at the advancement of human improvement and happiness'. For as Stewart rather primly concluded: 'It is this view of political economy that can alone render it interesting to the moralist, and can dignify calculations of profit and loss in the eye of the philosopher.'[1] Few people would regard the *Wealth of Nations* simply as a work on 'trade and finance', though Stewart's corrective is still relevant as a reminder that the book was the most striking attempt to sustain a peculiarly Scottish line of philosophical and historical inquiry into one of the most important features of modern civilisation, considered as a process, namely the spreading network of commercial relationships, with all its consequences for those questions whose place on the philosophical agenda was guaranteed by virtue of their centrality to earlier modes of political and moral discourse. It is certainly consonant with the view maintained here that Stewart later found it necessary to explain the defensive tone adopted in his memoir by reference to the intolerant mood created in Britain by the French Revolution.[2]

[1] 'Account of the Life and Writings of Adam Smith', in *Collected Works*, ed. W. Hamilton, volume x, p. 59.

[2] 'I think it proper for me *now* to add, that at the period when this Memoir was read before the Royal Society of Edinburgh, it was not unusual even among men of some talents and information, to confound, seriously, the speculative doctrines of Political Economy, with those first principles of Government which happened unfortunately to agitate the public mind.' See *ibid.*, note G, p. 87, added in 1810.

Moreover, in spite of all the efforts to establish affinities between Smith and Burke, it would be difficult to claim that Burke adopted Smith's philosophical approach when he made his intemperate defence of economic liberty in *Thoughts and Details on Scarcity*, a pamphlet written only five years after Smith's death.[1]

For the present, however, it is only possible to point to the powerful, but by itself, circumstantial evidence provided by changes in the external environment – the French Revolution and the accumulation of pressing and more purely economic problems connected with the Napoleonic Wars in the form of rising food prices, growing population, heavy taxation, fears of monetary disorder, and increased public debt. If such problems cannot in themselves explain the change in method of approach, they probably licensed a new kind of urgency towards certain public issues which may have encouraged the use of narrower and more rationalistic applications of what we now think of as economic reasoning. *Prima facie* at least, it was not an atmosphere which encouraged the kind of balance which Smith set out to achieve, though this should not be taken to imply that those who regarded themselves as his economic successors desired to emulate him in this respect.

Reverting in conclusion to Sheldon Wolin's hypothesis mentioned at the outset, that the history of the social sciences can be seen as entailing the rise of society and economy at the expense of polity, it would seem that Smith should not be linked quite so firmly to the a-political vision of the later liberals and radicals whom Wolin cites. Judged by classical standards, Smith's politics may appear to be heavily attenuated but it has by no means disappeared. In fact, to close on a more assertive note, it must be said that, whatever else it might be, the publication of the *Wealth of Nations* does not mark the moment at which Adam Smith's science of political economy can be observed escaping from anything – it is certainly not escaping from the eighteenth-century science of politics.

[1] For comment see J. R. Poynter, *Society and Pauperism* (1969), pp. 24, 52–5.

Bibliography

Although the distinction between primary and secondary sources is a little artificial in a work of this kind, it may still be of some help to the reader. Hence all seventeenth- and eighteenth-century sources are listed as primary, while the rest are denoted as secondary.

PRIMARY SOURCES

Blair, Hugh. Review of Hutcheson's *System of Moral Philosophy* in *Edinburgh Review*, No. 1, 1755.

Buchan, David Erskine, 11th Earl of. 'Letter to the Editor on Dr Adam Smith', *The Bee or Literary Weekly Intelligencer*, 8 June 1791, pp. 164–7.

Essays on the Lives and Writings of Fletcher of Saltoun and the Poet Thomson, London, 1792.

Letters on the Impolicy of a Standing Army, London, 1793.

[Carlyle, Alexander]. *A Letter to His Grace the Duke of Buccleuch on National Defence with Some Remarks on Dr. Smith's Chapter on that Subject, in Book entitled 'An Inquiry into the Nature and Causes of the Wealth of Nations'*, London, 1778.

Carlyle, Alexander. *Autobiography. The Life of Dr. Alexander Carlyle of Inveresk, 1722–1805*, London, 1910.

Federalist Papers, The. Sesquicentennial edition, Washington, 1937.

Ferguson, Adam. *An Essay on the History of Civil Society*, ed. Duncan Forbes, Edinburgh, 1966.

Hume, David. *A Treatise of Human Nature*, ed. L. A. Selby-Bigge, Oxford, 1888.

Essays, Moral, Political and Literary, ed. T. H. Green and T. H. Grose, 2 volumes, Oxford, 1963.

History of Great Britain, ed. D. Forbes, Pelican Classics edition, 1970.

Letters of David Hume, ed. J. T. Y. Greig, 2 volumes, Oxford, 1932.

Hutcheson, Francis. *A System of Moral Philosophy*, as reproduced in the *Collected Works*, volumes v and vi, Hildesheim, 1969.

Kames, Henry Home, Lord. *Sketches of the History of Man*, Edinburgh, 1774.

Locke, John. *Two Treatises of Government*, ed. P. Laslett, Cambridge, 1963.

   The Works of John Locke, London, 1823.

Millar, John. *A Historical View of the English Government*, 3rd edition, London, 1803.

Molesworth, Robert. Introduction to Francis Hotman, *Franco–Gallia*, London, 1721.

Montesquieu, Charles Secondat, Baron. *The Spirit of the Laws*, New York, 1949.

Smith, Adam. *The Theory of Moral Sentiments*, ed. D. D. Raphael and A. L. Macfie, Oxford, 1976.

   An Inquiry into the Nature and Causes of the Wealth of Nations, ed. R. H. Campbell and A. S. Skinner; textual ed. W. B. Todd, Oxford, 1976.

   Lectures on Jurisprudence, ed. R. L. Meek, D. D. Raphael, and P. G. Stein, Oxford. 1977.

   The Early Writings of Adam Smith, ed. J. R. Lindgren, New York, 1966.

   Lectures on Rhetoric and Belles Lettres, ed. J. R. Lothian, London, 1963.

   The Correspondence of Adam Smith, ed. Ernest Campbell Mossner and Ian Simpson Ross, Oxford, 1977.

Stewart, Dugald. *Account of the Life and Writings of Adam Smith* in his *Collected Works*, ed. Sir William Hamilton, Edinburgh, 1858, volume x.

SECONDARY SOURCES
BOOKS

Bailyn, Bernard. *The Ideological Origins of the American Revolution*, Cambridge, Mass, 1967.

   The Origins of American Politics, New York, 1968.

Beard, Charles. *An Economic Interpretation of the Constitution of the United States*, New York, 1913.

Bloom, Edward A. and Bloom, Lillian D. *Joseph Addison's Sociable Animal*, Providence, Rhode Island, 1971.

Bowley, Marian. *Studies in the History of Economic Theory before 1870*, London, 1973.

Brown, Robert E. *Charles Beard and the Constitution*, 1956.

Burrow, John W. *Evolution and Society: A Study in Victorian Social Theory*, Cambridge, 1966.

Campbell, Thomas D. *Adam Smith's Science of Morals*, London, 1971.

Comte, Auguste. *The Positive Philosophy of Auguste Comte*, Freely Translated and Condensed by H. Martineau, London, 1854.

Corry, Bernard A. *Money, Saving and Investment in English Economics, 1800–1850*, London, 1962.

Cropsey, Joseph. *Polity and Economy: An Interpretation of the Principles of Adam Smith*, The Hague, 1957.

Cumming, Robert D. *Human Nature and History: A Study of the Development of Liberal Political Thought*, 2 volumes, Chicago, 1969.

Dickinson, H. T. *Bolingbroke*, London, 1970.

Dickson, P. G. M. *The Financial Revolution in England: A Study in the Development of Public Credit, 1688–1756*, London, 1967.

Dunn, John. *The Political Thought of John Locke; An Historical Account of the 'Two Treatises of Government'*, Cambridge, 1969.

Durkheim, Emil. *Montesquieu and Rousseau*, Ann Arbor, Michigan, 1965.

Erskine-Hill, Howard. *The Social Milieu of Alexander Pope: Lives, Example and the Poetic Response*, New Haven, 1975.

Fay, C. R. *Adam Smith and the Scotland of His Day*, Cambridge, 1956.
The World of Adam Smith, Cambridge, 1950.

Fink, Zera S. *The Classical Republicans*, Evanston, 1945.

Forbes, Duncan. *Hume's Philosophical Politics*, Cambridge, 1976.

Giarizzo, Giuseppe. *David Hume politico e storico*, Turin, 1962.

Grampp, William D. *Economic Liberalism*, 2 volumes, New York, 1965.

Greene, Jack P. (ed.). *The Reinterpretation of the American Revolution; 1763–1789*, New York, 1968.

Halévy, Elie. *La Formation du radicalisme philosophique*, volume I, *La Jeunesse de Bentham*, Paris, 1901. Translated into English as *The Growth of Philosophical Radicalism*, London, 1934.

Hayek, Friedrich A. *Individualism and Economic Order*, London, 1948.
The Constitution of Liberty, London, 1960.
Studies in Philosophy, Politics, and Economics, London, 1967.

Hirschman, Albert O. *The Passions and the Interests*, Princeton, 1977.

Hollander, Samuel. *The Economics of Adam Smith*, Toronto, 1973.

Johnson, James W. *The Formation of English Neo-Classical Thought*, Princeton, 1967.

Kammen, Michael. *Empire and Interest; The American Colonies and the Politics of Mercantilism*, New York, 1970.

Kettler, David. *The Social and Political Thought of Adam Ferguson*, Ohio, 1965.

Koebner, Richard. *Empire*, Cambridge, 1961.

Kramnick, Isaac. *Bolingbroke and his Circle: The Politics of Nostalgia in the Age of Walpole*, Cambridge, Mass., 1968.

Lehmann, William C. *John Millar of Glasgow, 1735–1801*, Cambridge, 1960.

McCulloch, J. R. (ed.). *A Select Collection of Scarce and Valuable Tracts and Other Publications on the National Debt and the Sinking Fund*, London, 1857.

Macpherson, Clyde B. *The Political Theory of Possessive Individualism*, Oxford, 1962.

Marx, Karl. *Capital*, 3 volumes, Moscow, 1965.
Theories of Surplus Value, part I, Moscow, 1969.

Meek, Ronald L. *Social Science and the Ignoble Savage*, Cambridge, 1976.

Nicholson, John S. *A Project of Empire*, London, 1909.

O'Brien, Denis P. *J. R. McCulloch: A Study in Classical Economics*, London, 1970.

Pocock, John G. A. *Politics, Language and Time*, New York, 1973.
The Machiavellian Moment: Florentine Political Thought and the Atlantic Republican Tradition, Princeton, 1975.

Poynter, J. R. *Society and Pauperism; English Ideas on Poor Relief, 1795–1834*, London, 1969.

Rae, John. *Life of Adam Smith*, London, 1895.

Reisman, D. A. *Adam Smith's Sociological Economics*, London, 1976.

Ricardo, David. *The Works and Correspondence of David Ricardo*, ed. by Piero Sraffa in 11 volumes, Cambridge, 1951–73.

Richter, Melvin. *The Political Theory of Montesquieu*, Cambridge, 1977.

Robbins, Caroline. *The Eighteenth-Century Commonwealthman; Studies in the Transmission, Development and Circumstances of English Liberal Thought from the Restoration of Charles II until the War with the Thirteen Colonies*, New York, 1968.
(ed.), *Two English Republican Tracts*, Cambridge, 1969.

Rossiter, Clinton. *Seedtime of the Republic; The Origin of the American Tradition of Liberty*, New York, 1953.

Rothblatt, Sheldon. *Tradition and Change in English Liberal Education; An Essay in History and Culture*, London, 1976.

Rotwein, E. (ed.), *David Hume: Writings on Economics*, Edinburgh, 1955.

Schlatter, Richard. *Private Property; The History of an Idea*, London, 1951.

Schumpeter, Joseph A. *History of Economic Analysis*, London, 1954.

Scott, W. R. *Francis Hutcheson*, London, 1900.
Adam Smith as Student and Professor, Glasgow, 1937.

Skinner, Andrew S. (with Thomas Wilson) (ed.), *Essays on Adam Smith*, Oxford, 1976.
(with T. Wilson) (ed.), *The Market and the State*, Oxford, 1976.

Spiegel, Henry W. *The Growth of Economic Thought*, Englewood Cliffs, 1971.

Stephen, Leslie. *History of English Thought in the Eighteenth Century*, Harbinger paperback edition, New York, 1962.

Stourzh, Gerald. *Alexander Hamilton and the Idea of Republican Government*, Stanford, 1970.

Tawney, Richard H. *Religion and the Rise of Capitalism*, London, 1926.

Taylor, W. L. *Francis Hutcheson and David Hume as Predecessors of Adam Smith*, Duke, North Carolina, 1965.

Tucker, G. S. L. *Progress and Profits in British Economic Thought, 1650–1850*, Cambridge, 1960.

Venturi, Franco. *Utopia and Reform in the Enlightenment*, Cambridge, 1971.

Viner, Jacob. *Guide to John Rae's Life of Adam Smith*, New York, 1965.

Western, John R. *The English Militia in the Eighteenth Century: The Story of a Political Issue, 1660–1802*, London, 1965.

Wilson, Thomas (with Andrew S. Skinner) (ed.). *Essays on Adam Smith*, Oxford, 1976.

(with A. S. Skinner) (ed.). *The Market and the State*, Oxford, 1976.

Winch, Donald N. *Classical Political Economy and Colonies*, London, 1965.

Wolin, Sheldon. *Politics and Vision; Continuity and Innovation in Western Political Thought*, Boston, 1960.

Wood, Gordon S. *The Creation of the American Republic, 1776–1787*, New York, 1972.

ARTICLES, CHAPTERS AND CONFERENCE PAPERS

Adair, Douglas. 'The Tenth Federalist Revisited', *William and Mary Quarterly*, VIII (1951) 48–67.

'"That Politics May be Reduced to a Science"; David Hume, James Madison, and the Tenth *Federalist*', *Huntington Library Quarterly*, XX (1956–7) 343–60.

Barrington, D. 'Edmund Burke as an Economist', *Economica*, XXI (1954) 252–8.

Benians, E. A. 'Adam Smith's Project of an Empire', *Cambridge Historical Journal*, I (1925) 249–83.

Black, Robert D. Collison. 'Smith's Contribution in Historical Perspective', in T. Wilson and A. S. Skinner (eds.), *The Market and the State*, Oxford, 1976.

Blaug, Mark. 'The Economics of Education in English Classical Political Economy: A Re-Examination' in A. S. Skinner and T. Wilson (eds.), *Essays on Adam Smith*, Oxford, 1976.

Bourke, Paul F. 'The Pluralist Reading of James Madison's *Tenth Federalist*', *Perspectives in American History*, XI (1975) 271–95.

Branson, Roy. 'James Madison and the Scottish Enlightenment', mimeographed paper presented at the Fourth International Congress on the Enlightenment, Yale, 1975.

Coats, A. W. 'Changing Attitudes to Labour in the Mid-Eighteenth Century', *Economic History Review*, II (1958) 35–51.

'Adam Smith's Conception of Self-Interest in Economic Affairs', *History of Political Economy*, VII (1975) 132–6.

Cropsey, Joseph. 'On the Relation of Political Science and Economics', *American Political Science Review*, LIV (1960) 3–64.

'Adam Smith and Political Philosophy', in A. S. Skinner and T. Wilson (eds.), *Essays on Adam Smith*, Oxford, 1976.

Cumming, Robert D. 'The Four Stages Theory' in *Political Economy and Political Theory*, ed. C. B. Macpherson, mimeographed, Conference for the Study of Political Thought, 1974.

Douglas, Paul H. 'Smith's Theory of Value and Distribution', in J. M. Clark *et al.*, *Adam Smith, 1776–1926*, Chicago, 1928.

Dunn, John. 'The Identity of the History of Ideas', *Philosophy*, XLIII (1968) 85–116.

'The Politics of Locke in England and America in the Eighteenth Century', *John Locke: Problems and Perspectives*, ed. John W. Yolton, Cambridge, 1969.

Dunnes, W. L. 'Adam Smith and Burke: Complementary Contemporaries', *Southern Economic Journal*, VII (1941) 330–46.

Forbes, Duncan. 'Scientific Whiggism: Adam Smith and John Millar', *Cambridge Journal*, VII (1954) 643–70.

Review of 'David Hume, politico e storico', by G. Giarizzo in *The Historical Journal*, VI (1963) 280–95.

'Sceptical Whiggism, Commerce and Liberty', in A. S. Skinner and T. Wilson (eds.), *Essays on Adam Smith*, Oxford, 1976.

Goldsmith, M. M. 'Mandeville and the Spirit of Capitalism' in *Political Theory and Political Economy*, ed. C. B. Macpherson, mimeographed, Conference for the Study of Political Thought, 1974.

'Public Virtue and Private Vices: Bernard Mandeville and English Political Ideologies in the Eighteenth Century', *Eighteenth-Century Studies*, IX (1976), 477–510.

Heilbroner, Robert L. 'The Paradox of Progress: Decline and Decay in the *Wealth of Nations*', in A. S. Skinner and T. Wilson (eds.), *Essays on Adam Smith*, Oxford, 1976.

Howell, Wilbur S. 'Adam Smith's Lectures on Rhetoric: An Historical Assessment', in A. S. Skinner and T. Wilson (eds.), *Essays on Adam Smith*, Oxford, 1976.

Kettler, David. 'History and Theory in the Politics of Adam Ferguson', in *The Year 1776 in the History of Political Thought*, ed. J. G. A. Pocock, mimeographed, Conference for the Study of Political Thought, Chicago, 1976.

Kramnick, Isaac. 'Sophisters, Economists and Calculators: Bourgeois Radicalism in the Age of Burke', in *The Year 1776 in the History of Political Thought*, ed. J. G. A. Pocock, mimeographed, Conference for the Study of Political Thought, 1976.

Lamb, R. 'Adam Smith's Concept of Alienation', *Oxford Economic Papers*, XXV (1973) 275–85.

   'Adam Smith's System: Sympathy not Self-Interest', *Journal of the History of Ideas*, XXXV (1974) 671–82.

Lane, F. C. 'At the Roots of Republicanism', *American Historical Review*, LXXI (1966) 403–20.

Leslie, Margaret. 'In Defence of Anachronism', *Political Studies*, XVIII (1970) 433–47.

Lowenthal, D. 'Montesquieu and the Classics: Republican Government in *The Spirit of the Laws*', in J. Cropsey (ed.), *Ancients and Moderns*, 1964.

Macfie, Alec L. 'The Scottish Tradition in Economic Thought', in his *The Individual in Society*, London, 1967.

McNulty, P. J. 'Adam Smith's Concept of Labour', *Journal of the History of Ideas*, XXXIV (1973) 345–66.

Meek, Ronald L. 'The Scottish Contribution to Marxist Sociology', in *Economics and Ideology and Other Essays*, London, 1967.

   'Smith, Turgot, and the "Four Stages' Theory"', *History of Political Economy*, III (1971) 9–27.

   'Political Theory and Political Economy, 1750–1800', in *Political Theory and Political Economy*, ed. C. B. Macpherson, mimeographed, Conference for the Study of Political Thought, 1974.

Middendorf, John H. 'Johnson on Wealth and Commerce', in *Johnson, Boswell and their Circle*, Oxford, 1965.

Mizuta, H. 'Moral Philosophy and Civil Society', in A. S. Skinner and T. Wilson (eds.), *Essays on Adam Smith*, Oxford, 1976.

Moore, James. 'Hume's Political Science and the Classical Republican Tradition', in *The Year 1776 in the History of Political Thought*, ed. J. G. A. Pocock, mimeographed, Conference for the Study of Political Thought, 1976.

Morgan, Robert. 'Madison's Theory of Representation in the Tenth *Federalist*', *Journal of Politics*, XXXVI (1974) 852–85.

Mossner, Ernest C. *Adam Smith: The Biographical Approach*, David Murray Lecture, University of Glasgow, 1969.

Pascal, Roy. 'Property and Society: The Scottish Historical School of the Eighteenth Century', *The Modern Quarterly*, I (1938) 167–79.

Phillipson, Nicholas. 'Culture and Society in the Eighteenth Century Province: The Case of Edinburgh and the Scottish Enlightenment', in Lawrence J. Stone (ed.), *The University in Society*, Princeton, 1974, volume II, pp. 407–48.

Pocock, John G. A. 'Virtue and Commerce in the Eighteenth Century', *Journal of Interdisciplinary History*, III (1972) 119–34.

Raphael, D. D. 'Hume and Adam Smith on Justice and Utility', *Proceedings of the Aristotelian Society*, N.S., LXXII (1972–3) 87–103.

Robbins, Caroline. '"When is it that Colonies may turn Independent"; An Analysis of the Environment and Politics of Francis Hutcheson 1669–1746', *William and Mary Quarterly*, XI (1954) 214–51.

Robbins, Lionel. 'Hayek on Liberty', *Economica*, XXVIII (1961) 66–81.

Rosenberg, Nathan. 'Some Institutional Aspects of the *Wealth of Nations*', *Journal of Political Economy*, LXVIII (1960) 537–70.

'Adam Smith on the Division of Labour: Two Views or One?', *Economica*, XXXII (1965) 127–39.

'Adam Smith, Consumer Tastes, and Economic Growth', *Journal of Political Economy*, LXXVI (1968) 361–74.

'Adam Smith on Profits – Paradox Lost and Regained', in A. S. Skinner and T. Wilson (eds.), *Essays on Adam Smith*, Oxford, 1976.

Ross, Ian S. 'Political Themes in the Correspondence of Adam Smith', *Scottish Tradition*, No. 5 (1975).

Seeman, M. 'On the Meaning of Alienation', *American Sociological Review*, XXIV (1959) 783–91.

Shackleton, Robert. 'Montesquieu, Bolingbroke, and the Separation of Powers', *French Studies*, III (1949) 25–38.

Skinner, Andrew S. 'Economics and History: The Scottish Enlightenment', *Scottish Journal of Political Economy*, XII (1965) 1–22.

'Natural History in the Age of Smith', *Political Studies*, XV (1967) 32–48.

Adam Smith and the Role of the State, Glasgow, 1974.

'Adam Smith and the American Economic Community', *Journal of the History of Ideas*, XXXVII (1976) 59–78.

'Adam Smith on the Origin, Nature and Functions of the State', mimeographed paper given at the International Political Science Association meetings in Edinburgh, 1976.

'Adam Smith: An Economic Interpretation of History', in A. S. Skinner and T. Wilson (eds.), *Essays on Adam Smith*, Oxford, 1976.

Skinner, Quentin. 'Meaning and Understanding in the History of Ideas', *History & Theory*, VIII (1967) 3–53.

'Some Problems in the Analysis of Political Thought and Action', *Political Theory*, II (1974) 277–303.

'The Principles and Practice of Opposition: The Case of Bolingbroke versus Walpole', in N. McKendrick (ed.), *Historical Perspectives, Studies in English Thought and Society*, London, 1974.

Stevens, D. 'Adam Smith and the Colonial Disturbances', in A. S.

Skinner and T. Wilson (eds.), *Essays on Adam Smith*, Oxford, 1976.

Stigler, George J. 'Smith's Travels on the Ship of State', in A. S. Skinner and T. Wilson (eds.), *Essays on Adam Smith*, Oxford, 1976.

Tarlton, Charles D. 'Historicity, Meaning and Revisionism in the Study of Political Thought', *History and Theory*, XII (1973) 307–28.

Thomas, K. V. 'The Social Origins of Hobbes's Political Thought', in K. C. Brown (ed.), *Hobbes Studies*, Oxford, 1965.

Viner, Jacob. 'Adam Smith and *Laissez-Faire*', in *The Long View and the Short: Studies in Economic Theory and Policy*, Glencoe, Illinois, 1958.

'Adam Smith', in *The International Encyclopaedia of the Social Sciences*, Glencoe, Illinois, 1968.

Walton, Craig. 'Political Economy and Republican Virtue: The Tragedy of the American Constitution', mimeographed paper presented at the Fourth International Congress on the Enlightenment, Yale, 1975.

West, E. G. 'Adam Smith's Two Views of the Division of Labour', *Economica*, XXXI (1964) 23–32.

'The Political Economy of Alienation, Karl Marx and Adam Smith', *Oxford Economic Papers*, XXI (1969) 1–23.

'Adam Smith and Alienation', in A. S. Skinner and T. Wilson (eds.), *Essays on Adam Smith*, Oxford, 1976.

'Adam Smith's Economics of Politics', *History of Political Economy*, VIII (1976) 515–39.

Wolin, Sheldon. 'Hume and Conservatism, *American Political Science Review*, XLVIII (1954) 999–1016.

Wood, N. 'The Value of Asocial Sociability: Contributions of Machiavelli, Sidney, and Montesquieu', in M. Fleisher (ed.), *Machiavelli and the Nature of Political Thought*, New York, 1972.

Index

Smith, Adam (*cont.*)
  liberty, 13, 48, 81, 97–8, 172–3;
  taxation, 53, 129, 137–8, 153–4;
  voting rights, 40, 53, 63, 169–70,
  181; Whig and Tory, 44, 52
  writings, references throughout to
  Theory of Moral Sentiments; Lectures on Jurisprudence; Wealth of Nations; Essays on Philosophical Subjects, 9; Lectures on Rhetoric and Belles Lettres, 9, 96, 175; Letter to Editors of Edinburgh Review,
  17n
Social sciences, history of, 6, 20, 34, 35, 184
'Sociology', 6, 20, 22, 37, 56, 85–6, 177;
  of civic ethics, 36
Solon, 31, 160, 170
Spiegel, H. W., 15n
Spinoza, Baruch, 16
Standing armies, 8, 32–3, 60, 62, 64, 100, 102, 103, 105–13; *see also under* Smith, Adam
Steele, Richard, 73
Stephen, Leslie, 28
Steuart, Sir James, 72
Stevens, D., 147n
Stewart, Dugald, 4, 24–5, 44n, 59, 147, 185, 186
Stigler, George J., 165–8, 171
Stourzh, G., 31n, 34n, 36n, 162n
Sulla, 60
Swift, Jonathan, 72

Tamerlane, 59
Tarlton, C. D., 183n
Tawney, R. H., 18n
Taylor, W. L., 46n, 48n
Thomas, K. V., 164n
Toland, John, 31
Townshend, Charles, 8, 147n
Trenchard, John, 31
Tucker, G. S. L., 143n

Utilitarianism, 14, 181, 184

Venturi, Franco, 40n, 44
Viner, Jacob, 3n, 14n, 24n, 42n, 88n, 93, 134, 144n, 159
'Virtue' (public spirit), 12, 30, 37, 73, 84, 87, 106–7, 161, 171, 174–5, 177; *see also* 'Corruption'

Walpole, Sir Robert, 32, 121, 122, 129n
Walton, C., 163n
Wedderburn, Alexander, 147, 149, 156
West, E. G., 84n, 86n, 169n
Western, J. R., 104n
Whiggism, 'Real', 31, 46, 48, 65; 'sceptical', 39–41; 'vulgar', 39, 41, 65, 95, 129, 177
Winch, D. N., 147n
Witenagemot, 61
Wolin, Sheldon, 21–2, 171n, 187
Wood, G. S., 31n, 179n
Wood, N., 158n

Cambridge Studies in the History and Theory of Politics

Editors: Maurice Cowling, G. R. Elton, E. Kedourie, J. G. A. Pocock, J. R. Pole and Walter Ullmann

A series in two parts, studies and original texts. The studies are original works on political history and political philosophy while the texts are modern, critical editions of major texts in political thought. The titles include:

Texts

Liberty, Equality, Fraternity, by James Fitzjames Stephen, edited with an introduction and notes by R. J. White

Vladimir Akimov on the Dilemmas of Russian Marxism 1895–1903. An English edition of 'A Short History of the Social Democratic Movement in Russia' and 'The Second Congress of the Russian Social Democratic Labour Party', with an introduction and notes by Jonathan Frankel

J. G. Herder on Social and Political Culture, translated, edited and with an introduction by F. M. Barnard

The Limits of State Action, by Wilhelm von Humboldt, edited with an introduction and notes by J. W. Burrow

Kant's Political Writings, edited with an introduction and notes by Hans Reiss; translated by H. B. Nisbet

Karl Marx's Critique of Hegel's 'Philosophy of Right', edited with an introduction and notes by Joseph O'Malley; translated by Annette Jolin and Joseph O'Malley

Lord Salisbury on Politics. A Selection from His Articles in 'The Quarterly Review' 1860–1883, edited by Paul Smith

Francogallia, by François Hotman. Latin text edited by Ralph E. Giesey. English translation by J. H. M. Salmon

The Political Writings of Leibniz, edited and translated by Patrick Riley

Turgot on Progress, Sociology and Economics: A Philosophical Review of the Successive Advances of the Human Mind on Universal History. Reflections on the Formation and Distribution of Wealth, edited, translated and introduced by Ronald L. Meek

Texts concerning the Revolt of the Netherlands, edited with an introduction by E. H. Kossmann and A. F. Mellink

Regicide and Revolution: Speeches at the Trial of Louis XVI, edited with an introduction by Michael Walzer; translated by Marian Rothstein

George Wilhelm Friedrich Hegel: Lectures on the Philosophy of World History: Reason in History, translated from the German edition of Johannes Hoffmeister by H. B. Nisbet and with an introduction by Duncan Forbes

A Machiavellian Treatise, by Stephen Gardiner, edited and translated by Peter S. Donaldson

The Political Works of James Harrington, edited by J. G. A. Pocock

Studies

1867: Disraeli, Gladstone and Revolution: The Passing of the Second Reform Bill, by Maurice Cowling

The Social and Political Thought of Karl Marx, by Shlomo Avineri

Men and Citizens: A Study of Rousseau's Social Theory, by Judith Shklar

Idealism, Politics and History: Sources of Hegelian Thought, by George Armstrong Kelly

The Impact of Labour 1920–1924: The Beginnings of Modern British Politics, by Maurice Cowling

Alienation: Marx's Conception of Man in Capitalist Society, by Bertell Ollman

The Politics of Reform 1884, by Andrew Jones

Hegel's Theory of the Modern State, by Shlomo Avineri

Jean Bodin and the Rise of Absolutist Theory, by Julian H. Franklin

The Social Problem in the Philosophy of Rousseau, by John Charvet

The Impact of Hitler: British Politics and British Policy 1933–1940, by Maurice Cowling

Social Science and the Ignoble Savage, by Ronald L. Meek

Freedom and Independence: A Study of the Political Ideas of Hegel's 'Phenomenology of Mind', by Judith Shklar

In the Anglo-Arab Labyrinth: The McMahon–Husayn Correspondence and Its Interpretations 1914–1939, by Elie Kedourie

The Liberal Mind 1914–1929, by Michael Bentley

Political Philosophy and Rhetoric: A Study of the Origins of American Party Politics, by John Zvesper

Revolution Principles: The Politics of Party 1689–1720, by J. P. Kenyon

John Locke and the Theory of Sovereignty: Mixed Monarchy and the Right of Resistance in the Political Thought of the English Revolution, by Julian H. Franklin